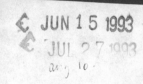

SAMUEL WEBER is a member of the Humanities Center, The Johns Hopkins University.

This radically new reading of *La peau de chagrin* presents a case for Balzac as a modern rather than a traditional, realist writer. Using the principles and languages of Marx, Derrida, Freud, Barthes, and others who have contributed to a redefinition of modern criticism, Samuel Weber presents a detailed and intricate explication of the text that challenges all standard interpretations of the novel.

Traditional readings of *La peau de chagrin*, and of Balzac in general, have pursued a message in the novel, a reality beneath the allegory. Weber demonstrates that Balzac's text can be grasped both as a *mise en scène* and as a play of representations that reflects no original truth, reality, or meaning beneath the text to which the representations can be referred and by which they can be authenticated. To unwrap Balzac in this manner is to discover that there is no thing inside, that there is only the 'wrapping.'

Weber's conclusions are not only startlingly original, but they also solve problems which have puzzled traditional readers of the novel since the earliest commentators of 1831. *Unwrapping Balzac* is a brilliant tour de force that will create controversy among Balzac scholars for years to come.

UNWRAPPING BALZAC
A Reading of
La Peau de Chagrin

Samuel Weber

UNIVERSITY OF TORONTO PRESS

Toronto Buffalo London

© University of Toronto Press 1979
Toronto Buffalo London
Printed in Canada

University of Toronto Romance Series 39

Library of Congress Cataloging in Publication Data

Weber, Samuel, 1940 –
  Unwrapping Balzac.

  (University of Toronto romance series ; 39)
  Includes bibliographical references and index.
  1. Balzac, Honoré de, 1799-1850. Peau de chagrin. I. Title. II. Series:
  University of Toronto. University of Toronto romance series ; 39.
  PQ2167.P6W4   843'.7   79-21801
  ISBN 0-8020-5446-3

This book has been published with the help of a grant from the Canadian Federation for
the Humanities , using funds provided by the Social Sciences and Humanities
Research Council of Canada, and from the Andrew W. Mellon Foundation to University
of Toronto Press.

Contents

Unwrapping Balzac

1

Introduction

Balzac is unmodern. The history of literature has generally denied his work the dialectical position of its namesake, *La Divina Commedia*. Today, *La Comédie humaine* is regarded as the close of an epoch, marking the culmination of a traditional form of narrative fiction that is separated from what follows it categorically, by a qualitative leap as it were, a break that ostensibly resists mediation.

Thus, when Gérard Genette ponders the origins of what he calls 'l'expérience littéraire moderne,' he turns to the 'silence de Flaubert' as the decisive turning point. By his refusal of the expressive function of language, Genette writes, Flaubert becomes 'le premier à contester profondément, quoique sourdement, la *fonction narrative*, jusqu'alors essentielle au roman.'[1] 'Jusqu'-alors': to determine Flaubert as the start of something new requires, explicitly or implicitly, the predetermination of the tradition from which he distinguishes himself. This reference is made casually, easily, and in passing: 'L'abondance des descriptions ne répond donc pas seulement chez lui [Flaubert], comme chez Balzac par exemple, à des nécessités d'ordre dramatique ... .'[2] The Other, whose negation permits a certain modernity to assert its specificity, to identify and to establish itself, in short to take (its) place, is Balzac: 'Par exemple.'

But the example, which seems at first merely an exchangeable illustration, recurs, most frequently in Genette's criticism and elsewhere, where the effort is made to distinguish the essence of our modernity, as it is articulated in fiction. For instance, Genette describes Flaubert's characteristic use of detail by emphasizing that it employs 'non pas seulement ... le détail utile, significatif, comme chez Balzac, mais ... le détail gratuit et insignifiant ... .'[3]

It is not only Genette who takes the opposition, Balzac/Flaubert, for granted. Indeed, one can wonder whether this opposition has ever been seriously questioned, so pervasive it seems to have been in literary history and criticism. One of its most forceful articulations has been that of Georg Lukács, whose *Balzac and French Realism* takes its point of departure in the question: 'Is Balzac or Flaubert the culmination [*die Spitzenerscheinung*], the typical classic of the 19th Century?'[4] Of course, the terms in which Lukács poses this opposition – realism versus naturalism, narration versus description, totality versus fragmentation, etc. – are as far removed from those of recent French Structuralism as his evaluation and preferences are from those of Genette. What is worth remarking, however, is that despite such divergences, both critics agree in regarding the two writers as personifying an antithesis that pits tradition and modernity against one another, separated by an apparently unbridgeable chasm. The fact that Lukács appeals to a more general continuity involved in the socio-historical development of bourgeois culture, in order to bridge, or rather explain, the opposition, does not per se diminish the uncompromising nature of the choice to be made. Within the specific domain of literary aesthetics, the alternative, Balzac *or* Flaubert, remains absolute and ineluctable.

Nor is this to be found in Lukács alone. The Hungarian Marxist's interpretation of the relation Balzac/Flaubert as the sign of a profound crisis in literary history, but also in regard to society as a whole, is shared by Albert Béguin, whose *Balzac visionnaire*, together with his later prefaces, includes some of the most insightful comments yet written on Balzac. Although in an obvious sense Béguin's conception of Balzac as a visionary, rather than as a realist, appears to be diametrically opposed to that of Lukács, here again the two critics have much in common. For both, the two authors embody a critical turning point in the aesthetic and moral development of literature. Moreover, the two critics agree in their general evaluation of the opposition, although for different reasons. For Lukács, Flaubert marks the prevailing historical tendency of alienation and fetishism, subverting the values, moral and aesthetic, of a classical humanism oriented upon Goethe. Béguin, although at first conceiving of the crisis in more individualistic, psychological terms, later comes to emphasize increasingly the social aspects of the alternative.

Like Lukács, Béguin seeks to portray that alternative as entailing two discrete aesthetic options; as though to establish their mutual independence, and by implication the possibility of a choice between them, Béguin seeks to invoke a chronological (and, by implication, logical) distinction. 'Balzac,' he writes, is 'en quelque sorte antérieur à la malédiction flaubertienne'; that is, he is anterior to the hubris of a literature that sees itself as being independent of any referential or representational function.[5] In Flaubert, 'les mots se libèrent de ce qu'ils avaient mission d'évoquer ... cela donne à toute une partie de l'œuvre de Flaubert son caractère dément ... .'[6] 'Ecrire pour écrire, il n'y a pas de vanité plus folle,' Béguin writes, and there can be no doubt that such 'folie' is meant to be taken quite literally.[7]

If, however, we read it literally enough, Béguin's construction of the Balzac/Flaubert relation in terms of a simple opposition, involving mutually independent and exclusive terms, begins to break down. According to Béguin's own description, *folie* emerges as something that is by no means the exclusive prerogative of Flaubertian literature, the result and nemesis of its self-referentiality. This becomes evident where it might least be expected, when Béguin is discussing not Flaubert, but the 'lois' that govern 'l'empire fermé du roman balzacien.' In that closed realm Béguin discovers – or should we say, stumbles upon – another *démence*, this time one that is unalterably and characteristically *balzacienne*: 'La démence fait craquer les os, les peurs et les colères rugissent plus fort que ne crient autour de nous les hommes.'[8] Of course, the Balzacian *démence* is quite different from that of Flaubert; by contrast with the latter, it is not the result of the hubris of art for art's sake, but precisely of the themes and things to which Balzac's fiction addresses itself. And yet – when, in a later text, the preface to *Facino Cane*, Béguin sets about describing the Balzacian madness in some detail, this opposition is, implicitly at least, called into question:

> La constante angoisse de Balzac une fois de plus se fait jour; jamais il n'a cessé de craindre la démence possible, de la sentir rôder autour de lui. Vivre la vie d'autrui, comme fait le romancier, il a pensé parfois que c'était un acte interdit, et que le privilège de cette vision insolite pouvait bien ressembler à la malédiction du délire mental. Mais il est un signe auquel se reconnaissent à coup sûr, chez Balzac, les instants où revenait cette peur profonde; aussitôt qu'il y fait allusion, il se reprend brusquement, écartant la fâcheuse pensée par le même réflexe de défense qui lui fit dire un jour: 'La mort est inévitable, oublions-la!'[9]

Far from being peculiar or restricted to the form of autonomous, self-referential writing (Flaubert), *démence* is here described as endemic to writing *tout court*. Even in its most 'traditional' forms, the process of reference and representation, of mimetic substitution, constitutes a threat to the writing subject, the *romancier*, by engaging him in a series of replacements and dislocations that threaten the stability of his 'own' place. If, however, *démence* is *already* inherent in traditional forms of fiction, then the 'anteriority' of Balzac with respect to the Flaubertian 'curse' takes on a different aspect. Instead of being construed as a simple opposition or alternative, both Flaubertian and Balzacian modes of writing begin to appear as diverse responses to a common problem: the displacement of the (writing) subject in and through the process of writing itself. Instead of the antithesis, Balzac contra Flaubert, we are confronted by a pair, Balzac *and* Flaubert: two names designating two modes of *defence* against a single threat.

Béguin himself, of course, is emphatic in condemning Flaubert's 'atroce macération de sa chair,' as being 'comme un suicide fictif.'[10] And yet, if the problem resides in the writing of fiction itself, then Flaubert can be seen as fighting fire with fire. What, however, of Balzac's defence? Confronted by the danger of losing his place, 'il se reprend brusquement,' Béguin asserts. Yet he does not add *where*, to what place of safety Balzac might withdraw if what he is fleeing inheres in the process of writing itself ('vivre la vie d'autrui'). Will not every attempt at withdrawal, insofar as it remains within the medium of literature, only reproduce the menace?

The only solution that can be envisaged would be the construction of a place that is at once both outside the sphere of fictional substitution, and yet sufficiently close to command the scene. Yet is this not one, if not indeed *the* function of the *Comédie humaine*? By designating a world of fiction that claims to transcend the individual works: a world with its own, relatively autonomous and consistent laws, with its specific topography and chronology, its recurring characters and interrelated events, the *Comédie humaine* can be seen as the attempt to put fiction in its (proper) place. The fictional world of representation is thus enclosed, framed within limits which seem to situate, and thus to control, what otherwise might become a most disconcerting series of dislocations and substitutions. And, once fiction is put in *its* place, then the subject (whether as reader, author, or as subject matter) can be certain of where he, she or it stands.

To put fiction in its place, in this sense, requires the reference to a place that is both outside and yet inside, and this can only be the site of the author, Balzac. This explains, at least in part, why initiation into the work of Balzac has often been indicated by the use of the proper name of the author to designate the initiates: namely, as *Balzaciens*. This only makes obvious what is required in order to delimit fictional texts as a *work*, and a *world*: the reference to a transcendent subject, which itself is deemed to be non-fictional since it must dominate and delimit the realm of fiction.

The implications of this reference are nowhere more evident than in André Allemand's study, *Unité et structure de l'univers balzacien* (1965). As the title indicates, unity and structure are considered to be largely equivalent. Their basis, however, is conceived in reference to a subject that is ultimately theological in character. As Allemand puts it,

*Balzac ne dispute pas à Dieu le droit de gouverner son vaste empire. Il pré-
tend seulement être en mesure d'exercer un droit analogue, dès l'instant où
il est parvenu à concevoir la réalité sous une autre forme.*[11]

The subjective reference implied by a conception of fiction as 'totalization'
and as 'unification' - in short, as work and as world - necessitates the theological model of the Creator, as the Identity or Being that unfolds in and as
'l'univers balzacien.' 'Concevoir la réalité sous une autre forme' is still to conceive of reality: not as an empirical or natural world, to be sure, but nevertheless as a self-contained, coherent whole. And the driving force by which the
substitutions of fictional representation are said to constitute themselves into
a totality is death: 'La mort, le néant, le rien, c'est la totalité achevée.'[12] As in
the philosophy of Hegel, where mortality is interpreted as the movement by
which the finite, natural individual negates its own finitude, death in Allemand's reading of Balzac becomes the means by which fictional representation
limits and delimits its own fictionality.[13] For if fiction can, as Allemand
argues, totalize itself in and as the *Comédie humaine*, this implies that the
process of totalization itself is non- (or perhaps meta-) fictional. To identify a
series of fictions as comprising a totality requires the reference to a transcendent, authorial subject, a consciousness in which the critic, who reaffirms it,
also partakes.

Death, inevitable as it is for the individual, is thus, in a sense, 'forgotten.'
And if such a forgetting corresponds to one aspect of the Balzacian text, to
identify that aspect with the text in its entirety is to forget more than death -
or, perhaps, less. For assertions such as 'La mort est inévitable, oublions-là!'
are - as the exclamation point indicates - articulations of a *desire*, and at the
same time, as Béguin has suggested, of a *fear*. To overlook the form in which
such fears and desires are uttered, the form of a certain *narration*, is to con-
flate the *desire* (fear) of narration with the *reality* of the text. Or rather, it is
to treat the text *as* a reality, as a coherent, meaningful discourse that ultimately simply says what it means, which is what the Author meant (as reiterated
by the Critic, his porte-parole). Again, there can be little doubt that to read
the texts of Balzac in this manner, to read as *porte-parole* and as *Balzacien*, is
to respond to one of the most insistent and most powerful solicitations of the
text, one that is evident, for instance, in those characteristic interventions of
the Narrator (Author), addressing himself directly to the Reader, in order to
invoke a world apparently familiar to and shared by Author and Reader alike.
And yet, to respond in such a manner is to equate *énoncé* and *énonciation*,
and thereby to overlook the way in which such utterances are themselves
inscribed, part and parcel, in a context of relationships that they do not necessarily command.

The inscription of a title – 'La Comédie humaine' – in a series of texts, fictional and non-fictional, does not in itself suffice to establish the point of view of totalization as that which organizes and structures those texts, any more than their various cross-references suffice to construct that totality. What the reader is confronted with is nothing more or less than indices, not of the process of totalization, but of the *project* and of the *desire* of such a process. That the two are not identical is what a reading like Allemand's tends to ignore. For Georges Poulet, however, this non-identity constitutes the very essence of Balzac's writing. At its centre is the 'homme de désir,' whose being is precisely defined not by self-fulfilment, but by self-projection towards an impossible goal.[14] The Balzacian man of desire is a person 'qui, éternellement, se projette au-délà de son être.'[15] Since such desire is barred from reaching its object, what ensues is a work that possesses a highly ambivalent character. On the one hand, it appears as an 'entrecroisement de plus en plus riche de rapports,' spreading itself out spatially, as it were; on the other hand, its very extension in space gives it a dilated, inflated quality, 'une sorte de gonflement interne.'[16] This does not mean that Balzac is simply pompous, vapid, or vacuous, but rather that in the innermost being of his work, there is not a hard core of meaning but something more elusive, more difficult to grasp or to define, neither entirely saturated and meaning-ful, nor wholly empty, neither whole, nor hole.

Poulet cites the following passage, from *Les Proscrits*, as exemplifying 'la dernière attitude' of the Balzacian man of desire:

> *Je vis une grande ombre. Debout et dans une attitude ardente, cette âme dévorait les espaces du regard, ses pieds restaient attachés par le pouvoir de Dieu sur le dernier point de cette ligne où elle accomplissait sans cesse la tension pénible par laquelle nous projetons nos forces lorsque nous voulons prendre notre élan, comme des oiseaux prêts à s'envoler. Je reconnus un homme. ... Par chaque parcelle de temps, il semblait éprouver sans faire un seul pas la fatigue de traverser l'infini qui le séparait du paradis où sa vue plongeait sans cesse.*[17]

The citation concludes Poulet's essay (in *La distance intérieure*), as though the passage *spoke for itself.* And it is true that, in the context of Poulet's reading, its meaning is unmistakable: it designates what Poulet has described as the *finality* of Balzacian desire: 'l'espace final est fait de séparation. Le temps final est fait d'attente.'[18] Cut off from attaining its object, Balzacian desire is left with nothing but the eternal reiteration of its own yearning, a process of repetition that transforms movement into stasis, scene into tableau.

And yet, in reading this scene precisely as a tableau, does not Poulet, knowingly or unknowingly, assume one of the positions inscribed in the text, thus privileging one of its elements? For the text does not speak for itself – it is *spoken*, by a narrator ('Je vis une grande ombre ... ') whose position is hardly one of critical neutrality. The speaker, of course, is none other than Dante, grand poet in exile, recounting, somewhat compulsively, a scene that could easily be taken as a reflection of his own condition. Nor is it without significance that the story ends with return *in sight*, to be sure in a flourish suggestive of the conclusion of an opera buffo. For what Poulet's reading assumes is that there is, or can be a *last word* to Balzacian desire, a 'dernière attitude,' a *final* time and space, once and for all. And wherever such finality prevails, even if it is that of 'separation' and unfulfilled yearning, reconciliation and reappropriation are always in the offing. For the very assertion of a last and final state implies, at least for the critical discourse that makes the assertion, an overcoming of estrangement in which the authorial word comes into its own – in the end. Such an implication, however, only echoes and repeats the desire of the narrator, or rather the desire of narration, without interpreting it or placing it into relation with other aspects of the text.

In *Les Proscrits*, for instance, one of those aspects surely involves the nature of that 'ombre' described by Dante. What Poulet omits from his otherwise lengthy citation is a reference to the physicality of the figure ('tous ces muscles tressaillaient et haletaient; par chaque parcelle de temps etc.').[19]

In thus omitting the physicality of desire, Poulet can all the more easily assume the position earlier mentioned, that of the insider-outsider, looking down upon the (static) scene. *Incessant* exertion becomes *eternal* repetition, (Balzac: 'sans cesse'; Poulet: 'éternellement'), as the situation coalesces into an object of sight, upon which the eyes of critic and reader can fix and dwell ('où sa vue plongeait sans cesse,' writes Balzac of *his* hero).

By thus assuming (in both senses of the word) the position of a transcendental spectator, Poulet hypostasizes the position of the Narrator, thus conceived as Author and Creator, outside the desire that is represented. And in general, to read a text as though it were something visual, almost inevitably involves such an assumption, and such an hypostasis. But this kind of sight must blind itself to those aspects of the text that call its own site, its position, into question; for instance, to those aspects of its subject – desire – that are not simply accessible to simple perception, such as the *force* that imposes that final separation, or the traces of tension it leaves behind. 'Le malheureux était si horriblement écrasé par je ne sais quelle force,' continues the narrator in *Les Proscrits*; and yet he has already identified that force ('ses pieds restaient attachés par le pouvoir de Dieu sur le dernier point de cette ligne où elle accomplissait sans cesse la tension pénible ... ').[20] 'Le pouvoir de Dieu' in turn has its own, particular history, one which Dante does not forget to tell. Honorino, the exemplary man of desire according to Poulet, is condemned to damnation because of the sin of suicide. Following the death of his beloved Térésa, he takes his own life in order to rejoin her. The scene of separation is thus the consequence of a desire for reunion that merges with a desire for death.

'La mort est inévitable, oublions-la!' To portray desire as eternal striving, as separation and hope, surely entails an attempt to forget death not at all unlike that which moves the writings of Balzac. The question, however, remains: how are those writings moved, what figure do they trace? The phrase immediately preceding that cited by Poulet seems to provide a ready answer: 'Là, sur la dernière ligne circulaire qui appartenait encore aux fantômes que je laissais derrière moi, semblable à des chagrins qu'on veut oublier, je vis une grande ombre.'[21] The 'dernière ligne circulaire' describes a pattern of movement that traditionally would enable us to 'forget' death, or (the same thing) to comprehend it. And yet, if the Balzacian narrator never entirely succeeds in leaving those phantoms behind, 'semblable à des chagrins qu'on veut oublier,' it is because there is always *another chagrin* whose story is waiting to be told. And a strange, irresistible compulsion drives the narrator to tell the tale:

> – Arrêtez! s'écria Godefroid, je ne saurais vous regarder, vous écouter davantage! Ma raison s'égare, ma vue s'obscurcit. Vous allumez en moi un feu qui me dévore.
> – Je dois cependant continuer, reprit le vieillard ... .[22]

2

'La très spirituelle épigraphe du livre ...'

La Peau de chagrin, like Les Proscrits, was published in 1831 among the three volumes of Romans et Contes philosophiques. The novel was an immediate success, something that its author had helped to prepare. In an advertisement for himself published in La Caricature under the name of Alexandre de B ... , Balzac recommended his book, among other reasons,

> parce que la vie humaine y est représentée, formulée, traduite comme Rabelais et Sterne, les philosophies et les étourdis, les femmes qui aiment et les femmes qui n'aiment pas la conçoivent; drame qui serpente, ondule, tournoie, et au courant duquel il faut s'abandonner, comme le dit la très spirituelle épigraphe du livre.[1]

In what follows let us endeavour to follow this recommendation, and to abandon ourselves to the undulations of this serpentine drama – abandoning ourselves not passively, however, but with extreme and minute attention to the movement of the text. And let us begin with that 'very spiritual epigraph' itself.

It is, as indicated, taken from Sterne's celebrated novel, Tristram Shandy and, in the process, it undergoes a change which merits attention. In Tristram Shandy, the figure depicts a gesture, a flourish made by Trim with his walking stick, punctuating a discourse on the values of celibacy:

> Whilst a man is free, – cried the corporal, giving a flourish with his stick thus –

> *A thousand of my father's most subtle syllogisms could not have said more for celibacy.*[2]

Throughout *Tristram Shandy*, ironic effects are produced from the manner in which the context or situation subverts the intended meaning of words, with the inexorability of a chemical process: an element, a word, is released into an atmosphere which immediately combines with and corrodes it, dissolving its 'original' meaning to form a new one, often at cross purposes with the speaker's intention. Through a certain context, the textuality and texture of language is revealed. Trim's flourish is not spared this fate. Instead of raising Toby's spirits, it undermines them for the attack on Widow Wadman; moreover, the notion it is intended to indicate, freedom, is itself one of those words whose meaning is continuously being undermined throughout the novel, as Trim's own comments demonstrate:

> *If Tom had not married the Widow, or had it pleased God after their marriage, that they had but put pork into their sausages, the honest soul had never been taken out of his warm bed, and dragg'd to the Inquisition ... .*[3]

Toby's celibacy, his destiny, is as much a matter of his free choice as was the wound he suffered at the battle of Namur. Yet Trim's eloquent flourish, punctuating and interrupting the unilinear, univocal chain of rhetoric, suggests in its very ambiguity something like freedom, transforming the stick from an aid to walking (both Trim and Toby are lame) into a magic 'wand' ('The corporal had unwarily conjured up the Spirit of calculation with his wand').[4] This wand is no longer a simple instrument in the hands of its owner; rather, it seems on the verge of escaping from his control, not by becoming a thing but by virtue of its multiple significance, an ambiguity which 'unwarily' conjures up the Spirit of calculation. The figure that it traces in the air may, through its irregular circling upwards, represent a certain flight, and yet it is a flight which is subverted by its very quality as an inscription; this movement, all of its airiness notwithstanding, is going nowhere.

From Shandy Hall to the Paris of 1830, however, Trim's magic walking stick does undergo a radical transformation: it is both brought back down to earth and yet given new wings. From a wand which describes the figural contours of a certain space, open-ended, it is turned over on its side, and metamorphosed into a serpent, whose curse is to crawl on its stomach and eat dust its life long. From an ambiguous gesture punctuating a chain of discourse, it becomes a simple representation, a symbol, whose function is precisely to safeguard, not interrupt, the continuity of that chain. Although Balzac did not intend the figure to depict a serpent – it first appeared in the Houssiaux edition after his death – there seems little doubt that he would have approved of the change.[5] As we have already read, in 1831 he described the novel as a 'drame qui serpente, ondule, tournoie, et au courant duquel il faut s'abandonner ... .' The reader's abandonment to the stream of the narrative, constantly parodied in *Tristram Shandy*, is now the explicit desideratum. Whereas Sterne begins his novel with a reductio ad absurdum of causality, and with it of the linearity upon which all conventional narration depends, in order then precisely to explode that linearity by exploiting the (non-linear) ambiguity of the linguistic sign itself, Balzac's writing remains pledged to just that linearity, whether as the continuum of the 'drame,' its 'courant,' or as the symbol which speaks for itself, without fear of contradiction: 'comme le *dit* la très spirituelle épigraphe du livre.' The Kantian problematic of the Third Antinomy, the relation between causality and freedom, which forms Sterne's point of departure (in this respect, Kantian *avant la lettre*) remains a distant prospect, something to be confronted at the end, if at all, in a universe where 'tout s'enchaine ... tout mouvement y correspond à une cause, toute cause se rattache à l'ensemble.'[6]

Hence, in contrast to Sterne, whose thematization of language indicates his indebtedness to the tradition of English nominalism, the intellectual horizons of Balzac are situated rather within the tradition of continental rationalism. For Balzac as for Leibniz, the chain of causality implies both a continuum and an immanence in which 'l'ensemble se represente dans le moindre mouvement,' and this continuity of representation, the monad, has as its aesthetic corollary, the symbol. Like the monad, the symbol possesses within itself its own articulation; its significance is its potential, and spontaneous, unfolding. Thus, quite apart from the particular symbolic significance of the serpent, which will emerge in due course, it represents the symbolic function as such. In contrast to Trim's airy and silent flourish, the serpentine epigraph seeks to speak for itself.

3

Work and Play

Vers la fin du mois d'octobre dernier, un jeune homme entra dans le Palais-Royal au moment où les maisons de jeu s'ouvraient, conformément à la loi qui protège une passion essentiellement imposable. Sans trop hésiter, il monta l'escalier du tripot désigné sous le nom de numéro 36.[1]

The novel begins with an 'end' and an 'opening': the scene is precisely situated, 'vers la *fin* du mois d'octobre dernier ... au moment où les maisons de jeu *s'ouvraient* ... .' This opening scene describes, is itself described, with a paradoxical mixture of precision and indeterminacy. The anonymity of the 'jeune homme' stands in marked contrast to the numerical precision with which the scene is situated in time, as in space. The novel begins, as it were, with the day itself, yet it is the dawn of a passion which is 'essentiellement imposable,' subordinated to a Law, which fixes the time and the place: the 'tripot désigné sous le nom de numéro 36.' The young man is unnamed; the casino, site of a certain *passion*, has a name: 'numéro 36.' It is a name designated by a law which, as tax or registration, is a law of number, of indeterminate precision: of a certain indeterminacy, and a certain precision. This law has its history. The numbering of houses was made mandatory for Paris in 1805, as part of the administrative reforms of the Napoleonic regime. Yet over a half-century afterwards, it still evoked opposition on the part of the population. According to a report written in 1864, 'if you ask one of the inhabitants of this suburb (Saint-Antoine) for his address, he will always give you the name of his house, and not the cold, official number.'[2] In *Modeste Mignon,*

written several years after *La Peau de chagrin*, Balzac describes the effects of
this growth in administrative control through numeration. The passage deserves to be cited at length:

> *Essayez donc de rester inconnues, pauvres femmes de France, de filer le
> moindre petit roman au milieu d'une civilisation qui note sur les places
> publiques l'heure du départ et de l'arrivée des fiacres, qui compte les
> lettres, qui les timbre doublement au moment précis où elles sont jetées
> dans les boîtes et quand elles se distribuent, qui numérote les maisons, qui
> configure sur le rôle-matrice des Contributions les étages, après en avoir
> vérifié les ouvertures, qui va bientôt posséder tout son territoire représenté
> dans ses dernières parcelles, avec ses plus menus linéaments, sur les vastes
> feuilles du Cadastre, oeuvre de géant ordonnée par un géant! Essayez donc
> de vous soustraire, filles imprudentes, non pas à l'oeil de la police; mais à
> ce bavardage incessant qui, dans la dernière bourgade, scrute les actions les
> plus indifférentes, compte les plats de dessert chez le préfet et voit les
> côtes de melon à la porte du petit rentier, qui tâche d'entendre l'or au
> moment où la main de l'Economie l'ajoute au trésor, et qui, tous les soirs,
> au coin du foyer, estime le chiffre des fortunes du canton, de la ville, du
> département!*[3]

The universalization of administrative control, bringing with it the quantifica-
tion of all spheres of life, subordinates the individuals to the nameless, numerical whole, which in turn, precisely by virtue of its anonymity, can only be
described by metaphor: 'oeuvre de géant, ordonnée par un géant.' This system
of control, whose mark is the number, achieves the possession of all individual things and persons by their registration or representation: that 'quality' or
singularity which had made representation possible while at the same time
resisting and limiting it, is (as number) reduced to its most general, abstract
form, that of pure identity which by virtue of its very 'purity' can be represented and hence possessed at will: ' ... qui va bientôt posséder tout son territ-
oire représenté dans ses dernières parcelles, avec ses plus menus linéaments,
sur les vastes feuilles du Cadastre ... .'

The form that this representation takes is that of a certain *inscription*, 'sur
les vastes feuilles de Cadastre.' Numeration and notation are inseparable, and
mark the rhythm of this world: 'qui note ... qui compte ... qui les timbre ...
qui numérote ... qui configure ... qui va bientôt posséder.' It is no accident
that this description of possession culminates in the possession of the means
of possession, of money and of a certain 'Economie': 'qui tâche d'entendre
l'or au moment où la main de l'Economie l'ajoute au trésor, et qui ... estime
le chiffre des fortunes de canton ... .' This 'Economy' extends its control to
the very 'dessert chez le préfet et voit les côtes de melon à la porte du petit

rentier,' to the very food – or, more precisely, to the very *dessert* and *hors d'oeuvres* – of life, and it embraces both the 'hors d'oeuvre du petit rentier' and the 'oeuvre de géant.' What is perhaps more significant, however, is the complicity between the anonymity of this 'oeuvre de géant' who controls his realm through inscription, and the anonymity of the narrator, present in the paratactical, cumulative syntax of a description which is never simply descriptive, but which *expresses* a speaker as well, which is enunciation no less than designation: a voice filling the void of a certain silence – that of inscription – source and product of a metaphor supplanting a number and supplicating a name.

A similar narrative 'intervention' occurs at the beginning of *La Peau de chagrin*; its context helps to elucidate the origin and function of the Balzacian metaphor. Having entered the building, the young man is involved in a brief exchange: he is forced to relinquish his hat, 'dont heureusement les bords étaient légèrement pelés,' and receives in turn 'une fiche numérotée en échange de son chapeau'(12). The exemplary significance of this exchange is formulated by the narrator in a direct address to the reader:

> *Quand vous entrez dans une maison de jeu, la loi commence par vous dé-*
> *pouiller de votre chapeau. Est-ce une parabole évangélique et providen-*
> *tielle? N'est-ce pas plutôt une manière de conclure un contrat infernal avec*
> *vous en exigeant je ne sais quel gage? (11)*

The exchange is the result of the law which subsumes name under number: here its purpose, the narrator ironically speculates, may be to 'savoir le nom de votre chapelier ou le vôtre ... si vous l'avez inscrit sur la coiffe' – inscription would thus be betrayal, abandonment of oneself to the law – or perhaps simply 'pour prendre la mesure de votre crâne et dresser une statistique instructive sur la capacité cérébrale des joueurs? Sur ce point, l'administration garde un silence complet' (12). This *silence*, which as we have seen is constitutive of the Law, provokes the eloquence of the narrator:

> *Mais, sachez-le bien, à peine avez-vous fait un pas vers le tapis vert, déjà*
> *votre chapeau ne vous appartient pas plus que vous ne vous appartenez à*
> *vous-même: vous êtes au jeu, vous, votre fortune, votre coiffe, votre canne*
> *et votre manteau. A votre sortie, le Jeu vous démontrera, par une atroce*
> *épigramme en action, qu'il vous laisse encore quelque chose en vous ren-*
> *dant votre bagage (12).*

We understand now why the exchange which initiates the young man into the *salon de jeu* can be called 'un contrat infernal': the 'gage' it demands is not merely to be measured in terms of his possessions, of his property, but of the *propre* as such: 'déjà votre chapeau ne vous appartient pas plus que vous ne

vous appartenez à vous-même: vous êtes au jeu, vous ... .' Small wonder that
the *salon* itself is the scene of a certain *impropriety*, that its 'parquet est usé,
malpropre' (14). And the culmination of this *jeu*, the demonstration of its
totality, is the return of the hat as one leaves, a vestige of the *property* that
has been lost, the 'return' on the original 'investment,' the conclusion of the
exchange. This final, silent gesture of the *jeu* is 'une atroce épigramme en action,' made eloquent and significant through the metaphor. No less than the
Law, with which it stands in deep complicity, the *jeu* inscribes: its signature
is an exchange. The scene of that exchange, which is the *jeu* 'même,' is the
salon:

> *Essayez de jeter un regard furtif sur cette arène, entrez! ... Quelle nudité!*
> *Les murs, couverts d'un papier gras à hauteur d'homme, n'offrent pas une*
> *seule image qui puisse rafraîchir l'âme. Il ne s'y trouve même pas un clou*
> *pour faciliter le suicide. Le parquet est usé, malpropre. Une table oblongue*
> *occupe le centre de la salle. La simplicité des chaises de paille pressées au-*
> *tour de ce tapis usé par l'or annonce une curieuse indifférence du luxe*
> *chez ces hommes qui viennent périr là pour la fortune et le luxe (13-14).*

Shabby, soiled, bare, the *salon de jeu* 'n'offre pas une seule image qui puisse
rafraîchir l'âme.' This poses particular problems for the author, whose task, as
Balzac writes in his 'Preface' to the first edition of the novel, involves a certain reproduction:

> *L'art littéraire ayant pour objet de reproduire la nature par la pensée, est le*
> *plus compliqué de tous les arts. Peindre un sentiment, faire revivre les cou-*
> *leurs, les jours ... voilà toute la peinture.*[4]

The writer, to accomplish this task,

> *est obligé d'avoir en lui quel miroir concentrique où, suivant sa fantaisie,*
> *l'univers vient se réfléchir; sinon, le poète et même l'observateur n'existent*
> *pas; car il ne s'agit pas seulement de voir, il faut encore se souvenir et em-*
> *preindre ces impressions dans un certain choix de mots et les parer de toute la*
> *grâce des images ou leur communiquer le vif des sensations primordiales.*[5]

Yet, confronted with the peculiar 'nature' of the *salon de jeu*, the art which
has as its object the reproduction of nature is obviously faced by a dilemma.
For the *salon* is not merely bare, it is threadbare: the 'tapis vert,' a sad re-
minder of the lush greenery of 'nature,' is worn out, 'usé par l'or'; what col-
ours are there to be revived in a room whose walls are covered 'd'un papier
gras'? The *salon de jeu*, in its drabness, is typical of the problem which, according to Balzac, confronts the writer whose task is to depict contemporary
subjects:

Enfin, les auteurs ont souvent raison dans leurs impertinences contre le temps présent. Le monde nous demande de belles peintures? où en seraient les types? Vos habits mesquins, vos révolutions manquées, vos bourgeois discoureurs, votre religion morte, vos pouvoirs éteints, vos rois en demi-solde, sont-ils donc si poétiques qu'il faille vous les transfigurer?[6]

The 'transfiguration' of this world, it is clear, will demand a power which is anything but 'éteint,' a 'roi' not 'en demi-solde,' a discourse distinct from that of 'bourgeois discoureurs,' a grandeur not contaminated by 'vos habits mesquins'; in short, precisely that *Moi* already implied in the naming of this world as '*vos*': '*vos* habits mesquins, *vos* révolutions manquées,' and yet a *Moi* for which that world is not radically Other, since, 'il faut encore *se souvenir,*' in order to recapture and communicate 'le vif des sensations primordiales.' Yet the barren, shabby *salon de jeu* assumes in its very drabness and nudity, a certain primordial quality. The lush phenomenality which is stripped away permits a certain essence to shine through; this is precisely the difference between evening and morning in the *Salon*. At night there predominates the plenitude of a harmonious whole:

Les salles sont garnies de spectateurs et de joueurs ... Si la passion y abonde, le trop grand nombre d'acteurs vous empêche de contempler face à face le démon du jeu. La soirée est une véritable morceau d'ensemble où la troupe entière crie, où chaque instrument de l'orchestre module sa phrase (13).

The 'démon du jeu' is inseparable from the passion

qui distingue le mari nonchalant de l'amant pâmé sous les fenêtres de sa belle. Le matin seulement arrivent la passion palpitante et le besoin dans sa franche horreur (13).

If the evening gamblers 'viennent y chercher des distractions,' like 'vieillards indigents qui s'y trainent pour s'y réchauffer,' their ecstasy is naïve: their passion seeks an *object* on which to warm itself. The morning gambler has his fire within:

Mais comprenez-vous tout ce que doit avoir de délire et de vigueur dans l'âme d'un homme qui attend avec impatience l'ouverture d'un tripot? ... En ce moment, vous pourrez admirer un véritable joueur qui n'a pas mangé, dormi, vécu, pensé, tant il était rudement flagellé par le fouet de sa martingale, tant il souffrait travaillé par le prurit d'un coup de trente et quarante. A cette heure maudite, vous rencontrerez des yeux dont le calme effraye, des visages qui vous fascinent, des regards qui soulèvent les cartes et les dévorent (13).

The purity of the *jeu* is that of a passion which tolerates no object, except for its agent, its subject; the gambler: if his eyes devour the cards upon which his fate depends, he himself is devoured by his passion, and, paradoxically enough, he thereby becomes the incarnation of that passion, of the *jeu*. The *petit vieillard*, who takes the young man's hat, illustrates this incarnation:

> *Cet homme, dont la longue face blanche n'était plus nourrie que par les soupes gélatineuses de d'Arcet, présentait la pâle image de la passion réduite à son terme le plus simple. Dans ses rides, il y avait trace de vieilles tortures, il devait jouer ses maigres appointements le jour même où il les recevait. Semblable aux rosses sur qui les coups de fouet n'ont plus de prise, rien ne le faisait tressaillir. ... C'était le Jeu incarné (12).*

This incarnation, which permits the *démon du jeu* to be contemplated face to face, and which lends the scene its peculiarly allegorical quality, is paradoxically only manifested through a *disincarnation*, the slow process by which the gamblers are driven and consumed by passion, a process in which this decomposition itself is manifest, negatively, in the furrows it traces: 'dans ses rides, il y avait trace de vieilles tortures ... ,' an *inscription* as significant as it is fatal (and which, it may be noted in passing, is itself the trace of a tradition that culminates in Kafka's *Strafkolonie*). This 'image de la passion réduite à son terme le plus simple' is 'pâle' precisely for this reason: if it is an image, it is less as representation or reproduction of an entity than as inscription, trace, or mark. That this human ruin, (dis)incarnation of the *jeu*, is held together by 'les soupes gélatineuses de d'Arcet' indicates more than simply the flimsy transparence which afflicts all substance in the corrosive atmosphere of the *salon de jeu*.

The naming of Jean-Pierre-Joseph d'Arcet (1777-1844), or rather of his most widely known discovery and project: the synthesis of gelatine, which he hoped (erroneously) might provide a cheap source of nutrition, stands out in the anonymous, self-absorbed world of the casino as an example of what Baudelaire praised as Balzac's 'goût prodigieux du détail.'[7] The detail is indeed prodigious for it establishes a link between the world of the salon and the world outside. D'Arcet's ill-fated efforts quite literally to hold body and soul together (in addition to his work on gelatine, he was known for his research on glue, developed from hides), serve to underscore that their dissociation, so evident in the figures of the gamblers, is by no means limited to the world of the salon. Common to both gamblers and non-gamblers is a social process that consumes the physical existence and energy of individuals, while at the same time producing power of quite another kind. In the salon, this power goes by the name of the JEU, or the 'démon du jeu.' Outside, it has other names.

One of the most interesting of those names is spelled out in a text written some thirty years after *La Peau de chagrin*, and yet which in many respects deals with similar scenes and processes, albeit in a mode generally classified as 'non-fictional.' In this text we also find the story of an unwitting hero, who, without fully realizing the consequences, finds himself involved in a contract whose fatal consequences he dimly anticipates. Like the young man on the threshold of the casino, who enters it 'sans trop hésiter,' this other hero is led on towards his destiny, 'timid, hesitant, like someone bringing his own hide to market and who has nothing to expect but – the tannery.'[8]

The hesitant hero is, of course, the worker, who is being led from the apparently idyllic sphere of circulation and exchange, populated by free and equal individuals, contractual partners, to the infernal sphere of production, in the text that tells the story called *Capital*. Among other things, that story relates how, in the capitalist mode of production, body and soul necessarily grow further and further apart, and how in the process a new and quite transcendent 'soul' comes into being: the soul of what Marx describes as 'value,' incarnated (and also disincarnated) in the commodity. If the 'themes' of the initial pages of *Capital* bear a striking ressemblance to those of *La Peau de chagrin* (not the least of which relates to the important and ambivalent function of surfaces: skin, hide, envelopes, fabrics, garments that protect and conceal), Marx's discussion of the interaction of circulation, exchange, and production, above all in regard to the commodity, can serve to elucidate the curious phenomena that characterize the *salon de jeu*.

In the latter we find, as already noted, individuals driven and consumed by a passion, the object of which is less than clear: 'Toujours en opposition avec lui-même, trompant ses espérances par ses maux présents, et ses maux par un avenir qui ne lui appartient pas' – Balzac's description of the gambler could apply to the worker as well. The difference, of course, is that the latter is constrained to sell his labour power in order to survive, that is to perpetuate his physical existence, whereas what drives the gambler is something other than simple self-preservation. And yet, is self-preservation really so simple? Can it be thought of as a merely physical or 'natural' matter, entailing primarily biological survival? For Marx, at least, the answer is univocal: if the entire realm of economics presupposes something called 'need,' the latter cannot be construed as being purely 'natural,' but is mediated by society, culture, history. Thus, Marx begins his discussion of the commodity both by asserting its relation to *need*, and by stressing that such needs can also include imagination and desire:

> *A commodity is, in the first place, an object outside us, a thing that by its properties satisfies human needs [Bedürfnisse] of some sort or another. The nature of such wants, whether for instance they spring from the stomach or from fancy, makes no difference.*[9]

Thus, even in the apparently straightforward case of the worker (and who, to-day, would still adhere to such a conviction?), the external constraints of self-preservation which compel him to sell his labour power, are doubtless less 'ex-ternal' – in the sense of 'natural' or 'biological' – than has often been supposed. Even at its most rudimentary level, that of 'need,' self-preservation implies a distinct project of subjective self-fulfilment, which in turn is mediated not simply by natural, but also by cultural, social, and historical as well as individual factors. If Marx therefore leaves the category of need deliberately vague and suspended (although making quite clear that it founds all discourse on economic matters) it is surely because such discourse is incapable of articulating and determining the category from which it derives. Other discourses will be necessary, and one of them may well be the multifaceted discourse of narrative fiction that confronts us in *La Peau de chagrin*.

Thus, despite the obvious differences separating the 'needs' of the worker and the constraints to which he is subjected (the subject of *Capital*), from those of the gamblers, the fact that Balzac describes the latter also as *besoin* ('la passion palpitante et le besoin dans sa franche horreur') may well be indicative not of terminological imprecision but of great perspicuity. For there is good reason to suspect that what determines 'need,' whether those of the workers or those of the gamblers, is a project of self-fulfilment governed by the project of a subject finally coming into its own, realizing its Self and recovering its essence. If such were the case, then the figure of the gambler would be only a more direct expression of the project already implied in 'self-preservation' and 'need' – in short, in 'economics' as the speculative project of reappropriation. Like the worker, only in more concentrated form, the inveterate, matutinal gambler would then embody the ambivalent passion of such an ambiguous project.

The gambler, then, as opposed to the worker, is engaged in the speculative process of circulation and exchange, without the mediation of objects of use, which is precisely what distinguishes the evening from the morning gambler. The latter operates wholly within the compass of his own desires and dreams, indifferent to the objects that surround him, except insofar as they speak the language of that desire. But however silent that language may be, as language it still requires a mediating medium: the casino is *almost* bare, but not quite; indeed its very threadbare appearance indicates the presence of the one thing that counts: the 'tapis' is 'usé par *l'or*.' The indispensable mediating phenomenon which consumes all others is money. The workers, who don't have it, cannot gamble (although the mass popularity of lotteries would argue for the contrary). The gamblers do, in one sense, have it, although they are perhaps more truly 'had' by it. This sort of ambiguity, involving the question of how money can be possessed, and how it functions, leads us inevitably into the workings of what Marx calls the 'commodity world,' and hence necessitates a brief recapitulation of his analysis of the commodity.

The commodity is a good produced not for consumption by its producer but to be exchanged and hence consumed by another. It is a product of labour, and as such, by definition, it must satisfy a need or a desire; it must have a use value, but its use value is mediated by exchange and by the market. If goods, such as commodities, can be exchanged despite their physical differences, the source of their commensurability is (Marx follows Ricardo on this point) the fact that a certain quantity of labour has been invested in their production. This labour, however, is not simply that of the actual, individual producer; it entails society as a whole, inasmuch as the exchange of commodities implies that at any given time, in the given group to which the exchangers belong, there is an overall reserve of energy that can be expended on the production of goods (ie, on the satisfaction of needs). The exchangeability of goods, as commodities, presupposes what Marx calls 'socially necessary labour' as that which renders the different goods commensurable with one another, and thus regulates their specific exchange value.

But in order for goods to be exchanged on a large scale, there must also be a vehicle of exchange, a medium of circulation, as opposed to direct barter. This is, of course, money, which represents the dual nature of the commodity in the fulness of its contradictory structure. Money is both *one* commodity among others, inasmuch as it is gold or silver, and at the same time *primus inter pares*, since it stands over against all other commodities as that which represents their value of exchange in general, and thus allows for their circulation.

In other words, and this brings us back to the casino, money is both a good with a use value, and an exchange value; and as the latter, it is the direct expression or embodiment of that socially necessary labour that constitutes value. Money, in short, is both substance and (objectified) energy. By virtue of this dual function, in the developed commodity world it becomes counterproductive simply to possess money, to hold on to it as does the miser Gobseck. To keep it is to lose it, to have it lose its force and vitality, just as the dying Gobseck is surrounded by the putrefying carcasses of the commodities he has hoarded. The 'life' of money can only flourish in the medium of circulation and speculation that confers it with its particular value. Money, as Marx writes in the *Grundrisse* (the notebooks preparatory to *Capital*), can be 'realized only by being thrown back into circulation,' by being made 'to disappear in exchange for the singular, particular modes of wealth. ... For the accumulating individual, it is lost, and this disappearance is the only possible way to secure it as wealth.'[10]

This is why neither labour as such nor the effort to retain wealth can directly manifest the law of value: the latter only fulfils itself in a movement of disappearance and reappearance, involving the expense of energy and its transformation into objects, which in turn change into energy. The overall result might be described as a movement of *consumptive production*: individual beings and entities are consumed, dissolve, or expend themselves in a process of circulation and exchange; out of that process, however, a new subject seems to emerge, one which appears to have the 'occult quality of positing value by virtue of being value.'[11] The circulation of commodities is not merely circular, for it implies the accumulation and production of value (and thus, of energy), and this, according to Marx, entails a paradox not to be explained at the level of experience restricted to the sphere of circulation and exchange. It is only when we follow the hesitant labourer and the eager capitalist into the sphere of production that the 'secret' of surplus value can be discovered. It is, of course, the secret of the one commodity that can produce more value than it itself is worth: the commodity of labour power, sold to the capitalist by the labourer.

We shall have occasion, later, to return to this occult sphere of production. For the present, however, it may suffice simply to signal a certain similarity between commodity production and value form as analyzed by Marx and the features which characterize the salon de jeu at the beginning of *La Peau de chagrin*. In each case, we are confronted with scenes of speculation (in all senses of the term) in which the passionate effort to accumulate wealth and power results in its opposite, the slow but ineluctable consumption of the speculators. Both workers and gamblers are confronted by phenomena that are no less worn and threadbare, but as such all the more transparent as signs and envelopes of a power that transcends the individuals it consumes. Workers and gamblers are both driven by a *need* that is not clearly distinguishable from a *passion*, since its goal is inseparable from the preservation of the self (although with the gamblers the importance of direct use value clearly recedes before the reveries of power as such, without intervening, mediating objects). For both, a contract is established in their respective spheres of circulation and exchange, but it is a contract made over the heads of the contracting parties, as it were, and yet which will not be any less *binding*.

In short, the *salon de jeu* mirrors the law of consumptive production that prevails in the commodity world outside, while eliminating the mediation of use value (in accordance with the latter's subordinate rôle in the commodity). Only one feature would seem to be lacking in this allegorical frontispiece, not simply of the novel, but of the commodity world that sets its scene: if the hesitant young man who is to be the hero of the novel occupies a position analogous to that of the timid and timorous worker in Marx's description, the figure that leads him to his doom, the businesslike, zealous capitalist, appears to be missing.

Missing, that is, from the stage. And yet there is a figure in the wings whose presence is all the more powerful for its being hardly visible as such, a figure who directs the spectacle from a position offstage with the sureness and sovereignty that leave little doubt as to its authority. This figure is, of course, the Author-Narrator, who addresses his readers in order to situate them vis-à-vis the scene, and in so doing necessarily situates himself. Can there be any doubt that this figure (or rather, since it is never manifest as such, or represented), this *voice*, emanates from a subject who alone can lay claim to all property rights to the text we are about to read, the scene we are about to see? If reading a text has anything to do with following a leader, it is this voice that we shall have to follow.

4

The Entry

The young man, as he enters this scene, is deaf to the eloquence of its stillness: 'l'inconnu n'écouta pas ce conseil vivant (le petit vieillard), placé là sans doute par la Providence,' and announced to the reader by the narrator: 'comme elle a mis le dégoût à la porte de tous les mauvais lieux' (12). Indeed, it is his deafness which allows him, the outsider, to enter a cosmos which, for those who hear its voice, has neither entry nor exit:

> Il entra résolument dans la salle, où le son de l'or exerçait une éblouissante fascination sur les sens en pleine convoitise (12).

The entry of this 'jeune inconnu,' who bears his anonymity aloft like a torch, is no less the entry of the reader, who is ushered in by the narrator: 'Quand vous entrez dans une maison de jeu ... ' (11) 'Essayez de jeter un regard furtif sur cette arène, entrez!' (13) That the 'vous' can embrace both the 'jeune inconnu' and the equally nameless reader is legitimized by the universality of the Law under whose protection the *salon de jeu* stands, the law of value.
Yet the young man, like the reader, must be an outsider in order to enter: he must come from outside and retain a certain alterity. The young man, like the reader, provides the *difference*, without which the perpetual circularity of the *salon de jeu* would collapse into total indifference. Yet this entry is anything but simple: if it provides a moment, a standpoint, from which the infinite repetition of the *jeu* can be depicted as a *tableau*, a snapshot, the entry itself is already contaminated by the scene which it does not merely introduce, but

organizes. After entering the building, 'sans trop hésiter,' the young man enters the *salon* itself three times, in a triple-take, as it were, in slow motion, during which time the *salon* is described: he enters *'résolument dans la salle,'* then enters again: 'au moment où le jeune homme entra dans le salon, quelques joueurs s'y trouvaient déjà' (14) – the moment of the photograph – and finally, it is precisely at the crucial moment of the *jeu* itself that the young man opens the door:

> *le* tailleur *et le* banquier *venaient de jeter sur les pentes ce regard blême qui les tue, et disaient d'une voix grêle: 'Faites le jeu!' quand le jeune homme ouvrit la porte (15).*

This 'entry' is thus not a simple *event*, and if it permits the *salon* to present itself, it in turn manifests a certain complicity with the *salon*. That the young man is not a total outsider, that his entry is no simple beginning, is indicated not by the mere repetition of the 'event,' but by its inner structure, which, in its very affirmation, reveals an inherent discordance. The young man enters the building *'sans trop* hésiter,' that is, with a certain hesitation; he enters the *salon* itself 'résolument,' that is, overcoming a certain resistance. This ambiguity is grasped at once by the gamblers, experts in discerning the still voice which animates the Sign: 'Au premier coup d'œil, les joueurs lurent sur le visage du novice quelque horrible mystère' (15); this silent communication designates the newcomer as no simple novice:

> *Comme, lorsqu'un célèbre criminel arrive au bagne, les condamnés l'accueillent avec respect, ainsi tous ces démons humains, experts en tortures, saluèrent une douleur inouïe, une blessure profonde que sondait leur regard, et reconnurent un de leurs princes à la majesté de sa muette ironie, à l'élégante misère de ses vêtements (16, my emphasis).*

The origin and significance of that *'blessure profonde'* is mysterious, and will remain so until the young man recounts his history in the second part of the novel; yet it is already clear that the 'douleur inouïe,' 'sa muette ironie,' 'l'élégante misère de ses vêtements,' and above all, the profundity of that *'blessure,'* make the anonymous young man not merely a novice but 'un célèbre criminel,' a Prince – *primus inter pares.* Yet this prince is also an Infant; prince by virtue of being an infant, *in-fans* in 'la majesté de sa *muette* ironie,' and in years. If this 'ange sans rayons' is, in a certain sense wayward ('égaré dans sa route,' 16), what distinguishes him most emphatically from 'tous ces démons humains' is the fact that he still has a *'route;'* and if his past has been one of struggle, unlike the joueurs, he is as yet neither whipped nor stripped:

Cette figure avait encore vingt-cinq ans, et le vice paraissait n'y être qu'un accident. La verte vie de la jeunesse y luttait encore avec les ravages d'une impuissante lubricité. Les ténèbres et la lumière, le néant et l'existence s'y combattaient en produisant tout à la fois de la grâce et de l'horreur (16, my emphasis).

If we recall the sense in which money, the medium of the *jeu*, is itself the representation of a certain vital struggle, of the expense of energy aimed at the (re-)production of life as living presence, this young man and the conflict he embodies appear as the counterpart and adversary of the demonic sovereign of the *jeu*. And yet, the infancy of the young man reaches the point where his masculinity recedes before a more original innocence:

Tous ces professeurs émérités de vice et d'infamie, semblables à une vieille femme édentée prise de pitié à l'aspect d'une belle fille qui s'offre à la corruption ... (16).

The fact that this confrontation, the 'belle fille qui s'offre à la corruption,' and the 'vieille femme *édentée*,' is subsumed under the unity of a certain femininity, indicates again that this vital struggle takes place within the complicity of the adversaries, an *entente* between 'la verte vie de la jeunesse' and the force which ravages it, 'une impuissante lubricité.' This complicity between innocence and corruption, virtue and vice, grace and horror, purity and impurity is already manifest in the appearance of the young man (although it is eloquent in the metaphors that appearance suggests): 'Ses mains, jolies comme des mains de femme,' are yet 'd'une douteuse propreté; enfin, depuis deux jours il ne portait plus de gants' (16). Deprived of its protective covering, an original innocence reveals itself, yet only at the cost of its corruption: the *propre* appears, and thereby is soiled, becomes *malpropre:*

Si le tailleur et les garçons de salle eux-mêmes frissonnèrent, c'est que les enchantements de l'innocence florissaient par vestiges dans ces formes grêles et fines, dans ces cheveux blonds et rares, naturellement bouclés (16, my emphasis).

'Blonds et rares,' like the 'pièce d'or qu'il avait à la main' and which he will shortly throw – 'sans calcul sur le tapis' – the young man confronts the corruption of the *jeu* with the vestigial innocence of his 'green life,' of his flesh, hair, with a purity which is the diametrical opposite, and yet counterpart, of the sordid barrenness of the *salon*, of the 'tapis *vert*, usé par l'or.' And when he moves through the silent, immobile room, in which the only other sound and movement is that of gold, to cast his bet, he prepares a sacrifice which is at once a defiance (*sans calcul*) of the *jeu*, whose 'rules' he thus violates. The desperate vitality of the young man, his blindness to the signs of the *jeu*, indicate not the passion of 'sens en plein *convoitise*,' the passion of pure possession, but another desire, whose figure is, in all senses, a certain *abandonment*, ('jeta sans calcul'). A young Italian, 'aux cheveux noirs, au teint olivâtre,' whose 'tête méridionale respirait l'or et le feu' (14), whose very vital element and substance is the *jeu*, following its rules, listening for its hints (who 'paraissait écouter des pressentiments secrets qui crient fatalement à un joueur: "Oui! – Non!" [14]) – this young Italian grasps the challenge and violation of the *jeu*, and 'saisit avec le fanatisme de la passion une idée qui vint lui sourire ... porta sa masse d'or en opposition au jeu de l'inconnu' (17). He reads correctly, wins, and then explains:

> – *J'ai entendu, dit-il, une voix qui me criait dans l'oreille: 'Le Jeu aura raison contre le désespoir de ce jeune homme.' – Ce n'est pas un joueur, reprit le banquier; autrement, il aurait groupé son argent en trois masses pour se donner plus de chances (18).*

The *banquier* is right and wrong. Unlike the gamblers, the young man, as we shall soon be told, comes to the casino not to speculate but *to learn*, not to acquire a fortune but to discover his fate. The absence of calculation in his throw, in contrast to those who listen for the voice of the *jeu*, expresses total self-abandonment to an incalculable Chance, to the necessity of a destiny. If the young man merits the name of 'prince,' it is because what he risks is not 'mere' money, not a representation, but his very life, his Self, and in so doing he participates more profoundly even than the inveterate gamblers in the essence of the *jeu* ('vous êtes au jeu, vous ... ' exclaims its *porte-parole*, the narrator). And indeed, having lost his bet, the young stranger departs with 'l'air d'un Anglais pour qui la vie n'a plus de mystères.' Yet his *jeu* is not finished even if its trajectory has already been traced: the infinite circularity of a certain circulation is not so much broken as bracketed, and the 'passion palpitante' that reigns in the casino accompanies the young man, as he exits, whistling its song and sealing its pact:

> *Le jeune homme passait sans réclamer son chapeau; mais le vieux molosse, ayant remarqué le mauvais état de cette guenille, la lui rendit sans proférer une parole; le joueur restitua la fiche par un mouvement machinal, et descendit les escaliers en sifflant di tanti palpiti d'un souffle si faible qu'il entendit à peine lui-même les notes délicieuses (18, my emphasis).*

It is a beginning, 'vers la fin ... ' and *tanti palpiti* still separate that 'souffle si faible,' scarcely audible, from the final silence. But this silence is already present: in the *salon*, in the *infancy* of the young man, and in a narrative voice, which, for all its resonance, can only make itself heard through the mute metaphoricity of a *text*.

5

Postponement

The scene in the *salon de jeu* is played *avant-scène*, a pantomime in front of the curtain, a *prelude* in the most emphatic sense, anticipating the actual 'drama,' which begins as the young stranger steps out into the street, having acquired that fatal certainty he had sought. If the young man's destiny has been sealed in the *salon*, he must leave it in order to accomplish that destiny: in the *salon*, we remember, 'il ne s'y trouve même pas un clou pour faciliter le suicide.' Existence, in the *salon de jeu*, admits no radical distinction between life and death, living and dying converge. Death loses its alterity when life appears as a process of self-consumption: the wrinkles of the old man, incarnation of the *jeu*, no less than the traces on the felt surface of the gambling table, are the features, the negative manifestation of a living death. Yet in the closed circulation of the *salon de jeu*, where nothing can be *lost*, life has become not merely self-consumption, but production as well: consumptive production, from the point of view of the individual – gamblers and things – but from the point of view of the whole, of the *jeu* itself, productive consumption. Life thus becomes, as Benjamin observed of the German Baroque *Trauerspiel*, the production of corpses, and the growing corpse is the *presentation of death*.[1] If suicide is inconceivable in this world, it is because death is perennially present, *alive* in the *passion de jeu*. To accomplish his destiny, the young man must leave this magic circle. For him, death and life still form an alternative, the combat of 'le néant et l'existence,' and if his fate is sealed by the *jeu*, it still requires his active acceptance – a leap into the

Seine – to be realized. *His* death, unlike that of the gamblers, will have the form of an *event*, indeed of a *fait divers*:

> *Chaque suicide est un poème sublime de mélancholie. Où trouverez-vous, dans l'océan des littératures, un livre surnageant qui puisse lutter de génie avec cet entrefilet:*
>> *'Hier, à quatre heures, une femme s'est jetée dans la Seine du haut du Pont des Arts.'*
>> *Devant ce laconisme parisien, les drames, les romans, tout pâlit (18-19, my emphasis).*

For the suicide, as for the gambler, death involves a certain disappearance, yet with a crucial distinction: the living corpse of the aged gambler is the sign of a wasted life, but it is a life which has burned itself out, consumed by the passion of gambling. The suicide, precisely by putting an 'end' to *her* life, conserves it in its enigmatic integrity as a meaningful mystery, the aura of which survives in a newspaper report that is no less 'indéchiffrable' than the corpse which the young man intends to 'produce':

> *Une mort en plein jour lui parut ignoble, il résolut de mourir pendant la nuit, afin de livrer un cadavre indéchiffrable à cette Société qui méconnaissait la grandeur de sa vie (20).*

The distance between the sign and what it designates, between the 'entre-filet' and the woman suicide, between the 'cadavre indéchiffrable' and 'la grandeur de sa vie,' measures the space 'entre une mort volontaire et la féconde espérance dont la voix appelait un jeune homme à Paris' (18); this distance does not merely separate, it constitutes the grandeur of an enigma in the resonance of a *voice*: that which announces the hopes of a young man in Paris and which echoes in the silence of a self-inflicted death, life determining its own end, its 'end' as its 'own.'

It is this vocal continuity, permeating a certain death, that enables the narrative voice to pass continuously from the apotheosis of suicide to the inner voice of the young man's meditation:

> *L'inconnu fut assailli par mille pensées semblables, qui passaient en lambeaux dans son âme, comme des drapeaux déchirés voltigent au milieu d'une bataille (19).*

If the narrative discourse appeared to emanate from a point outside the *Salon de Jeu*, while setting its scene, here narration and narrative converge and merge in a life meditating upon its own end. The fact that it is the voice of this life which endows such meditation with a certain coherence is highlighted and set off by an ominous inscription that the young man reads as he stands gazing at the Seine:

> *Il frissonna tout à coup en voyant de loin, sur le port des Tuileries, la bar-*
> *aque surmontée d'un écriteau où ces paroles sont tracées en lettres hautes*
> *d'un pied: SECOURS AUX ASPHYXIES (19).*

That this warning is announced by 'un écriteau,' which itself seems strangely to embody the danger of a certain asphyxiation, suggests a significance beyond its immediate effect. The latter is, however, important enough, since it entails a deferral of the young man's intentions ('une mort en plein jour lui parut ignoble' [20]) which will allow the novel to unfold. The text thus is inscribed in the space of a postponement, a deferred asphyxiation.

Alone, wandering through the streets of Paris, the young man reflects upon his value:

> *Mort, il valait cinquante francs; mais vivant il n'était qu'un homme de*
> *talent sans protecteurs, sans amis, sans paillasse, sans tambour, un véritable*
> *zéro social, inutile à l'Etat, qui n'en avait aucun souci (20).*

'Sans tambour' he is reduced to silence in a world that speaks in the metonymic language of value. Reduced to itself, without money, property, or patron, the young man's life is worthless, but it is not extinct. Rather, it is reduced to pure punctuality, to sheer potential that slumbers like the coals of a fire ready, at the proper instant, to burst into flame. That instant comes when the young man hears a familiar sound:

> *Il se prit à sourire, remit philosophiquement les mains dans ses goussets, et*
> *allait reprendre son allure d'insouciance où perçait un froid dédain, quand*
> *il entendit avec surprise quelques pièces retentir d'une manière véritable-*
> *ment fantastique au fond de sa poche. Un sourire d'espérance illumina son*
> *visage, glissa de ses lèvres sur ses traits, sur son front, fit briller de joie ses*
> *yeux et ses joues sombres. Cette étincelle de bonheur ressemblait à ces feux*
> *qui courent dans les vestiges d'un papier déjà consumé par la flamme; mais*
> *le visage eut le sort des cendres noires, il redevint triste quand l'inconnu,*
> *après avoir vivement retiré la main de son gousset, aperçut trois gros sous*
> *(20).*

This 'find' and the conflagration of happiness it provokes are symptomatic of the fact that the apparently aimless wandering of the young man is also a search: and the gesture of his hand, reaching into the pocket to remove three sous – too little to help – the gesture of discovery followed by that of throwing away ('l'inconnu jeta sa monnaie à l'enfant et au vieux pauvre') – repeats and anticipates the *jeu* of possession and abandonment which we shall come to recognize as the articulation of a desire.

But the young man's wandering is marked by a second discovery:

En arrivant à l'étalage d'un marchand d'estampes, cet homme presque mort rencontra une jeune femme qui descendait d'un brillant équipage. Il contempla délicieusement cette charmante personne, dont la blanche figure était harmonieusement encadrée dans le satin d'un élégant chapeau. Il fut séduit par une taille svelte, par de jolis mouvements. La robe, légèrement relevée par le marchepied, lui laissa voir une jambe dont les fins contours étaient dessinés par un bas blanc et bien tiré (21).

'Image du luxe,' this woman appears also as a luxurious manifestation of the image itself, just as the gambling casino, reducing phenomena to sheer transparency, consumed the image in its very fulfilment. Here, the transparency of the image is resolved in a decisive manner, by a certain *investment*: the woman is lavishly clothed in garments that reveal the *contours* of what they conceal and protect ('lui laissa voir une jambe dont les fins contours étaient dessinés par un bas blanc et bien tiré'). And, if we recall the young man's worn-out hat and frayed gloves, and the nude *malpropreté* of the casino, we see that the essence of this image, the image of luxury, is not so much transparency as a certain translucence. Its archetype is doubtless the veil. This also explains the function of money in the hands of the young woman: as in the casino, the coins 'étincelèrent et sonnèrent sur le comptoir,' on the shop counter, however, they do not disappear in the infinite circulation of the *jeu* but instead are exchanged, transformed into a tangible commodity: the lithographs purchased by the woman. If, as we see, a certain *inscription* is present even here – stressing the continuity with that of the casino, the permanence of a certain *jeu* – there is nevertheless at least a semblance of substantiality, albeit only that of a *representation*: the engraving. As opposed to its function in the gambling casino, where the link between money and life-consuming passion is legibly marked in the features of the gamblers, as the visible, tangible representation of labour power (= value), here in the shop, money is translucent, not transparent. Like the clothes of its possessor, who, we will have occasion to remember, is a woman, the 'essence' of money is *veiled*, what appears is only its power to appropriate, its purchasing power, and not the mortal expense of forces that is its origin.

If money can function as the fetish par excellence, it is because of the privileged relation it bears to the sphere of phenomenality as such. Since it is both one commodity among others (as a product of labour meant to be exchanged), and also the universal means and medium of exchange, money appears both as the essence of phenomenality (it is 'present' in and as the 'beautiful value-soul' [Marx] of all commodities), and as the antithesis of phenomena: to hold on to it, as to a thing, is to lose it. In and of itself, isolated from circulation and exchange, from speculation, money can therefore be described by Marx as nothing more than a 'pure figment of the imagination' ('ein reines Hirngespinst,' or 'festgehaltene blosze Einbildung').[2] This in turn reflects the fact that the essence of money cannot be articulated or restricted to the sphere of phenomenality: what money represents is something invisible as such, and unrepresentable: the expenditure of energy that constitutes value, and constitutes it as a *social* relation. And yet, the goal of that relation remains attached to something that invites representation, imagination, and comprehension, even while eluding them: the goal of self-fulfilment.

The result is inevitably a paradoxical incitement to represent the unrepresentable, or, as in the case of the young man, to uncover what appears to be a mystery, by raising the veils that seem to conceal it:

> *Le jeune homme ... échangea vivement avec la belle inconnue l'œillade la plus perçante que puisse lancer un homme, contre un de ces coups d'œil insouciants jetés au hasard sur les passants (21).*

But, as in the casino, the young man is short-changed: and thus, the mystery – and the story – are preserved.

6

The Store

Il voulut se soustraire aux titillations que produisaient sur son âme les réactions de la nature physique, et se dirigea vers un magasin d'antiquités dans l'intention de donner une pâture à ses sens, ou d'y attendre la nuit en marchandant des objets d'art (22).

The scene which now confronts the young man is the antipode of and thus inextricably tied to the *salon de jeu*. He is overwhelmed at first by the chaotic plenitude, 'un tableau confus, dans lequel toutes les œuvres humaines et divines se heurtaient' (23). The tableau is as confused as the casino is clear, as full as the latter is empty: 'c'était une espèce de fumier philosophique auquel rien ne manquait' (23), these 'trois salles gorgées de civilisation' (24) where 'le commencement du monde et les évènements d'hier se mariaient avec une grotesque bonhomie' (23). Life in all its fullness, nature as well as culture, 'œuvres humaines et divines,' confronts the spectator, who feasts his eyes on the living spectacle which unfolds before him:

Des crocodiles, des singes, des boas empaillés souriaient à des vitraux d'église, semblaient vouloir mordre des bustes, courir après des laques ou grimper sur des lustres (23).

Here, in this first image, the central paradox of the store emerges: the creatures of nature appear on the verge of devouring those of art, and yet nature is only present *as* art, 'œuvres divines,' but still *œuvres*. The representations, the *biens culturels*, which confront the spectator *appear* to be the re-presentation, revivification of the original life they represent, but the appearance is deceptive, the life of these objects is mere appearance, 'une vie trompeuse.' It is not nature which devours art, but art which consumes and annihilates nature: representation is the death of the living presence it represents. The very materiality of the objects, which permits them to appear and to represent, marks the unbridgeable gap between the vitality of nature and the fatality of culture. Cuvier alone has accomplished the poetic task of reviving the representation and resurrecting the past:

> *Il est poète avec des chiffres, il est sublime en posant un zéro près d'un sept. Il réveille le néant sans prononcer des paroles artificiellement magiques; il fouille une parcelle de gypse, y aperçoit une empreinte, et vous crie: 'Voyez!' Soudain les marbres s'animalisent, la mort se vivifie, le monde se déroule! (29)*

Cuvier performs his magical task without pronouncing 'des paroles *artificiellement* magiques,' without *words* at all: his magic is authentic because it adds literally nothing, 'en posant *un zéro* près d'un sept'; the zero itself, the addition which is pure because it adds nothing except itself as pure act, performs the magical and poetical act of awakening the dead. The *voice* which accomplishes 'cette épouvantable résurrection' says nothing but merely calls attention to, directs a glance at an *imprint*, and the dead material, 'les marbres s'animalisent.' To be 'poète avec des chiffres' is to neutralize the alterity of representation, of words as well as things, in the pure neutrality of the sign that adds nothing of its own but merely signifies: zero. And yet, this zero which revives the past and wakes the dead is also fatal, the resurrection is 'épouvantable' because it is 'une sorte d'Apocalypse rétrograde.' By resurrecting the past it buries the present, and even if this buried present can now itself be resurrected in a future, a certain voice protests:

> *En présence de cette épouvantable résurrection due à la voix d'un seul homme, la miette dont l'usufruit nous est concédé dans cet infini sans nom, commun à toutes les sphères et que nous avons nommé LE TEMPS, cette minute de vie nous fait pitié. Nous nous demandons, écrasés que nous sommes sous tant d'univers en ruine, à quoi bon nos gloires, nos haines, nos amours; et si, pour devenir un point intangible dans l'avenir, la peine de vivre doit s'accepter? Déracinés du présent, nous sommes morts jusqu'à notre valet de chambre entre et vienne nous dire: 'Madame la Comtesse a répondu qu'elle attendait monsieur' (30).*

Crushed under the sheer weight of this 'épouvantable résurrection due à la voix d'un seul homme,' it is significantly enough another voice, that of a servant, announcing the presence of a woman ('Madame la Comtesse ... attendait'), which saves the present. Yet, for the moment no countess is waiting and no valet is there to announce her arrival: there is only the young man confronted by the apocalyptic accumulation of works, and after a short while he begins to lose his bearings: 'il voulut choisir ses jouissances; mais à force de regarder, de penser, de rêver, il tomba sous la puissance d'une fièvre due peut-être à la faim qui rugissait dans ses entrailles' (24). Perhaps it is this very hunger which leads him to attempt to absorb the very life of the objects he observes:

> *Il s'accrochait à toutes les joies, saisissait toutes les douleurs, s'emparait de toutes les formules d'existence en éparpillant si généreusement sa vie et ses sentiments sur les simulacres de cette nature plastique et vide. ... Poursuivi par les formes les plus étranges, par des créations merveilleuses assises sur les confins de la mort et de la vie, il marchait dans les enchantements d'un songe. Enfin, doutant de son existence, il était comme ces objets curieux, ni tout à fait mort, ni tout à fait vivant (27).*

The attempt is a failure because these objects are only 'simulacres,' a second nature, but one which is 'plastique et vide.' It is a world of representations, situated 'sur les confins de la mort et de la vie,' and the only undeniable reality is the fatal expense of energy that they embody, an expense which the young man repeats in his futile effort to absorb their apparent vitality, while succeeding only in dissipating his own ('en éparpillant si généreusement sa vie'). Thus, despite initial appearances, the second nature of this shop is bathed in a light not unlike that of the *salon de jeu*:

> *Quand il entra dans les nouveaux magasins, le jour commençait à pâlir; mais la lumière semblait inutile aux richesses resplendissant d'or et d'argent qui s'y trouvaient entassées.*
>
> *Les plus coûteux caprices de dissipateurs morts sous des mansardes après avoir possédé plusieurs millions, étaient dans ce vaste bazar des folies humaines. Une écritoire payée cent mille francs et rachetée pour cent sous, gisait auprès d'une serrure à secret dont le prix aurait suffi jadis à la rançon d'un roi. Là, le genie humain apparaissait dans toutes les pompes de sa misère, dans toute la gloire de ses gigantesques petitesses.*
>
> *... Enfin c'était des travaux à dégoûter du travail, des chefs-d'œuvre accumulés à faire prendre en haine les arts et à tuer l'enthusiasme (27-8).*

The sun that shines here is the same as in the *Salon de Jeu*, the anti-physis which is 'd'or et d'argent.' And here as there, this *or-argent* is the symbol and sign of vital energy expending itself in a certain labour, one which appears to be the (re)-production of living presence but which is, in fact, its consumption.

These objects, as representations of culture and as commodities, are the signs not so much of life as of death. At first there is an apparently endless struggle:

> Il étouffait sous les débris de cinquante siècles évanouis, il était malade de toutes ces pensées humaines, assassiné par le luxe et les arts, oppressé sous ces formes renaissantes qui, pareilles à des monstres enfantés sous ses pieds par quelque malin génie, lui livraient un combat sans fin (28).

Then, finally, silence and darkness, as appearance itself disappears:

> Pendant un moment encore, les vagues reflets du couchant lui permirent d'apercevoir indistinctement les fantômes par lesquels il était entouré; puis toute cette nature morte s'abolit dans une même teinte noire (31, my italics).

Thus, despite the evident differences between the plenitude of the shop and the nudity of the casino, the verdict of the Jeu is confirmed by this 'nature morte' which 's'abolit,' portending the suicide it announces: 'La nuit, l'heure de mourir était subitement venue' (31). And again, as in the salon de jeu, there appears the figure of a 'petit vieillard':

> Tout à coup, il crut avoir été appelé par une voix terrible, et il tressaillit comme lorsque au milieu d'un brûlant cauchemar nous sommes précipités d'un seul bond dans les profondeurs d'un abîme. Il ferma les yeux, les rayons d'une vive lumière l'éblouissaient: il voyait briller au sein des ténèbres une sphère rougeâtre dont le centre était occupé par un petit vieillard qui se tenait debout ... (31).

This old man, whose summons will be echoed by another voice, even closer to the edge of the abyss into which the young man feels himself hurled, takes full possession of his guest, just as the vieillard of the gambling casino was himself possessed by the Jeu. The antiquaire, however, will not take from the young man, but give. First, he confronts him with Raphael's portrait of Jesus, which dispels the phantoms and recalls a certain reality:

> A l'aspect de cette immortelle création, il oublia les fantaisies du magasin, les caprices de son sommeil, redevint homme, reconnut dans le vieillard une créature de chair, bien vivante, nullement fantasmagorique, et revécut dans le monde réel (34).

If the objects in the shop are the tombs and monuments of the living presence they only re-present; if they, and their owner, who himself appears as 'le Peseur d'or ... sorti de son cadre' (32), embody the death of reality, spectral and phantasmatic, it is no accident that precisely this one portrait should, for an instant, dispel the spectres to reveal 'une créature de chair, bien vivante, nullement fantasmagorique.' For it is a portrait which represents soul of representation itself, the incarnation of the divine, its presentation in the human, and the promise of a re-presentation – a resurrection – which will be not death but life, not a moment of absence but an eternity of presence. It is a manifestation, a phenomenon, which is at once its own source of light:

> La tête du Sauveur des hommes paraissait sortir des ténèbres figurées par un fond noir; une auréole de rayons étincelait vivement autour de sa chevelure d'où cette lumière voulait sortir (34).

And as its brilliance overcomes the shadows, which remain its *fond*, its *word* makes the silence eloquent and writes past and future into the space of its reverberation:

> Les lèvres vermeilles venaient de faire entendre la parole de vie, et le spectateur en cherchait le retentissement sacré dans les airs, il en demandait les ravissantes paraboles au silence, il l'écoutait dans l'avenir, la retrouvait dans les enseignements du passé (ibid.).

Yet this 'parole de vie' is itself short-lived; the old man brings the young spectator back to 'reality,' the reality of the shop:

> J'ai couvert cette toile de pièces d'or, dit froidement le marchand. Eh bien, il va falloir mourir! s'écria le jeune homme ... (34).

Everything in the store, including the sublime portrait of Raphael, is covered with gold. Here, as in the *salon de jeu*, money destroys a certain life in its immediacy and its individuality, and yet, paradoxically, appears itself as eternal life: incarnated first in the passion of gambling and here in the indestructible power of the antique dealer. 'Sec et maigre' like the old man in the *salon*, he is the precise counterpart of the incarnation of the *jeu*: the gamblers are *possessed*, the *marchand* possesses. Both are moved by a single passion, but whereas that passion confronts the gamblers as their Other, as the *passion de jeu* that consumes their vital energy, draining them dry, the *marchand* appears to have mastered his desire and harnessed its force, which no longer confronts him as an alien demon. His power derives from his possessions, which he possesses not simply as objects, as the living presence represented in the portrait of Jesus, but as commodities, whose value in gold 'represents' the death of all determinate incarnation (of 'concrete' labour), and yet, as such, the resurrection of a life which is abstract, universal, ubiquitous ('abstract' labour). To possess commodities, therefore, is to inhabit that world of signs which characterizes the commodity-language, the constant circulation between appearance and essence, representation and concept, object and money, use value and exchange value. Since the exchange value of a commodity is the abstraction from, the negation of its use value, the marchand must have the *'seconde vue'* required to perform that negation, to penetrate the phenomenal exteriority to the commodity-soul within, to decipher the commodity-sign, distinguishing use value as the 'arbitrary' signifier from exchange value as transcendental *signifié*. Yet what separates this *marchand* from his more prosaic counterparts is that he rightly grasps this *signifié*, whose manifestation is money, as being itself a *signifiant*: the true transcendental *signifié* is not simply value, money, but the 'abstract human' labour which produces it, and this labour is nothing other than the movement of a certain life, expending its vital energy in order to reproduce and reappropriate itself in the form of living presence. This is the movement – and desire – which possesses the gamblers and which the *marchand* has masterfully appropriated:

> *J'ai tout vu, mais tranquillement, sans fatigue; je n'ai jamais rien désiré, j'ai tout attendu. Je me suis promené dans l'univers comme dans le jardin d'une habitation qui m'appartenait (40).*

To possess without being possessed, to live without dying, to appropriate without being expropriated, this is the secret which the old man reveals to his listener:

> *Je vais vous révéler en peu de mots un grand mystère de la vie humaine. L'homme s'épuise par deux actes instinctivement accomplis qui tarissent les sources de son existence. Deux verbes expriment toutes les formes que prennent ces deux causes de mort: VOULOIR ET POUVOIR! Entre ces deux termes de l'action humaine, il est une autre formule dont s'emparent les sages, et je lui dois le bonheur et ma longévité. Vouloir nous brûle, et pouvoir nous détruit; mais SAVOIR laisse notre faible organisation dans un perpétuel état de calme. Ainsi le désir ou le vouloir est mort en moi, tué par la pensée; le mouvement ou le pouvoir s'est résolu par le jeu naturel de mes organes. En deux mots, j'ai placé ma vie, non dans le cœur qui se brise, non dans les sens qui s'émoussent, mais dans le cerveau qui ne s'use pas et qui survit à tout (39-40).*

If desire (*vouloir*) and power (*pouvoir*) are fatal, it is because they involve an expense which is condemned as uneconomical, a mortal waste of the store of vital energies. The gamblers in the casino and the young man's vertigo in the shop testify to the perils of such wasteful expense. But as an antidote to this unprofitable investment of energy the *marchand* proposes a certain *ideality*: 'Que reste-t-il d'une possession matérielle?' he demands rhetorically, and responds: 'une idée' (40). Yet in the commodity-world this 'idea' is more real, more effective than material reality itself: it is the idea of *value*, which is the invisible essence of the object as commodity and which transforms its material existence into an allegory of its essence. If value can be *represented* in a use value – or more adequately, in the universal equivalent, money – it itself, as abstract social labour, can never appear directly in the form of an entity. Thus, if the determinate object represents the expense of a certain energy, the exhaustion of a certain living being, value, the objectification of labour *in the realm of ideality* appears, *qua* objectification, to contain the secret of life. The possessor of value has at his disposal the energies of life without the fatal expense of their production. If we recall that labour, according to Marx (who here follows a tradition at least as old as Aristotle), is the production or realization of a representation, its objectification in and as *value* is the quintessential representation of that original, and originally deferred, presence which bears the name of 'life.' For the ideal commodity owner, and the *marchand* is clearly such a one, the significance of the commodity as a repository of value is ultimately not money but *life* itself. Hence, his concern is less with individual objects than with the (ideal yet real) whole they represent:

> *Oh! comment préférer de fébriles, de légères admirations pour quelque chairs plus ou moins colorées, pour des formes plus ou moins rondes; comment préférer tous les désastres de vos volontés trompées à la faculté sublime de faire comparaître en soi l'univers, au plaisir immense de se mouvoir sans être garrotté par les liens du temps ni par les entraves de l'espace,* au plaisir de tout embrasser, de tout voir, *de se pencher sur le bord du monde pour interroger les autres sphères, pour écouter Dieu? (41, my emphasis).*

True possession, in the commodity-world, is always possession of a representation: and since representations pertain to the realm of a certain ideality, they can be most adequately possessed intuitively:

> *Oh! savoir, jeune homme, n'est-ce pas jouir intuitivement? n'est-ce pas découvrir la substance même du fait et s'en emparer essentiellement? Que reste-t-il d'une possession matérielle? une idée. Jugez alors combien doit être belle la vie d'un homme qui, pouvant empreindre toutes les réalités dans sa pensée, transporte en son âme les sources du bonheur, en extrait mille voluptés idéales dépouillées des souillures terrestres. La pensée est la clef de tous les trésors, elle procure les joies de l'avare sans en donner les soucis. Aussi ai-je plané sur le monde, où mes plaisirs ont toujours été des jouissances intellectuelles (40).*

Intellectual, intuitive possession ('jouissances') provides for an expense which spares the physical forces of the speculator since it is, in essence, *imaginative*:

> *N'ayant jamais lassé mes organes, je jouis encore d'une santé robuste. Mon âme ayant hérité de toute la force dont je n'abusais pas, cette tête est en-*

core mieux meublée que ne le sont mes magasins. Là, dit-il en se frappant le front, là sont les vrais millions (40-1).

Thus gradually emerges the difference between the *marchand* and the gamblers. Both inhabit an imaginary world, a space of representation and of circulation; but whereas the gamblers are tormented and driven by their desire to possess, ultimately, the lineaments of luxury in the form of 'concrete' objects, the *marchand* knows that the safest and surest, indeed the only form of enduring possession is that which remains within the sphere of circulation and of representation, which resigns itself to possess its 'object' solely in its representations, by intuition, imagination, vision:

J'ai vu le monde entier. Mes pieds ont foulé les plus hautes montagnes de l'Asie et de l'Amérique, j'ai appris tous les langages humains, et j'ai vécu sous tous les régimes. J'ai prêté mon argent à un Chinois en prenant pour gage le corps de son père, j'ai dormi sous la tente de l'Arabe sur la foi de sa parole, j'ai signé des contrats dans toutes les capitales européennes, et j'ai laissé sans crainte mon or dans le wigwam des sauvages; enfin j'ai tout obtenu, parce que j'ai tout su dédaigner. Ma seule ambition a été de voir. Voir, n'est-ce pas savoir? (40)

Paradoxically, it is because the *marchand* has renounced a certain materiality that he is able to possess the *works* of human culture in commodity form, whereas the gamblers are condemned to live the mirage of wealth within the barren walls of the *salon de jeu*. Yet what perhaps is the most decisive difference between the gambler and the *marchand* is indicated by the latter's ability to avoid the consumption of a certain *chagrin:*

Ce que les hommes appellent chagrins, amours, ambitions, revers, tristesse, est, pour moi, des idées que je change en rêveries; au lieu de les sentir, je les exprime, je les traduis; au lieu de leur laisser dévorer ma vie, je les dramatise, je les développe; je m'en amuse comme de romans que je lirais par une vision intérieure (40, my emphasis).

The merchant's shop is thus not merely a collection of works but a work of art itself, to be read like a novel. The *marchand* is more than a collector, he is a creator, an author, and his voice fills *his* shop much like that other voice filled the *salon de jeu*, reading the scene 'par une vision intérieure,' announcing and assuring the meaning of its signs, developing them by a certain envelopment, divesting them of their 'natural skin' (Marx: *'Naturalhaut'*) to reveal their elusive value-soul, which unlike Goethe's *schöne Seele*, resides not in the security of an impermeable inwardness but on the surface of a certain circulation.

Yet there is one object in this entire store which eludes such development, which cannot be bought or sold, which founds and limits the circulation of all value as its origin and end. This object is the *marchand*'s response to the young man's despair – 'eh bien, il va falloir mourir!' – just as it is the answer of a certain life to the menace of death. And if it resists development, it is because its essence is to be a certain envelopment, product of a tannery which, as we have seen and will not cease to see, menaces the very life it is designed to protect. This object, which money cannot buy because it represents the origin of money and value themselves, is the *Naturalhaut* par excellence: the *peau de chagrin*.

7

The Truce of a Text

Like the commodity-fetish, the *peau de chagrin* appears to be a 'sensory-suprasensory' object. It is presented by the *marchand* to the young man after the latter has announced his imminent suicide. The talisman is thus introduced as an antidote to a death-wish. At the same time, among all the other objects in the shop, the skin has a privileged relation to life, which it does not merely represent, but *symbolizes*. 'Cette peau symbolique,' as the *marchand* calls it, fulfils in exemplary fashion the function of the symbol, defined by Hegel as:

> *an intuitive conception [eine Anschauung], whose essence or concept more or less coincides with the contents of what it expresses qua symbol.*[1]

If the symbol is characterized by a continuity of expression, the *peau de chagrin* is the exemplary expression of a certain life itself. As skin it both delimits and defines the life it covers, protects, and manifests. As the surface of the living being it is its most immediate and natural *expression*, the limit of its natural property and the condition of its existence in the world. It is no wonder, then, that the skin appears, at first glance, to be a living phenomenon, producing its own appearance, giving off its own light:

> *Par un phénomène inexplicable au premier abord, cette peau projetait au sein de la profonde obscurité qui régnait dans le magasin des rayons si lumineux, que vous eussiez dit une petite comète (36).*

The essence of living manifestation, the skin appears metonymically to have acquired the powers of the life it originally covered. And although this fetish is immediately demystified by the young man, who discovers after scrutinizing the skin that it only reflects light, the strange powers of the talisman remain no less real for being demasked, just as the fetish character of the commodity survives its theoretical analysis. The source of these powers, of the symbolic quality, is a *metonymy*: the skin is *what it is* by virtue of *where it is*: its essence is determined by its position as the exterior limit of a living interior, the defining borderline between proper and improper, own and other, life and non-life; yet it itself is part of the body it determines.

If it is a metonymic relation that constitutes the symbolism of the skin, this is also the source of the talisman's essential instability, indicated in the figure of the comet, which produces light while consuming itself. Condition of vital phenomenality, the skin also marks the crisis of this phenomenality, already announced in the initial and initiating exchange of the *salon de jeu*, an exchange which was also a *dépouillement* ('Quand vous entrez dans une maison de jeu, la loi commence par vous dépouiller de votre chapeau'). Indeed, the passion of the gamblers and the ravages of the *Jeu* are intimately linked to this *Naturhaut* precisely because it is both more and less than simply natural, as the young man soon discovers:

> *Il apporta la lampe près du talisman que le jeune homme tenait à l'envers, et lui fit apercevoir des caractères incrustés dans le tissu cellulaire de cette peau merveilleuse*, comme s'ils eussent été produits par l'animal auquel elle avait jadis appartenu *(37, my emphasis)*.

The skin is thus the bearer of a text, but of a text so intrinsically fused with its bearer that the inscription seems to emanate directly from the creature whose skin has now itself become a text which replaces and conserves its *author*. The skin is not merely a *Naturalhaut*, it is a *Naturaltext*, as the young man shortly discovers. To test the nature of the inscription he borrows the *marchand*'s stiletto – it is not the first time he has used such a knife, as we shall see – and tries to

> *entamer la peau à l'endroit où les paroles se trouvaient écrites; mais, quand il eut enlevé une légère couche de cuir, les lettres y reparurent si nettes et tellement conformes à celles qui étaient imprimées sur la surface, que, pendant un moment, il crut n'en avoir rien ôté (37).*

As soon as he begins to penetrate it, the young man discovers that the text is implanted in the skin, which thus reveals itself to have a certain depth; the text is indeed consubstantial with its bearer. And it is as ineffacable as the skin is indestructible – indestructible, that is, through external causes. For the destruction which the skin embodies comes from within, and its medium is *the word*.

First, the words engraved in the skin. Unlike that other manifestation of life, Raphael's portrait of Jesus in which 'les lèvres vermeilles venaient de faire entendre la parole de vie,' these words are *written*, detached from their author just as the skin is detached from its former wearer. These written words, moreover, must not simply be read: they must be translated, for as the *marchand* remarks, they are written in *Sanscrit*. Yet the text of the novel itself *represents* the text of the talisman in *Arabic*. The 'original' is thus not simply – be it through 'error' or 'design'[2] – obscured: the problem of its *representation*, of the text as representation, is thereby made manifest. The original words, which seem enigmatically to be the work of the animal whose skin now bears them, is described in one language, represented in another, and translated into a third. The very *solidity* of the *Naturaltext* appears thus to elude representation by a text which is not simply natural, the text of the novel.

Whatever the language of the original text may be, the young man reads and translates it. Yet his spoken translation itself is not merely represented; it is represented *as a text*, and, moreover, as one which slightly but decisively alters the *disposition* of its original:

لو ملكتنى ملكت الكل
و لكن عمرك ملكى
واراد الله هكذا
اطلب وستننال مطالبك
و لكن قسن مطالبك على عمرك
وهى هاهنا
فبكل مرامك استسنزل ايامك
أتريد فى
الله مجيبك
آمين .

This, we are told – by the young man or by the narrator? – 'voulait dire en français':

SI TU ME POSSEDES, TU POSSEDERAS TOUT.
MAIS TA VIE M'APPARTIENDRA. DIEU L'A
VOULU AINSI. DESIRE, ET TES DESIRS
SERONT ACCOMPLIS. MAIS REGLE
TES SOUHAITS SUR TA VIE.
ELLE EST LA. A CHAQUE
VOULOIR, JE DECROITRAI
COMME TES JOURS.
ME VEUX-TU?
PRENDS. DIEU
T'EXAUCERA.
SOIT!

Like 'the very spiritual epigraph of the book,' the text has become a visible representation of what it signifies: it has become a symbolic text. If the Arabic is far less clear in this respect, the disposition of the characters of the translation is now rigidly linear and represents both the contraction which is the destiny of the skin and of its possessor, and that valley in the shape of an 'inverted cone' into which the young man will descend in search of a certain origin.

Yet not less important is the fact that this text – its form and disposition – is a representation of a very remote degree: it represents the words of the young man, which, as translation, represent a reading of the 'original' text; this, in turn – be it Sanscrit or Arabic – is itself the written representation of the words of a living being. That the young man's words are not simply represented *in* a text – hardly to be avoided – but *as* a text, seems to testify to the process of representation involved. This process appears in the represented text as one of reduction or contraction of the surface, of the line to the point, of the phrase to the word. On the one hand, this transforms the linearity of discourse into a significant configuration, which, however, is itself no less determined by linearity. On the other hand, the reduction is ambiguous: it can be read either as impoverishment or as concentration. That it is the latter which is intended is indicated by the final word, upon which, as it were, the entire edifice rests. This word is both an exclamation, reproducing the accents of a *voice*, and an *imperative*, expressing a *will*. The will *to be*, to be *present*, to live as the possessor of everything: this is what animates this text, which we now see is the text of a contract. Or perhaps of a pact. For if the *marchand* begins by warning of 'ce contrat si fatalement proposé par je ne sais quelle puissance' (39) – thus recalling once again the 'contrat infernel' of the *Jeu* –

it is a pact that is concluded, or more precisely, 'signed': 'Vous avez signé le pacte, tout est dit' (42). This shift from contract to pact indicates the nature of the agreement concluded; the skin offers the power to possess all things in exchange for the vital energies of the possessor. The skin offers its property as magical 'means of production' and of possession in exchange for the vital substance of the producer. The relation to the capitalist mode of production becomes unmistakable.[3] For the act and institution which establishes the structural specificity of the capitalist mode of production is the labour *contract* in which the labourer agrees to sell his labour power in exchange for the means of his subsistance furnished by the capitalist. The contract fulfils its determination as an exchange of equivalents inasmuch as the labourer indeed receives the full *value* of his labour power: that is, the labour products necessary to reproduce that labour in the person of its bearer, the individual labourer. At the same time, the use value of this same labour power exceeds its exchange value, since the energy expended by the worker produces more goods than are needed to reproduce him. This unpaid surplus social labour produces the contradictory phenomena characteristic of the commodity-world: on the one hand, the consumption of the energies of the labouring class and the reduction of its members to agents of the process of production; on the other and in inverse proportion, the accumulation of wealth and of productive forces, forces which increasingly take the form of machinery. And within the sphere of circulation itself appears the phantasmagoria of money begetting money, the spontaneous generation of value: capital. If labour, and the process of production in general, were originally determined as human energy expended for the satisfaction of needs, for the maintenance and production of human life, the needs and life which effectively determine production in a capitalist society are the needs and life of *capital* itself, the transcendental subject-object, conserving and negating the dead labour of the past in its unrelenting production of new 'life,' in the form of surplus labour. If the contract which binds labour and capital 'skins' the worker, as Marx writes, it is because it sanctions a life that is dedicated to death, allowing the worker to temporarily postpone his demise at the price of his vital energies themselves. The labour contract provides for the *divestment* of the producer, who is reproduced only as the bearer of labour power, whose consumption is tolerated only insofar as it is *productive* consumption, and who as individual is thereby *consumed* in the process.

It is this tension, then, between individuals acting as though they were autonomous subjects, conscious of what they were and wanted, ends in themselves, and the truly effective subject that is not an individual but the law of value, which endows the *peau* with its talismanic powers. It is a phenomenon, an object that can be seen and touched, and yet its power can at most be adduced from the manner in which it defies the usual laws of material objects, for instance through the ineffacable text it bears. The skin is therefore the object not so much of a contract, insofar as this implies the relative autonomy and equality of the contracting parties, as of a *pact* which promises to appease desire directly, without the mediation of work. And yet, ironically enough (as with the gamblers), it is precisely the laws of commodity-production that structure the exchange from which work is conspicuously absent. The skin, essential manifestation of a certain consumption, will consume the subject of desire no less ineluctably than the work process consumes the labourer. Once again *desire* and *need* converge and merge in the terms of the pact no less than in the words of the young man as he impulsively exclaims: 'Eh bien, oui, je veux vivre avec excès. ... Oui, j'ai besoin d'embrasser les plaisirs du ciel et de la terre dans une dernière étreinte, pour en mourir' (41-2). 'J'ai *besoin* ... ' - a simple turn of phrase, to be sure, and yet indicative perhaps of the nature of his desire. And, 'serrant le talisman d'une main convulsive,' he commands 'un dîner royalement splendide ... .'

With the utterance of the wish, the pact is sealed, or as the old man solemnly declares: *signed*.

> *Vous avez signé le pacte, tout est dit. Maintenant, vos volontés seront scrupuleusement satisfaites, mais aux dépens de votre vie. Le cercle de vos jours, figuré par cette peau, se resserrera suivant la force et le nombre de vos souhaits, depuis le plus léger jusqu'au plus exorbitant. ... Après tout, vous vouliez mourir? eh bien, votre suicide n'est que retardé (42).*

The *peau de chagrin*, representation of a certain life at its very *limit*, impregnated with the *traces* of that life, with its *product* in the form of a *text*, metonymical symbol and symbolized metonymy, emerges as the fetish par excellence, in all senses of the term. Yet it is a fetish not in the simple sense of a product which obfuscates its true origins, for production is not effaced in the skin. Unlike the commodity, *this* fetish has its origins engraved in it, waiting to be read.[4] Which is not the same as to be seen or heard. If the skin is a fetish, it is precisely *because* its textuality appears as a product, an object to be possessed, consumed, perceived, and understood. The fetish which the skin *literally* embodies is the *embodiment of the letter*, the naturalization of the text, its ineffacability, embedded in a substance which is more than mere surface. It is the fetish of a certain mode of production if not of production itself. And by a strange necessity, the *means* of this production is the voice - one which effaces the text. 'Vous avez signé le pacte, tout est dit,' says the *marchand* after the young man has given voice to his desires. And indeed, 'tout est dit' with the possible exception of one thing: the *Dire* itself. The young man has spoken, but the pact is signed. The marchand has spoken, yet he too will not have the last word. Not because what he has said is wrong, but because it is more right than he knows. And because, as we begin to surmise, there can be no last word, no more than a first. The peace promised by the pact is in fact only the truce of a text. Violence is not ended but only deferred.

8

The Canard

Once again, the young man finds himself in the street, and again there is an obstacle in his path. He literally throws himself at it: 'En s'élançant de la porte du magasin sur la chaussée, il heurta trois jeunes gens qui se tenaient bras dessus, bras dessous.' After an exchange of 'gracieuses interpellations' – 'Animal! Imbécile!' – the young man receives his 'proper' name: 'Eh! c'est Raphael!' (43). The name of the painter marks the transition from the magic- al shop to the 'reality' outside: abrupt, and yet unfolding in the continuity of a desire and of its articulation, the commodity-world. Raphael will have good reason to be surprised, not at 'l'accomplissement de ses souhaits,' but at 'la manière naturelle par laquelle les évènements s'enchaînaient' (42). The chain of events is as natural and as continuous as the *peau* itself, and like it also the subject of an exchange. Taillefer, Raphael is informed by his friends, a rich banker 'qui ne sachant que faire de son or, veut le changer en esprit' (45), has decided to found a newspaper to that end, and to inaugurate the project is holding a great banquet that very evening, at which Raphael's first wishes ('vivre avec excès') will be fulfilled.

The fact that the *peau*, symbolic fusion of *pouvoir* and *vouloir*, should exercise its magic powers by means of the *press* is anything but accidental; for the press, no less than the talisman, is a place where power and desire converge, and this not merely in its external, social function but in its inner- most structure as well. And if the former is the more evident, the social func- tion of the press cannot be understood without insight into its inner structure.

Only then can the chain be traced which leads Raphael to the excess which is the birth and death of his desire.

The social circumstances are familiar enough:

> *Or donc, le pouvoir s'est transporté, comme tu sais, des Tuileries chez les journalistes. ... Le gouvernement, c'est-à-dire l'aristocratie de banquiers et d'avocats qui font aujourd'hui de la patrie comme les prêtres faisaient jadis de la monarchie, a senti la nécessité de mystifier le bon peuple de France avec des mots nouveaux et de vieilles idées, à l'instar des philosophes de toutes les écoles et des hommes forts de tous les temps (44-5).*

The principle of total exchangeability, hallmark of the commodity-world, articulates itself in the press. And the form of this articulation is antithetical: Balzac's *Monographie de la presse parisienne*, written in 1842, begins by noting the antithesis of a certain appropriation:

> *L'ordre gendelettre (comme gendarme) s'étant constitué en société pour défendre ses propriétés, il devait en resulter, ce qui résulte en France de beaucoup d'institutions, une antithèse entre le but et les résultats: on pille plus que jamais les propriétés littéraires.*[1]

Not merely 'les propriétés littéraires' are pillaged, but 'le propre' itself, according to a dialectic which we have already seen at work in the commodity-world. Balzac's characterization of the 'Directeur-rédacteur-en-chef-propriétaire-gérant' can be extended to the Press as a whole:

> *Cet individu, qui offre toujours une des quatre faces de son quadruple titre, tient du propriétaire, de l'épicier, du spéculateur, et,* comme il n'est propre à rien, il se trouve propre à tout *(my emphasis).*[2]

La Presse - 'hoax perpétuel contre les hommes et les choses,'[3] incarnated in a *Directeur* who 'n'est plus un homme, ni une chose'[4] - is the site of a certain seduction. 'Neither man nor thing,' and betrayal of both, this indicates the secret of its power over its readers:

> *Peut-être les abonnés sont-ils plus inexplicables que les journaux et que les journalistes. Les abonnés voient leurs journaux changeant de haines, pleins de bienveillance pour tels hommes politiques contre lesquels ils faisaient feu tous les jours, vantant aujourd'hui ce qu'ils dépréciaient hier, s'alliant avec ceux de leurs confrères qu'ils boxaient la veille ou l'an dernier, plaidant des thèses absurdes, ils continuent à les lire, à s'y abonner avec une intrépidité d'abnégation qui ne se comprendrait pas d'homme à homme.*[5]

Not *d'homme à homme*, but perhaps *d'homme à femme*:

> *La presse, comme la femme, est admirable et sublime quand elle avance un*
> *mensonge, elle vous lâche pas qu'elle ne vous ait forcé d'y croire; et elle*
> *déploie les plus grandes qualités dans cette lutte où le public, aussi bête*
> *qu'un mari, succombe toujours.*[6]

The power of the press thus seems inseparable from a certain desire; and the most significant convergence of desire and journalism is the *feuilleton*, which thrives only in Paris and which gives the *capital* its distinctive quality:

> *C'est un rêve perpétuel. On y consomme les hommes, les idées, les systèmes,*
> *les plaisanteries, les belles œuvres et les gouvernements, à faire envie au*
> *tonneau des Danaides.*[7]

If the feuilleton is luxury in language, Paris is the feuilleton in action. And the principle of that action is the convergence of total exchangeability with total consumption. Émile explains this to Raphael:

> *Pour nous, la patrie est une capitale où les idées s'échangent et se vendent*
> *à tant la ligne où tous les jours amènent de succulents dîners, de nombreux*
> *spectacles; où fourmillent de licencieuses prostituées, où les soupers ne*
> *finissent que le lendemain (45).*

Yet since the exchangeability and consumption are total, the fate of the journalist tends to resemble that of 'le pêcheur à la ligne ... le rédacteur qui vit, comme le pêcheur, de sa ligne.'[8] The squandering of energies exhausts the squanderer, the consumers are consumed:

> *Chaque jour, il use les qualités les plus précieuses de l'esprit à sculpter une*
> *plaisanterie en une ou deux colonnes; il découpe ses phrases en pointes, il*
> *s'épuise à donner les fleurs de son esprit dans cette espèce de mauvais lieu*
> *de l'imagination, appelé le petit journal. Il s'aperçoit trop tard de ses dis-*
> *sipations; mais souvent il a fini par devenir la dupe de ses plaisanteries, il*
> *s'est inoculé les ridicules après les avoir ridiculisés, comme un médecin*
> *meurt de la peste.*[9]

Taillefer's orgy will have a similar end, 'la Mort souriant au milieu d'une famille pestiférée ... les miasmes d'une orgie!' (160). Yet above all, this fate is the very one which the press imposes upon literature. And here again it is not merely its institutional power to influence the financial success of books which is decisive: the corruption goes far deeper, to the very source and articulation of literary desire itself; it is this which makes the press, and above all, the feuilleton, a 'mauvais lieu de l'imagination.'[10] If Balzac could describe the imagination as a concentric mirror which reflects the world, the press has smashed this mirror:

> *Le publicisme était un grand miroir concentrique: les publicistes d'aujourd'-*
> *hui l'ont mis en pièces et en ont tous un* morceau *qu'ils font briller aux*
> *yeux de la foute (my emphasis).*

These fragments glitter with the sumptuous brilliance of a banquet: yet those
who consume them, like Lucien de Rubempré in *Les Illusions perdues*, are
inevitably short-changed. The banquet of journalism thrives on

> *la turbulence des premiers désirs littéraires, et les joyeusetés dangereuses de*
> *gamins de Paris. ... Là se trouve tout le sel du journalisme, un esprit con-*
> *stamment original, dépensé en feux d'artifice dont les carcasses (les motifs)*
> *sont cependant et comme toujours hideuses.*[12]

Like its vital principle, money, journalism is a banquet which devours its
guests in accordance with the law of productive consumption, the hidden
motor of the sphere of self-preservation, of 'history' as the realm of necessity,
and of its culmination in the phantasmagoria of capitalist accumulation. If
individuals disappear, the mass of subscribers must grow since it is axiomatic
that 'tout journal qui n'augment pas sa masse d'abonnés, quelle qu'elle soit,
est en décroissance.'[13] And this growing giant, the 'public' – not without relation to that 'géant' of total registration and enumeration: 'œuvre du géant
ordonné par un géant' – is nourished by a Press which, it should not be forgotten, resembles nothing so much in its ruses and seductions as a *woman*:
one which feeds its public while feeding off it, and spawning in addition to its
readers a whole caste of agents: journalists, those 'gamins de Paris,' who, as
Balzac writes, are frequently 'des fils des familles ruinés.'[14] One such son is
Raphael de Valentin.

Taillefer's dinner, at which the promiscuity of the *Magasin d'Antiquités* is
reduced to its less sublimated form of voracious desire, is distinguished from
the preceding scenes inasmuch as it is not merely dramatic, literary, and
artistic ('un livre et un tableau' [52]), but also musical: a concert. Or, to be
more precise, an opera; it is here that the voice enters the scene. Beginning
with the silent spectacle of a luxury in which 'les paroles furent assez rares,'
the 'second acte' is ushered in with a gradual crescendo, becoming 'quelque
peu bavard' as speaking and eating merge: 'Chacun mangea en parlant, parla
en mangeant,' until 'l'orgie seule déploya sa grande voix, sa voix composée de
cent clameurs confuses qui grossissent comme les crescendo de Rossini' (51).
The stage of antithetical struggle is soon reached – 'cette mêlée de paroles ...
comme au milieu d'un combat' (52) – and then surpassed as all articulation
disappears in the cacophonous confusion:

> *Il n'y eut plus alors de paroles distinctes. ... Cette assemblée en délire hurla,*
> *siffla, chanta, cria, rugit, gronda. ... Les ressemblances animales inscrites*

sur les figures humaines, et si curieusement démontrées par les physio-
logistes, reparaissent vaguement dans les gestes, dans les habitudes du corps
(61).

The room is filled with ideas, opinions, silks, jewels, and foods, all united in a
tumultuous confusion which at its height merges with silence in strange copu-
lation: 'Le silence et le tumulte s'étaient bizarrement accouplés' (63). And
this silence marks the moment at which the guests, dinner finished, are about
to pass to new morsels:

C'était une haie de fleurs mêlées de rubis, de saphirs et de corail; une cein-
ture de colliers noirs sur des cous de neige, des écharpes légères flottant
comme les flammes d'un phare, des turbans orgueilleux, des tuniques
modestement provocantes (64).

Confronted with this new manifestation of *luxe*, there is a momentary silence;

Ces hommes sans frein furent subjugués tout d'abord par la puissance
majestueuse dont est investie la femme (65).

Then, slowly, the guests prepare to sample 'ces beautés choisis,' and the orgy
revives with an heroic cadence:

Mais bientôt quelques rires éclatèrent, le murmure augmenta, les voix
s'élevèrent. L'orgie, domptée pendant un moment, menaça par intervalles
de se réveiller. Ces alternatives de silence et de bruit eurent un vague res-
semblance avec une symphonie de Beethoven (65).

But the women who confront Raphael and Emile are true daughters of *La
Presse*: Aquilina is 'leste, souple, et sa vigueur supposait l'agilité d'une pan-
thère, comme la mâle élégance de ses formes en promettait les voluptés
dévorantes' (66). Her 'male elegance' complements the femininity of Raphael:
but if he is a Prince, sacrificing his innocence to the corruption of the *Jeu*, and
now to the Press, she, with her friend, Euphrasie, is its incarnation; a

monstre qui sait mordre et caresser, rire comme un démon, pleurer comme
les anges ... puis en un moment rugir, se déchirer les flancs, briser sa pas-
sion, son amant; enfin, se détruire elle-même comme fait un peuple in-
surgé ... (66).

Yet even more than Aquilina, it is Euphrasie who incarnates devouring desire:
'Donnez-moi des millions, je les mangerai; je ne voudrais pas garder un centime
pour l'année prochaine' (69). Raphael's desire to 'vivre avec excès' finds its
consummation in Euphrasie, yet her words shock and frighten him:

Vivre pour plaire et régner, tel est l'arrêt que prononce chaque battement de mon cœur. La société m'approuve; ne fournit-elle pas sans cesse à mes dissipations? (69)

Something in the two courtisanes is profoundly alien to the prospective journalists. Euphrasie's defiance of the economy of life, her total self-abandonment to a circulation which allows her to appear in the present and assures her disappearance when her resources·are exhausted – all this shocks her male listeners and confirms how little Raphael has truly assumed the pact he has 'signed.' Emile speaks for them both and for the economy of investment: 'Ne crains-tu pas de payer tout cela un jour?' And Euphrasie answers:

Eh bien ... au lieu d'entremêler mes plaisirs de chagrins, ma vie sera coupée en deux parts: une jeunesse certainement joyeuse, et je ne sais quelle vieillesse incertaine pendant laquelle je souffrirai à mon aise (70).

Her clear-cut division of youth from age, pleasure from 'chagrin,' life from death exemplifies both the dream and the nightmare of a certain self-preservation, conceiving itself as the reproduction and accumulation of living presence: a dream, because it successfully separates (as simple alterity) presence from absence, life from death; a nightmare, because it is the affirmation of a death that limits all possible accumulation and investment, mixing death and life, pleasure and pain even more intimately. Raphael, confronted by his own project, reacts as he did to the luminous mystery of the talisman: he searches for its cause. 'Qu'as-tu donc souffert pour penser ainsi?' he asks the courtisane. The question is probably symptomatic: it convokes narration in order to ward off the impending danger of a certain consumption. Euphrasie's answer, in any case, anticipates the story Raphael will tell: 'J'ai été quittée pour un héritage, moi!' (69) It is just such a heritage that Raphael will never be able to quit, or to requite, as we shall soon learn. But Raphael has already made the decisive gesture: his question will now permit him to raise his voice, in telling his own story. This story, to be sure, no less than the novel as a whole, will be, in all senses (and nonsenses) of the word: a *canard*. But this is no reason for not taking it seriously. On the contrary, in his *Monographie* Balzac reveals that it is precisely the *canard* whose history and destiny has most fully revealed the essence of the Press, and its power. Of course, Balzac's discussion is itself something of a *canard*:

Fixons bien l'étymologie de ce mot de la presse. L'homme qui crie dans Paris l'arrêt du criminel qu'on va exécuter, ou la relation de ses derniers moments, ou le bulletin d'une victoire, ou le compte rendu d'un crime extraordinaire, vend pour un sou le feuillet imprimé qu'il annonce, et qui se nomme un canard en termes d'imprimerie. Cette profession de crieur va diminuant. Après avoir brillé sous l'ancienne monarchie, sous la Révolution

> *et sous l'Empire, la classe patentée des crieurs-jurés compte aujourd'hui
> peu d'individus. Le* journal, *lu aujourd'hui par les cochers de fiacre sur leur
> siège,* a tué cette industrie. *La relation du fait anormal, monstrueux, im-
> possible et vrai, possible et faux, qui servait d'élément aux* canards, *s'est
> donc appellée dans les journaux* un canard, *avec d'autant plus de raison
> qu'il ne se fait pas sans plumes, et qu'il se met à toute sauce (my emphasis,
> except for* un canard).[15]

The newspaper has not merely killed the 'industrie,' it has eliminated the *canards* themselves, for whom the printed text was simply the aid and appendage
of the living voice of the crier. The living voice has been transformed into
dead newsprint, *les canards* into *un canard*. The human voice, guarantee of a
certain truth even in announcing the improbable, has been supplanted by the
text: the improbable has become the hoax. The voice, separated from its
original mission, 'se met à toute sauce' as text: the mouth which is thus suggested does not speak: it swallows. And the cause of this, it should be noted,
is the 'plume': originally, 'naturally,' intended to protect, it has become a
means of inscription, leaving the *canard* exposed and vulnerable to its *pointe*.
That Raphael should feel compelled to tell his story at the very moment
when, reaching its climax, the voice of the orgy falls silent, is doubtless his
attempt to avoid the fate of the *canards*. By raising his voice, however, he
cannot help but become one.

9

A Burst of Laughter

The retrospective structure of the Balzacian narrative has often been noted. The 'present' emerges as an 'effect,' as the symptom and product of a cause, of an original presence *hors scène*, whose priority is no less logical than chronological. G. Poulet writes of 'un monde supérieur et antérieur, un monde non plus de déterminations, mais de déterminance.' The effect of this realm of 'déterminance' upon the Balzacian protagonist is that 'ce qu'il *devient* a de moins en moins d'importance en comparaison de ce qui le fait devenir.'[1] The present and its phenomena appear increasingly to be epiphenomenal; they tend to efface themselves as signs pointing to an invisible referent, anterior and superior, origin and cause, prior to all manifest sense and sensibility: a pre-sense. This prior instance, which thus commands the narrative structure and the discourse of its readers, is implicit in what may be termed the enigmatic aspect of the present, beginning significantly with the anonymity of the young man, but it is often enough explicit in other Balzacian texts: 'les causes de la vie, la vie avant la vie,' 'pre-existent text,' 'first principle' – the formulations are well known and could be easily extended into an impressive list. Perceptive readers and critics of Balzac who thus identify the presence of this original 'déterminance' are supported by the heavy weight of such evidence, implicit and explicit.

At the same time, however, such criticism remains commanded by the discourse it interrogates: it fulfils the role of *porte-parole* by responding to the work. This critical responsability, however, responds to a work whose authority is rarely problematized. Instead, and necessarily, the origin of that authority is reiterated, its function described. Necessarily, because the authority of critical discourse – its *truth* – is inseparable from the truth of its 'object': the literary work. The originality of the latter founds the value of the former. It is this authority of the origin, and of the discourses (narrative and critical) that it legitimizes, that are solicited and shaken by the textuality of the text. And, in particular, by the text we are reading. *La Peau de chagrin* not only reveals the predominance and power of a certain origin: it displays the desire of that pre-existent text. The novel thereby confronts us with the mise-en-scène of this desire. And that mise-en-scène takes the form of a narration.

For the *Peau de chagrin* is not merely the story of Raphael de Valentin: it is the story of Raphael telling a story, *his* story, the narration of his narration. The enigma of his present situation is elaborated by his own voice, enunciating the origin of his destiny, producing its meaning, bringing it to light and thus eradicating the last traces of his earlier anonymity. The advent of this narration, in the metonymic sequence of the text, is by no means purely adventitious: if it is not simply to be heard, but above all to be *read*, its place must be noted. This place is at the end of the novel's first section, entitled 'Le Talisman,' as night falls on Taillefer's orgy. 'The Talisman' is the description of an enigma: that of a desire seeking to fulfil itself in a world where fullness is phantasmagorical. The apparent 'progression' from the emptiness of the gambling casino to the plenitude of the dinner orgy, via the *magasin d'antiquités*, reveals itself to be the repetition of a circulation in which production is only a moment of consumption, in which the expense of vital energies is always short-changed, and no profitable investment is possible except for the eminently theoretical speculation of the *marchand*. It is a scene in which the fatality of the present foreshadows the mortality of the future, leaving only the past to redeem the life thus endangered. Euphrasie, *porteparole* of this fatality, allows Raphael only one possible response: 'Qu'as-tu donc souffert pour penser ainsi?' (69) Yet it is not in *her* past but in his own that Raphael will seek refuge from the fatal *usure* (the strange confusion of a certain accumulation – *usury* – and a certain disagregation or *wear and tear*). This gives him the opportunity to raise his voice and thereby break the silence which has haunted the casino, the store, and paradoxically even the orgy itself. If Raphael raises his voice it is to redeem the caducity of the present, to support and supplement that other voice – the discourse of the narrator – which has already enunciated that present as an enigma, as a sign whose referent is invisible but certain. Against and after the consumptive circulation of the casino, the shop, and the orgy – the circulation of the commodity-world – Raphael's voice announces the descent 'into the hidden places of production' (Marx) where the tannery is concealed.

With the advent of Raphael's narrative, the corrosive circulation of the commodity-world is no longer simply represented by a discourse which, however intimately involved it is with its 'object,' is nonetheless, in a certain sense, transcendent. With Raphael's narration, this world seems to speak for itself, to represent and to reproduce itself, re-membering and re-collecting itself as a process, reconstructing and reviving the presence of its past, and thus declaring the consumption of the present to be not a fatal expense, but the expression and manifestation of a living being: life reproducing itself. The *usure* which devours all entities – persons, phenomena, words – appears reappropriated in the living presence of a voice recounting the story of its life, endowing it with meaning and direction, explaining the tattered phenomena of its present as products of its past and ciphers of its future.

And yet, from its inception Raphael's narrative is haunted by the very *usure* it seeks to master:

– *Ah! si tu connaissais ma vie.*
– *Ah! s'écria Emile, je ne te croyais pas si vulgaire, la phrase est usée (73).*

The phrase with which Raphael seeks to ward off the menace of Euphrasie and to indicate the enigmatic depth of a life waiting to be revealed is already shop-worn, its value debased by use, as Emile protests. The latter thereby demonstrates his function as listener: to serve as what Marx, referring to the exchange of commodities, called the 'mirror of value' (*Wertspiegel*). Since the value of a commodity, the socially necessary labour required for its production, is never visible as such, it is only in relation to another, commensurable commodity that this value can appear. Its manifestation therefore must take the dissimulated form of a mirroring; the value-soul of one commodity can only appear in and as the mirror-image of another (or of the commodity that serves as medium of exchange and as universal equivalent: money). The dissimulation involved concerns the immediate form assumed by this mirror relationship: what appears at first glance to be a quality of the things involved – the commodities being exchanged or their surrogate, money – is in fact a social relationship constituted by 'abstract' but socially necessary labour. As is well known, Marx described this process of dissimulation as the 'fetishistic character of the commodity,' a category to which we shall have occasion to return.

Here, however, what is of interest is that the relation of (autobiographical) narration appears to have a structure not unlike that of the commodity. The value of the verbal signs emitted by the narrator, ostensibly telling the story of his own life (his property), is mediated by or dependent upon the response of the listener, who can either accept or question the utterances proferred. In the case at hand, Emile calls attention to the inflated (and hence, debased) value of the phrases used by Raphael. He thus underscores the particular problem of the inflation of certain forms of discourse through their use. This problem is endemic to language since the latter, as a form of representation (again, not unlike the commodity), is separated from what it represents (here, Raphael's previous suffering):

> *Cette longue et lente douleur qui a duré dix ans peut aujourd'hui se reproduire par quelques phrases dans lesquelles la douleur ne sera plus qu'une pensée, et le plaisir une réflexion philosophique (74).*

The quick and ready reproducibility of the past threatens the discourse that is about to recount it. The process of summoning up ten years of suffering menaces it to the very *quick*: 'Vue à distance, ma vie est comme rétrécie par un phénomène moral' (74).

Is it purely accidental that the first form in which Raphael's life is menaced by the contraction – *le rétrécissement* – otherwise promised by the talisman is associated here with the project of autobiographical narration, the subject recounting his life? Raphael's past shrinks in the phrases he utters to conjure it up just as the *peau de chagrin* will shrink his present and future with every desire he utters. In both cases that eminently reproductive organ which is the voice will reduce what it produces, the life of the subject. It is as though the expense of breath involves a certain fatality, consuming the life that expresses itself through it.

Small wonder, then, that the circumstances in which Raphael decides, or is driven, to raise his voice are as ambivalent as they are significant. For Raphael's narrative takes its departure in an 'éclat de rire' that is anything but joyous. It occurs at the height of the orgy, when noise has become silence, and reality begun to resemble a nightmare ('ils prirent les jeux de cette débauche pour les caprices d'un cauchemar où le mouvement est sans bruit, où les cris sont perdu pour l'oreille'). At this highly charged moment, Raphael suddenly bursts into laughter:

> *Raphael laissa tout à coup échapper un éclat de rire si brusquement intempestif, que son ami lui demanda compte de cette joie brutale (72).*

At the moment when reality and meaning are merged with unreality and absurdity, and when a certain loss threatens to prevail ('les cris ... perdus pour l'oreille'), Raphael feels compelled to recount his life. For the reader, as for the listener, Emile (who 'lui demanda compte ... '), it is his laughter that must be accounted for.

10

Patrimony

Raphael's narrative begins with his eighteenth year. The dominant figure of his youth was his father, 'chef d'une maison historique à peu près oubliée en Auvergne,' who left his native soil, 'vint à Paris pour y lutter avec le diable' (79). From the very first, Raphael's youth is cast under the shadow of struggle. And the 'devil' with whom his father struggles to save the fortunes of a 'maison historique' is nothing less than History itself. Having first succeeded 'sans grand appui à prendre position au cœur même du pouvoir [,] la Révolution renversa ... sa fortune; mais il avait su épouser l'héritière d'une grande maison, et s'était vu, sous l'Empire, au moment de restituer à notre famille son ancienne splendeur' (79). At this very moment, however, 'la Restauration, qui rendit à ma mère des biens considérables, ruina mon père' (80). M. de Valentin's fateful struggle with history to save his patrimony reveals a peculiar pattern: the self-same movement that impoverishes the father enriches the mother.

The balance, however, is meager: it barely suffices 'pour sauver l'honneur de notre nom' (80). The familial resources are clearly on the maternal side, while the family (paternal) *name* is haunted by debt. Ten years after the death of Mme de Valentin, that name is ruined by a *text*. When the family notary,

M. de Villèle exhuma, tout exprès pour nous, un décret impérial sur les déchéances, et nous eut ruinés, signai-je la vente de mes propriétés, n'en

*gardant qu'une île sans valeur, située au milieu de la Loire, et où se trouvait
le tombeau de ma mère (81).*

The physical demise of M. de Valentin follows closely upon his financial ruin,
which is also the ruin of his name, and which leaves his son, Raphael, 'onze
cent douze francs, produit net et liquide de la succession paternelle' (81). All
that remains of the maternal succession, considerably less *liquid*, is an island
situated in the middle of the Loire, site of the maternal tomb. Yet even in
ruin the maternal side of Raphael's heritage asserts its superiority over the
paternal: in the midst of the (natural) circulation of the Loire, the mortal remains of Raphael's mother are preserved. His patrimony, by contrast, itself
largely due to the resources of his mother, quickly dissolves in that other, less
natural circulation.

But the poverty of Raphael's patrimony is already evident in the depiction
of his father:

*Pour te révéler les tristesses de ma vie, il suffira peut-être de te dépeindre
mon père: un homme grand, sec et mince, le visage en lame de couteau, le
teint pâle, à parole brève, taquin comme une vieille fille, méticuleux
comme un chef de bureau (75).*

Raphael's father emerges, in the narrative of his son, as an ambivalent figure:
powerful, inspiring fear ('grand'), he is also 'sec et mince,' and in many respects recalls the old man of the *Salon de Jeu*. Like the gamblers, his visage
bears the imprint of a passion: Raphael tells of 'les chagrins dont l'empreinte
flétrissait la figure de mon père.' His appearance, marked by a certain pallor,
his taciturnity ('à parole brève'), recall the ravages of the *jeu* and the nudity
of the casino, devoured, no less than M. de Valentin, by the circulation of .
money and its laws. And like the gamblers, M. de Valentin's struggle and passion consist in an attempt to master that circulation. The very passion that
wears away the father also hones the traits of his face, 'en lame de couteau.'
Yet his most significant aspect appears when his son conjures up his image in
memory:.

*Je crois encore le voir devant moi. Dans sa redingote marron, où il se tenait
droit comme un cierge pascal, il avait l'air d'un hareng saur enveloppé dans
la couverture rougeâtre d'un pamphlet. Cependant, j'aimais mon père, au
fond, il était juste (75).*

'Au fond, il était juste' – yet it is precisely this 'fond' which the metaphors of
Raphael's description subvert. Raphael's use of metaphor in describing his
father, like the intrusions of discourse in the description of the *Salon de Jeu*,
is evoked and provoked by the very insubstantiality, the poverty of the phen-

omena which are to be depicted; this poverty, if it is not to be simple disappearance, absence, must be read as the transparency of a sign. The metaphors, like the voice, are *intended* to serve as a simple supplement deciphering the sign, penetrating it so as to reveal that which it signifies.

Yet the metaphors have their own logic, and they can be read as more than simple illustrations or ornaments of the figure designated as *M. de Valentin*. The two comparisons – the Easter candle and the pickled herring – have, quite apart from their visible shape, a common destiny: consumption. The herring is protected by its wrapping – which is, remarkably, a text: a reddish pamphlet – only to be eaten, to disappear into a mouth. The Easter candle is destined to be consumed by the flame. Yet here a decisive difference between the two kinds of consumption emerges: the pallor of the Easter candle produces a light which illuminates as it consumes. And it is no ordinary illumination, but one which promises the resurrection of man. If the candle is finally consumed and the light goes out, its promise remains, a promise which is intimately interwoven with the name of the son. For Raphael is not merely the name of the painter of the Saviour (in the *magasin d'antiquités*); the name itself signifies the same promise; it means in Hebrew 'God hath healed.'

Thus, if both herring and candle are consumed, it is in the name of an eternal life, redeeming the disappearance which is the very manifestation and destiny of M. de Valentin. Yet the full ambiguity of this promise, as it affects the father, is indicated in the *law* he imposes upon his son, a law that the latter appears to assume ('au fond, il était juste'). Above all M. de Valentin insists upon the 'laws of time and of space,' for which he demands a strict accounting:

> *Il me logea dans une chambre contiguë à son cabinet; je me couchais dès neuf heures du soir et me levais à cinq heures du matin; il voulait que je fisse mon droit en conscience. ... les lois du temps et de l'espace étaient si sévèrement appliquées à mes courses, à mes travaux, et mon père me demandait en dînant un compte ... rigoureux (75).*

The contiguity of father and son ('dans une chambre contiguë à son cabinet') appears as part of the draconic law which rules over both: the very posture of the father ('Il se tenait *droit* comme un cierge pascal') is mirrored in the son's course of study ('je fisse mon droit'). The father's proximity enforces the demands he imposes on his son, the demands, however, of a law that will destroy the legislator himself. If M. de Valentin demands a strict accounting from his son, he himself will ultimately be unable to make his own books balance.

Thus, the contiguity of father and son already repeats the parental matrimony, in all of its fateful ambivalence:

Figure-toi l'imagination la plus vagabonde, le cœur le plus amoureux, l'âme la plus tendre, l'esprit le plus poétique, sans cesse en présence de l'homme le plus caillouteux, le plus atrabilaire, le plus froid du monde; enfin marie une jeune fille à un squelette, *et tu comprendras l'existence dont les scènes curieuses ne peuvent que t'être dites ... (76, my emphasis).*

The inner wealth of the son, and first of all, his 'vagabond imagination,' is confined within a marriage in which Raphael assumes the position vacated by the death of his mother, while his father appears as the living allegory of death itself, 'un squelette.' If Raphael's father is thus metaphorically stripped to the bone, if the economy and legality that M. de Valentin embodies lead his name to the edge of ruin, this fatal patrimony leaves the son only one resort and re-source: the plenitude and wealth of the maternal succession, of a certain fem-ininity. The paternal skeleton must at all costs be re-covered, be it only with the *peau de chagrin.*

11

The Broken Net

Oh! quand je devrais t'endormir, je veux te raconter l'une des plus terribles joies de ma vie, une de ces joies armées de griffes et qui s'enfoncent dans notre cœur comme un fer chaud sur l'épaule d'un forçat (76).

With these words Raphael sets the scene of a fateful deviation. Hitherto, the son had restricted his desires to the reveries imposed upon him by the despotic regime of his father. To challenge this regime was to risk exile:

Vouloir m'écarter de la route uniforme que mon père m'avait tracée, c'eût été m'exposer à sa colère; il m'avait menacé de m'embarquer à ma première faute, en qualité de mousse, pour les Antilles (76).

The instruments by which the paternal tyranny enforced its law – the law of a certain economy – upon the son are appropriately enough themselves 'economic':

Jusqu'à l'âge de vingt ans, il ne laissa pas dix francs à ma disposition, dix coquins, dix libertins de francs, trésor immense dont la possession vainement enviée me faisait rêver d'ineffables délices ... (15).

This use of money by his father invests it with a fateful power for Raphael: by a metonymic displacement, money becomes identified with the pleasure it can procure ('coquins', 'libertins') so that its possession becomes synonymous with the satisfaction of desire. This desire, moreover, develops precisely in the shadow of a possession *denied* by the paternal law ('la possession vaine-ment enviée'). To have or not to have? – this becomes the decisive question. What thereby takes place within the psychic economy of the subject, Raphael, is correlative of that aspect of the commodity-world which Marx described as *fetishism*: the value of commodities is identified with their manifest, objectal existence instead of being grasped as a function of labour, that is, of a social activity. The fetishization of money, the visible manifestation of exchange value, is the consequence. Raphael's father possesses money: magically, since for his son that possession has no history; it is a mere fact; and *legitimately*, since it is the father who lays down the law for the son ('au fond il était juste').

Against this setting, a decisive scene unfolds. Raphael accompanies his father to a 'bal chez le duc de Navarreins, cousin de mon père' (76). His ap-pearance, which reflects the severity of the paternal economies, recalls (and foreshadows) his entry in the *salon de jeu:* 'J'avais un habit râpé, des souliers mal faits, une cravate de cocher et des gants déjà portés.' Such details, Raphael tells his listener, are essential 'pour que tu puisse parfaitement comprendre ma position' (76). What is this *position*?

'Je me mis dans un coin afin de pouvoir tout à mon aise prendre des glaces et contempler les jolies femmes' (76). Hiding his shabbiness, eating sweets, and looking at women from a corner, seeing and unseen – yet not entirely. There is one pair of eyes that he cannot escape: 'Mon père m'aperçut. Par une raison que je n'ai jamais devinée, tant cet acte de confiance m'abasourdit, il me donna sa bourse et ses clefs à garder' (77).

'Par une raison que je n'ai jamais devinée' – it would not be exaggerated to see in this the enigma of Raphael's entire existence. This gesture, with which M. de Valentin bestows his son with 'sa bourse et ses clefs,' with the means of making dreams reality, of radically altering his *position*, above all in regard to the father, overwhelms Raphael. It is as though through this single, inexplic-able act Raphael's father had placed the law into his son's hands and at the same time presented him with the possibility of its transgression:

> *Depuis un an, je me rêvais bien mis, en voiture, ayant une belle femme à mes côtés, tranchant du seigneur, dînant chez Véry, allant le soir au spec-tacle, décidé à ne revenir que le lendemain chez mon père ... (77).*

The dream of becoming a *Seigneur*, 'bien mis, en voiture, une belle femme à mes côtés' – and above all, 'ne revenir que le lendemain chez mon père': the act of radical infidelity, all this Raphael now holds in his hand, trembling:

> *J'avais estimé toute cette joie cinquante écus. ... J'allai donc dans un boud-oir où, seul, les yeux cuisants, les doigts tremblants, je comptai l'argent de*

> *mon père: cent écus! Evoquées par cette somme, les joies de mon escapade*
> *apparurent devant moi, dansant, comme les sorcières de Macbeth autour de*
> *leur chaudière, mais alléchantes, frémissantes, délicieuses (77).*

In Raphael's hands money dissolves into the 'fixated figment' (*festgehaltene Einbildung*) which according to Marx it really is. Objectively it can only function in relation to whatever it can be exchanged for. To hoard it, in a capitalist society, is to lose it.

But Raphael's speculation is not less radical, or even real, for being imaginary. He 'exchanges' his father's money for fantasies which, as images, represent that Presence which fascinates and tempts with the force of black magic. Moreover, it should be noted that the image which these forbidden joys take is fatally *feminine*: the witches which, through the mediation of Lady Macbeth tempt Macbeth to murder the man who has treated him with the very confidence that Raphael's father has just shown towards his son. The vitality and plenitude which this money thus represents for Raphael takes the form of a woman; the transgression which leads to her possession, however, is fatal for Macbeth, for M. de Valentin *père*, and, as we shall see, for his son.

Raphael takes the gamble. He decides to risk a wager at the 'fatal tapis vert' set up in the hall:

> *En proie à des angoisses inexprimables, je jetai soudain un regard translu-*
> *cide autour de moi. Certain de n'être aperçu par aucune personne de con-*
> *naissance, je pariai ... (77).*

The moment in which Raphael foresakes the paternal *via recta* to commit a speculation that can only be called 'criminal' is also the origin of that 'seconde vue' which plays such an essential role in the Balzacian aesthetic. The sentiment of guilt thus converges with the power of 'penetration':

> *De cette soirée date la première observation physiologique à laquelle j'ai dû*
> *cette espèce de pénétration qui m'a permis de saisir quelques mystères de*
> *notre double nature. Je tournais le dos à la table où se disputait mon futur*
> *bonheur, bonheur d'autant plus profond peut-être, qu'il était criminel ...*
> *malgré ... obstacles, par un privilège accordé aux passions qui leur donne le*
> *pouvoir d'anéantir l'espace et le temps, j'entendais distinctement les paroles*
> *des deux joueurs, je connaissais leurs points, je savais celui de deux qui re-*
> *tournait le roi comme si j'eusse vu les cartes ... (77-8).*

Raphael's 'crime,' his violation of the confidence and moral authority of his father endows him with what might be called an 'eidetic intuition,' the ability to accede to a realm of essences otherwise veiled by the phenomena of immediate perception. This transgression and the power of penetration that it confers also characterize the commodity owner, whose insight can pierce (*perceive*) the 'natural skin' of his wares in order to grasp their 'value-soul.'

But Raphael's newly-won vision, with which he can see 'qui retournait le roi,' does not prevent him from being seen by another *roi*, just at the critical moment:

> *Mon père passa devant moi tout à coup, je compris alors cette parole de l'Ecriture: L'esprit de Dieu passa devant sa face!* J'avais gagné *(78, my emphasis)*.

At the decisive moment, when there is no possibility any more of holding back – the dice have been thrown, les jeux sont faits – an image appears to witness the forbidden act. Raphael's father, appearing and disappearing, seems to Raphael like 'l'esprit de Dieux' about to give judgment. The next instant Raphael realizes that he has consummated the act: 'j'avais gagné.' There is no turning back now.

And yet can he – or we for that matter – be certain about what really has happened? The actual decision, the act itself, the turn of the card, has never been (re-) presented as such. It has taken place between the lines, as it were. If indeed it took place at all. The only actual witness is the very figure whose authority is thereby violated: Raphael's father.

In the absence of an answer, the effects of whatever has taken place are evident enough. If the Law has been violated, its authority seems all the more tyrannical: 'J'étais comme un condamné qui, marchant au supplice, a rencontré le roi' (78). Raphael's win seems to be a sign of vindication: the king is surprisingly benevolent and annuls the sentence of death. But immediately there appears a shadow of doubt, a certain *hasard*:

> *Par hasard, un homme décoré réclama quarante francs qui manquaient. Je fus soupçonné par des yeux inquiets, je pâlis et des gouttes de sueur sillonnèrent mon front. Le crime d'avoir volé mon père me parut bien vengé (78).*

Although he is subsequently exonerated, Raphael's guilt taints his luck, calling his breakthrough into question. For indeed, in breaking the law laid down by his father, in stealing from him, Raphael has sought to break through the constraints of a paternal tyranny, to break away from his patrimony. Yet the character of this attempted breakthrough is displayed by the metaphors in which it is described:

> *J'avais gagné. A travers le tourbillon d'hommes qui gravitait autour des joueurs, j'accourus à la table* en m'y glissant avec la dextérité d'une anguille qui s'échappe par la maille rompue d'un filet. *De douleureuses, mes fibres devinrent joyeuses (78, my emphasis).*

Raphael's breakthrough, which transforms the pain of his 'fibres' into joy, is only possible because of a *broken fiber,* 'par la maille rompue d'un filet,' through which he can slip into a realm of liberty, joy, and self-possession, with the dexterity of an eel, whose very figure and movement is that of an unbroken, linear continuity. Like the serpent of the frontispiece, this eel is another 'very spiritual epigraph' of the novel. Its spirit, here at least, is not difficult to identify. A paternal interdiction giving rise to a desire; the transgression of an *actus interruptus*; the guilt, but also the power that ensues and that involves a certain penetration: even without the eel slipping through that broken net, there could be little doubt that the scene being played out here is an *Urszene*, and that what is at stake is nothing less than the (maternal) phallus. In order even to begin to discuss its ramifications, however, I shall have to digress briefly and review the significance of the phallus as Freud analyzed it.

Commenting on the theoretical import of the phallus, Jacques Lacan writes:

> *Le phallus dans la doctrine freudienne n'est pas un fantasme, s'il faut entendre par là un effet imaginaire. Il n'est pas non plus comme tel un objet ... pour autant que ce terme tend à apprécier la réalité intéressée dans une relation. Il est encore bien moins l'organe, pénis ou clitoris, qu'il symbolise. Et ce n'est pas sans raison que Freud en a pris la référence au simulacre qu'il était pour les Anciens.*[1]

If the phallus is neither a phantasm, in the sense of an imaginary 'effect,' nor an object, nor finally a physical organ, but rather a *simulacrum* (understood as a representation that does not re-present anything that was, is, or will ever be *present*), it is because, Lacan continues, the phallus is

> *un signifiant ... déstinée à désigner dans leur ensemble les effets de signifié, en tant que le signifiant les conditionne par sa présence de signifiant.*[2]

The phallus as signifier derives from what Freud designated as the complex of castration (whereby 'complex' should be understood also as signifying *context*). The child 'discovers' castration when it perceives that the mother does not possess the organ it previously believed she had. The child subsequently interprets this perception as the perception of an absence, the result of a real act of castration. This act menaces the child as well, inasmuch as it desires to possess the mother. Its desire to possess what it has hitherto perceived to be the very origin and essence of life itself, its presence and plenitude – the mother – thus becomes a fatal temptation, at least as long as it *perceives* castration to involve the absence or loss of a possible, even indispensable presence: the maternal phallus. Until the child can renounce the wish to possess or to become what never was nor will have 'been' – the phallus – it remains subjected to the full and ambivalent force of 'castration.' Thus, phallus and castration are as inseparable as they are paradoxical. The phallus can be said to 'originate' in castration, but only in the sense that the latter, as Derrida has written, entails

> *l'affirmation de cette non-origine, le lieu vide et remarquable de cent blancs auxquels on ne peut donner sens, multipliant les suppléments de marque et les jeux de substitution à l'infini.*[3]

Constituted and de-constituted by castration, the phallus functions as an irreducible metaphor, referring not to a reality (castration), but to that which annuls and perpetuates all reference as an interminable text, a concatenation of signifiers that *articulates* (but never simply *expresses*) the movement of desire.

The movement of the eel through the broken link of the (paternal) net, on the contrary, also represents the 'phallus,' yet precisely not as that irreducible *difference* which constitutes the articulation of a text, but as *image*: the visible representation of a substantial, self-present object, coherent and continuous, self-identical in its movement, independent of the text (net) in which it is caught. The interstice, for this desire and its vagabond imagination, is the gateway to freedom, a hole through which to escape, an absence leading to presence. Visible *resemblance*, by which images such as a candle, a herring, a serpent, purse and keys, an eel become representations of the 'phallus,' indicates the wish to master the difference of articulation as negativity by determining the phallus as a phenomenon, an entity, a signified, rather than as a mark, trait, or trace. And this is why the *jeu des cartes* – a 'turn' located between[4] two presents without itself ever being present – cannot be seen, even by Raphael's penetrating double vision. And it is why this non-present is replaced by the apparition of the father, who bars the son's way to the plenitude of the phallus, and yet who himself appears as a figure of the Divine Spirit. Within the horizon of presence and absence, the paternal law no less than its *name* appears exclusively privative, a barrier to be overcome or a net to be broken through. As a skeleton to be covered, or a debt to be repaid. What is commonly called the 'phallic symbol' in fact *denies* the phallus precisely because its 'symbolism' is not that of the *signifier*, but rather that of the *image*, whose principle is that of visible likeness.

The irrecuperable investment of 'castration' is *denied* – we will soon explore the implications of this term – by a life seeking to reappropriate its expenses in a profitable investment: like a candle consuming itself in a light that promises eternal life; a herring to be eaten; money cast away in the hope of bringing a greater return. And yet ineluctably, at the 'end' of such efforts there is always the remarkable and fatal *rock* of castration:[5] a rock without substance, depth, or solidity – be it that of the cave or the corner, the valley

or the inter-val – or that of a 'mark' re-marking its 'self.' And it is the intuition of this fateful 'end' that leads Raphael inexorably to the *jeu*, which he
seeks to master with his double vision and yet which eludes his sight; which
he solicits for an answer to his destiny and yet where he finds only the echo
of his desire; which promises joy and liberation but only enthrals him all the
more inextricably in the paternal net from which he is seeking to escape.
Thus, his father rewards him for his theft by elevating him to full partnership
in his doomed struggle to save the family name, and as Raphael recalls, no
punishment could have been more enslaving:

> *Le jour où mon père parut en quelque sorte m'avoir émancipé, je tombai
> sous le joug le plus odieux ... je compris tous les chagrins dont l'empreinte
> flétrissait la figure de mon père (80).*

The fate of an apparent emancipation to full equality which in fact entails
merely another, more effective form of subordination, is hardly unknown in
the world of commodity-production. But in the specific psychic economy
that emerges here as the correlative of that production, it is becoming increasingly clear that 'si le joueur ne perd, il perdra.'[6]

12

The Matrix

Dix mois après avoir payé ses créanciers, mon père mourut de chagrin; il m'adorait et m'avait ruiné; cette idée le tua (81).

Raphael thus recounts how his father was ruined by the very legality he had sought to impose upon his son. This son is now an orphan:

Je n'avais ni parents ni protecteurs. Sans cesse arrêté dans ses expansions, mon âme s'était repliée sur elle-même ... le despotisme de mon père m'avait ôté toute confiance en moi ... je ne croyais pas que ma voix pût exercer le moindre empire. ... Malgré la voix intérieure qui doit soutenir les hommes de talent dans leurs luttes et qui me criait: 'Courage! marche!' ... je doutais de moi comme un enfant (82).

Orphaned, Raphael's situation is that of infancy in the most literal (etymological) sense: he lacks the power of making himself heard. Not that he does not have great things to say: it is their execution that lets him despair. He is incapable of carrying out what he carries within:

Porter des trésors dans une besace, et ne pouvoir rencontrer une enfant, quelque jeune fille curieuse pour les lui faire admirer! J'ai souvent voulu me tuer de désespoir (84).

Just as a value only exists in the commodity-world insofar as it circulates and augments itself (as capital), so here too a certain ability to circulate is required.

At this point in his narrative – the history of a voice haunted by silence – Raphael is once again interrupted by Emile, and the authority of his voice again called into question:

> – *Joliment tragique ce soir! s'écria Emile.*
> – *Eh! laisse-moi condamner ma vie, répondit Raphael. Si ton amitié n'a pas la force d'écouter mes élégies, si tu ne peux me faire crédit d'une demi-heure d'ennui, dors! Mais ne me demande plus alors compte de mon suicide qui gronde, qui se dresse, qui m'appelle et que je salue (84).*

By thus appealing to the curiosity of his listener, to his desire to know or discover, Raphael can demand an extension of his credit and thereby sustain the credibility of his voice, narrating his life from beginning to end: 'Dès ce moment [Emile] prêta toute son attention à Raphael en le regardant d'un air hébété' (84).

If Raphael thus effectively silences his sceptical listener, it is because the voice of the narrator, as Walter Benjamin has observed, derives its authority from its own death. In his essay on 'the Storyteller' Benjamin writes that 'death is the sanction of everything that the storyteller can tell. He has *borrowed* his authority from death' (my italics).[1] If I have stressed the word 'borrow' (geliehen), it is because the authority of the story-teller must be understood as originating elsewhere, and hence as entailing a debt that will have to be paid back at some time in the near or distant future. Raphael's narrative speculates upon (the value of) his own death, for this alone appears capable of sealing its meaning. In this respect, his narration repeats the pact he has made with the *peau de chagrin*: in exchange for his death, his life will be made worth living, his desires fulfilled. The struggle to impose himself by means of his voice is realized in the story he tells to a now docile, if not spellbound listener.

Raphael can now continue to tell the story of his efforts to be heard without fear of interruption:

> *Combien de fois, muet, immobile, n'ai-je pas admiré la femme de mes rêves, surgissant dans un bal ... (83).*

'Muet, immobile,' unheard and unheeded by the woman of his dreams – this is the situation Raphael vows to change. The scene which his desire envisages places him at its centre:

> *Je voulus me venger de la société, je voulus posséder l'âme de toutes les femmes en me soumettant les intelligences, et voir tous les regards fixés sur moi quand mon nom serait prononcé par un valet à la porte d'un salon (85).*

Again, Raphael becomes the image of his image: this time not the object of
the paternal glance but of 'tous les regards' - and the instrument of this attention is again a voice: that of a valet announcing his name. The servant obviates
the necessity for Raphael to raise his own voice; this is to be done for him.
Silent and yet eloquent, he shall be the object of all eyes. In this position, he
can possess and dominate the world and its women, or more precisely,
the Woman, 'la femme de mes rêves,' and thus escape the fatal 'torments
d'une impuissante energie qui se dévorait elle-même.' These energies, so
fatal when latent, must be put to work, externalized, directed, invested;
they must be put into circulation, *verwertet*, objectified in 'un ouvrage qui
pût attirer l'attention publique sur moi, me faire une fortune ou un nom' (87).
Just as in the commodity-producing society no necessary 'qualitative' relation
exists between the labour actually expended in production and the exchange
value of the commodity produced, Raphael's labour is designed to produce
'un ouvrage' which will *make his name* in the world, whose value is thereby
determined by a certain market, by its effect upon others, and in terms of the
recognition it procures for its producer. And the essence of this recognition is
the woman who alone can make Raphael's life worth living. Describing his as-
cetic existence while working on his 'ouvrage,' a 'wiser' Raphael speaks of his
labour as

> *ce sacrifice de tous les jours, ce travail de ver à soie inconnu au monde et
> dont la seule recompense est peut-être dans le travail même. ... Amant ef-
> féminé de la paresse orientale, amoureux de mes rêves, sensuel, j'ai tou-
> jours travaillé, me refusant à gouter les jouissances de la vie parisienne ...
> et la femme était cependant ma seule chimère, une chimère que je caressais
> et qui me fuyait toujours! Enfin ma vie a été une cruelle antithèse, un per-
> pétuel mensonge (92-3).*

Work is directed at a chimera no less phantasmatic than the 'figment' (*Gespinst*) of which Marx wrote and which he traced to the 'spectral objectivity'
(*gespenstige Gegenständlichkeit*) of the commodity. Yet here a new factor
emerges: this chimera is a woman, 'une chimère que je caressais et qui me
fuyait toujours!' Marx, in a revealing metaphor, also hints at the elusive, and
illicit, feminity of the commodity: 'The objectivity of the value of commodities differs from Dame Quickly inasmuch as we never know where it is to be
had.'[2] The desire of a certain labour pursues the chimera of a woman who is
not to be had, and yet whose femininity seems to found the very idea of possession and production itself. To avoid the 'cruel antithesis' and 'perpetual lie'
(which, we remember, also characterized the gamblers) Raphael develops a
plan which subordinates labour, the production of a masterwork, to the wager
which in a sense work has never ceased to be. This plan, Raphael relates, 'fut

comme un pari fait avec moi-même, et où j'étais le joueur et l'enjeu' (87). The Prince of Players simply substitutes a certain labour for the calculation of the gambling table, but the stakes remain the same.

Nonetheless, the substitution is not without importance since it situates Raphael, in contrast to the gamblers, squarely on the side of production, a move which his narration repeats and confirms. This too is part of a patrimony that forbids him to enter the casinos. The gamblers' antithesis, between an impoverished present and the dream of an affluent future, is now transformed into that of death and life, or the antithesis of *death-in-life*:[3] 'Je me bâtissais une tombe pour renaître brillant et glorieux. J'allais risquer de mourir pour vivre' (87). This antithesis, however, reveals the complicity of its two terms, death and life, within the horizon of production and of presence. Death is represented as a tomb, which does not merely represent the absence of life, but which houses its remains. If Raphael hopes to be reborn from this tomb to new glory, it is surely because his 'tomb' is intimately bound to that other tomb in which Mme de Valentin lies buried on an island in the Loire.

Again, the possibility of a certain production and rebirth is confounded with Raphael's maternal heritage. Yet, if we read further, we find that the very form of the antithesis, at least as it functions decisively in the Balzacian text, reflects the structure of the tomb. For the antithesis permits an irreducible exteriority (of two mutually exclusive terms) to appear as an indissociable interiority. Ultimately, the antithesis, like the tomb, allows the *presentation of absence* to take place, and hence it provides the basis for the system of representations that constitutes the Balzacian text. And if, as seems likely, the tomb which exemplifies the fundamental antithesis, that between life and death, is the tomb of Raphael's mother, we may begin to understand the full sense in which antithesis (and its related dualistic forms: alternative, antagonism, paradox) forms the *matrix* of the Balzacian text and the syntax of its desire.

The 'tomb' to which Raphael's desire leads him, the 'sépulcre aérien' which is to be the site of his labours to produce the work that will save, or make, his name, is the scene of the antithesis, or rather of a series of antitheses which we will now examine. Situated in the midst of Paris, the Saint-Quentin Hotel is a centre of tranquility, located in a street which 'n'aboutissait à rien et ne devait pas être très passante' (90). This dead-end street in the middle of Paris both expresses and articulates Raphael's desire and his destiny: the search for a centre and the voyage along a way whose end is dead. The street, like the hotel itself, is peopled solely by women and girls:

> *A l'angle de la rue de Cluny, je vis une petite fille d'environ quatorze ans*
> *qui jouait au volant avec une de ses camarades. ... Devant chaque porte,*
> *des femmes assises devisaient comme dans une ville de province par un*
> *jour de fête (90).*

This feminine scene – 'scène ravissante' – *province* in the midst of the city, on
a street that leads nowhere, invites depiction:

> *J'observai d'abord la jeune fille, dont la physionomie était d'une admirable*
> *expression, et le corps tout posé pour un peintre (90).*

And yet the purity and serenity of the ravishing scene is inseparable from its
poverty, and the poverty of Raphael, which forces him to seek refuge in a hotel, whose 'délabrement ... me fit espérer d'y rencontrer un gîte peu coûteux'
(90). No refuge escapes the law of exchange and its economy; the shadow of
Raphael's patrimony hangs over the dead-end street.

But no less important is the attitude it imposes upon Raphael within the
hotel. There he finds Mme Gaudin and her daughter, Pauline: the father of
the house is away, missing. Raphael soon takes his place and agrees to finish
her education – thus following in the steps of his illustrious predecessor,
Rousseau. But when he feels himself threatened by the very intimacy of the
household, it appears that the paternal laws are no less binding for the lover
than for the son:

> *Tromper une femme ou faire faillite a toujours été même chose pour moi.*
> *Aimer une jeune fille ou se laisser aimer par elle constitue un vrai contrat*
> *dont les conditions doivent être bien entendues. Nous sommes maîtres*
> *d'abandonner la femme qui se vend, mais non pas la jeune fille qui se*
> *donne, car elle ignore l'étendue de son sacrifice (95-6).*

The gift of virginity involves not simply *tromperie*, for the moral question is
equated with an economic one: to 'deceive' is to go bankrupt, and Raphael
seeks refuge from this menace by assuming the more secure role of a brother,
and an artist: it is the solution of the *Marchand* that he embraces:

> *Quand je rentrais, je trouvais Pauline chez moi, dans la toilette la plus mod-*
> *este; mais, au moindre mouvement, sa taille souple et les attraits de sa per-*
> *sonne se révélaient sous l'étoffe grossière. Comme l'héroïne du conte de*
> *Peau-d'Ane, elle laissait voir un pied mignon dans d'ignobles souliers.*
> *Mais ces jolis trésors, cette richesse de jeune fille, tout ce luxe de beauté*
> *fut comme perdu pour moi. Je m'étais ordonné à moi-même de ne voir*
> *qu'une sœur en Pauline ... (95).*

The treasures of Pauline become the perils of Raphael: the wealth of her femininity is less covered than revealed by 'l'étoffe grossière' that she wears. And the foot that peeks out from her 'ignobles souliers' recalls that other foot of Cathérine Lescault in *Le Chef-d'œuvre inconnu*, a reference that becomes all the more significant when Raphael continues:

J'admirais cette charmante fille comme un tableau, comme le portrait d'une maîtresse morte; enfin, c'était mon enfant, ma statue. Pygmalion nouveau, je voulais faire d'une vierge vivante et colorée, sensible et parlante, un marbre (95).

Raphael, this new Pygmalion, *inverts* the latter's desire, which is also that of Frenhofer and of the sculptor Sarrasine. Yet here, artistic representation does not simply hinder or replace possession of the object: it is its very condition. The virgin life which breathes and speaks carries with it not simply the promise of fulfilment but the menace of a fatal *faillite*. This all too living life conceals within itself the threat of death: to be possessed it must be transformed, represented as a statue, a marble, a tableau. And not merely represented, but represented as a loss: this 'luxe de beauté [qui] fut comme perdu' for Raphael is represented by him as a *dead mistress*. This representation itself is anything but innocent: it has the hidden form of a murder: the dead mistress, the lost luxury, takes the place of the living virgin which it corrupts, destroys, and conserves as its referent.

To avoid that *tromperie* which Raphael equates with bankruptcy (and whose fatal effects are represented in *Sarrasine* and *Le Chef d'œuvre inconnu*) a new deception is required: Raphael assumes the role of the Father ('c'était mon enfant') and the artist (' ... ma statue'). His child – work before the work he intends to produce – is the tomb of the life it represents: the portrait of a dead mistress.

Yet it is no simple tomb. Its essence, production of a vagabond imagination, entails a certain luxury: the luxury of a wrap, a veil, a *vestment* permitting the speculation of an imaginary investment to take place:

J'étais né pour l'amour impossible, et le hasard a voulu que je fusse servi par delà mes souhaits. Combien de fois n'ai-je pas vétu de satin les pieds mignons de Pauline, emprisonné sa taille svelte comme un jeune peuplier dans une robe de gaze, jeté sur son sein une légère écharpe en lui faisant fouler les tapis de son hôtel et le conduisant à une voiture élégante! Je l'eusse adorée ainsi (97).

The desire that produces this vestment (a word that here should also be read as a verb [*vétu*]) is that of the veil (again a genitive to be read both ways: as objective and subjective). Raphael, confined to the hotel, imprisons the body of Pauline, 'comme une jeune peuplier,' in a 'robe de gaze'; his gesture ('*jeté sur son sein* une légère écharpe') is that of the gamblers and of the artist: it will also be his last gesture. Throwing away in order to gain, imprisoning in order to escape ('la conduisant à une voiture élégante'), murdering in order to create, dying in order to live: these are the figures that describe the articulations of his desire. The imagination which wrapped M. de Valentin in a reddish pamphlet only to consign him to the devouring mouth is driven to cover and to veil a body, a foot, which it can only desire at a distance through the contiguity of a vestment which functions as a second skin, one whose depth allows for a penetration that does not destroy either the penetrator or the penetrated.

Yet if penetration is meant as an instrument of possession and appropriation, its destructive aspect is unmistakable:

> *J'aime à froisser sous mes désirs de pimpantes toilettes, à briser des fleurs, à porter une main dévastatrice dans les élégants édifices d'une coiffure embaumée. Des yeux brûlants, cachés par une voile de dentelle que les regards percent comme la flamme déchire la fumée du canon, m'offrent de fantastiques attraits (96).*

These 'fantastic attractions' define the power of the veil: what is veiled is not merely the female body: it is the very organ of sight itself – 'des yeux brûlants' – ardent behind a lace cover that protects them as the Easter candle did not, and that therefore invites the penetration of other eyes; behind the veil a woman, seeing, is barely seen. By metonymic extension, the veils themselves: the founding condition of this perceptive, imaginative penetration, become the object of desire. 'Ces voiles de volupteuses mousselines' become the negation of poverty, the essence of luxury and love, the origin of a certain *lux*, of a translucence which preserves the antithesis of opacity and transparence: purifying poverty of its stigmas, corrupting virgin purity, murdering a certain life. This veil is not merely a surface: it has volume and depth. It is the medium and milieu of passion:

> *Ah! vive l'amour dans la soie, sur la cachemire, entouré des merveilles du luxe qui le parent merveilleusement bien, parce que lui-même est un luxe peut-être (96, my emphasis).*

The luxury of these veils leads ineluctably to another *entourage*: that of the sovereign. This time, however, it is not a King, but a Queen:

> *Enfin, je veux revoir cette mystérieuse femme, mais éclatante, mais au milieu du monde, mais vertueuse, environnée d'hommages, vêtue de dentelles, étincelante de diamants, donnant ses ordres à la ville, et si haut placée*

et si imposante que nul n'ose lui adresser des voeux. Au milieu de sa cour, *elle me jette un regard à la dérobée, un regard qui dément ces artifices, un regard qui me sacrifie le monde et les hommes (96, my emphasis).*

This is the sacrifice Raphael is eager to accept: not that of the virgin but of the sovereign, the mysterious woman who is both at the centre, the mi-lieu of her court of luxury, and who reigns high above it: *souffleur* and *metteur-en-scène* at once: author and *vedette*; the sovereign who sacrifices the world 'et les hommes' to her lover, by a *glance*. It is the triumph of imagination and of the desire that informs it. The dead mistress is revived, circulating at the centre of her court and yet mysteriously remaining the same, mistress and manifestation of value no less than that other phantasm, money. Like money (and also like the *peau de chagrin*) she is unique in being, or having that which cannot be bought: a particular wrap.

En ne faisant rien de ce que font les autres femmes, en ne marchant pas, ne vivant pas comme elles, en s'enveloppant dans un manteau qu'elles ne peuvent avoir, *en respirant des parfums à elle, ma maîtresse me semble être bien mieux à moi ... (97, my emphasis).*

Again it is a certain vestment, a coat which she alone can have, that is the sign of her singular superiority, of her very sovereignty, placing her above those 'petites créatures' whom Raphael calls 'les portmanteaux de la mode.' Like Fœdora, this sovereign is the Mode itself, its essence and quintessence, enveloping herself in the wraps of her sovereignty. This Queen, protected and defined by her mantle, 'au milieu du monde,' and yet separated from it by her wrap, occupies its innermost centre and the pinnacle above it. Among the fatal circulation of commodities (things, persons, signs) she constitutes the ever-identical *Urphänomen*, the living presence which guarantees the legitimacy of the world of representations and the possibility of productive investment. This Queen incorporates the very image of that investment: this is her 'mystery.' For her very being, *in the vestment* of her robe, is accessible only to the speculation of the *regard*: it is, in essence, *speculative*.

After thus rereading the tomb, we can now rewrite the 'ravishing scene' as a scenario which is that of fetishism itself. The dead-end street scene, suggesting the provincial and rural origins both of Raphael as individual and of his society, provides the setting for a domestic drama which plays itself out in the interstices of the text it seeks to reduce to a tableau. The origin of this scenario is precisely the denial of the interstice: the denial of sexual difference articulated in the problem of castration. The discovery of castration is the discovery *tout court*: it is dis-covered through a certain uncovering of the body of the mother. The absence of the penis that the child has believed (desired) the mother to

possess confronts the subject of desire with the problem of *difference*. The
fetichist seeks to solve this problem by means of imagination alone. He denies
the evidence of his eyes and replaces it with a monumental construction that
is intrinsically antithetical. Freud gave this antithesis the name of denial (*Ver-
leugnung*) and explained it as follows:

> '*Skotomization*' *seems to me particularly unsuitable, for it suggests that the
> perception has been fully obliterated [glatt weggewischt worden], so that
> the result would be the same as when a visual impression falls on a blind
> spot in the retina. In the case we are discussing, on the contrary, we see
> that the perception has persisted and that a very energetic action has been
> exerted to keep up the denial of it. It is not true that the child emerges
> from his experience of seeing the female parts with an unchanged belief in
> the woman having the phallus. He retains this belief but he also gives it up;
> during the conflict between the dead weight of the unwelcome perception
> and the force of the opposite wish, a compromise is constructed such as is
> only possible in the realm of unconscious modes of thought – by the pri-
> mary process. In the world of psychical reality the woman still has a penis
> all the same [dennoch], but this penis is no longer the same as it once was.
> Something else has taken its place, has been appointed its successor, so to
> speak, and now absorbs all the interest which formerly belonged to the
> penis. But this interest undergoes yet another very strong reinforcement,
> because the horror of castration sets up a sort of permanent memorial to
> itself by creating this substitute. ... One can now see what the fetish
> achieves and how it is enabled to persist. It remains a token of triumph
> over the threat of castration and a safeguard against it; it also saves the
> fetishist from being a homosexual by endowing women with the attribute
> which makes them acceptable as sexual objects (my emphasis).[4]

The secret of the Balzacian antithesis (antithesis as the manifestation of a secret) can be retraced in this text of Freud to the conjunction *all the same*
(dennoch): 'the woman has a penis all the same, but this penis is no longer the
same ... .' *All the same:* this marks the function of the veil in the economy
of fetishistic desire. The difference (of the sexes) – all (is) the same. And
yet, not quite. All is different, all the same. Nature is untainted, and all
the same tainted. Virginity is pure, and all the same impure. The image is
absent, invisible, and all the same present. It is the veil that expresses
this antithesis and the secret it constitutes and confirms. The veil is the compromise ('a compromise is constructed') that promises. It also denies the 'non-
secret' of castration[5] in order to erect a monument to it ('a token,' *Denkmal*)
that is also a tomb in which the ruins of a certain (infantile) desire are preserved. Surrogate and sign ('Zeichen'), the fetish-veil seeks to inaugurate the

underivable substitution of 'castration' (this word should always be read within quotation marks) by an original substitution ('Etwas anderes ist an seine Stelle getreten') pointing to an original referent (the plenitude and presence of the maternal phallus, necessarily invisible). If this 'referent' is also the first cause, it is as inseparable from its 'effect,' its veil and vestment, as the *signifié* is from the *signifiant*. And this veil and vestment are not merely the product of a speculative-imaginary desire: they are also the work, as denial, of a *will*, of 'a very energetic action' which must be perennially repeated, even though it paradoxically (antithetically) takes the form of a unitary event. It is, therefore, no accident that Raphael, like Louis Lambert, writes a *Traité de la Volonté*, or that the dynamics of the Balzacian text assume the form of a *struggle*. It is, and must be, a hopeless struggle, a struggle without end, since it is only in and *as* struggle that the fetishistic *denial* can be maintained and castration mastered as negativity or absence. Yet this struggle, which is the very condition of all (productive) investment, is also its antithesis: a fatal expense, permanently denying the appropriation it promises, and compromises. The struggle is inevitably haunted by the bankruptcy it hopes to overcome and incessantly confirms.

The manifestation of this struggle – its lieu and milieu – is, above all, vestiary. The fetishistic denial of castration is played out at the level of perception, between the real and the imaginary; the lack of a certain appearance is perceived as the lack of what did not appear. This lack must therefore be invested (*besetzt*: cathected) with a vestment that preserves the vestiges of what it conceals, thus denying what for the fetishist can only be a mortal divestment. The choice of clothes as fetishes, Freud writes, 'fixes upon the scene of undressing as the last moment in which the woman could still be regarded as phallic.'[6] And yet the fetishization of clothes, he adds, has another, more functional aspect:

> In very subtle cases the fetish itself – its structure – has become the vehicle both of the denial as of the assertion of castration. This was the case with a man whose fetish was a suspensory belt such as can also be worn as bathing trunks. This piece of clothing covers the genitals as well as all genital differences. Analysis revealed that it could mean both that the woman is castrated, and that she is not castrated, and moreover it allows the supposition that the man may be castrated as well, for all these possibilities could be equally well concealed beneath the belt. ... Naturally, a fetish of this kind, constructed out of two opposing ideas [aus Gegensätze doppelt geknüpft], is especially resilient [hält natürlich besonders gut].[7]

Woven or knotted together out of oppositions, 'aus Gegensätze doppelt geknüpft,' the fetish displays the form of the Balzacian antithesis itself: the unity of inversions and reversals, the feminine masculinity of Raphael and the masculine femininity of the women he desires; the confusion of youth and age, of poverty and wealth, innocence and depravation; the inherent instability of images consuming themselves in order to produce the enigma of an invisible plenitude; the density and translucence of the luxurious veil, inviting penetration and possession and yet devouring and dispossessing the desire it thus solicits and evokes. And the medium of such inversion and reversals remains necessarily that of perception: of the glance and of the voice, promising through self-effacement the presence of a plenitude which can only be maternal. The irreducible *ambivalence* of 'castration' – its splitting and doubling – is thus reduced to an *antithesis* by the desire of (maternal) presence. Leading to the fetish is always the desire to untie that double knot, in order to see and to know (*voir et savoir*), and thus to dominate (*pouvoir*) what is behind the fetish. 'Behind' the fetish, however, is a desire captivated by its own image, and 'blind' to its own *jeu*. Which indicates why the antithesis must be the *matrix* of the Balzacian text; and why, like its image, the *peau de chagrin*, it is destined to *disappear*.

13

ʿCes riens qui ont tant de prix ...ʾ

If the antithesis is the matrix of this text, it is also the repudiation of a certain patrimony. Above all, of the paternal name, the name of the dead father, the trace of a mortal and inescapable indebtedness, the economy of an irrevocable expense. Up to the moment when he is confronted by Foedora – by her *name* – Raphael's efforts reflect a paternal economy which proscribes all speculation (as *jeu*) and which demands a rigorous accounting for every expense. The aim of this economy is inseparable from the paternal name, that M. de Valentin seeks to 'save' and that Raphael seeks to 'make.' Yet this paternal economy, which seeks to reduce its expenses to a minimum, is itself devoured by the circulation it seeks to master. This is also the fate of labour and of the labourer in capitalist production. The individual labourer is consumed by the process and relations of production which 'maintain' his life; and the role of labour itself diminishes with the development (and automation) of productive forces. The importance of living labour, and the 'value' of the class of labourers (the social costs of their reproduction) are progressively reduced and replaced by non-living means of production while surplus value is appropriated by speculators and investors.

In all senses then, labour, life reproducing itself, figure of a certain paternity, is supplanted by the laws and economy of exchange, speculation and investment. What Rastignac describes to Raphael as the 'théorie de la fortune' thus summarizes a history which is that both of the individual subject and of society:

Toi, tu travailles? eh bien, tu ne feras jamais rien. Moi, je suis propre à tout et bon à rien, paresseux comme un homard? eh bien, j'arriverai à tout. Je me répands, je me pousse, on me fait place; je me vante, on me croit; je fais des dettes, on les paye! La dissipation, mon cher, est un système politique (98).

Dissipation is a political system to be sure, but one of political *economy*: commodity-production as the production of value 'dissipates' the energies of those who labour in order to allow them to be reappropriated as capital, the value-producing 'property' of a non-productive class of speculators and investors. For this class 'dissipation' remains an investment, speculation in the sense of a *reflexive* movement. Rastignac speaks with the reflexive voice of money-begetting-money, spending itself and yet retaining and accumulating itself: 'je me répands, je me pousse, on me fait place; je me vante, on me croit ... .' The expense of this dissipation is productive and reproductive: if it is constituted by exchange, this exchange is directed towards the maintenance of life, the fulfilment of 'need,' the presentation of a living present. And this is why the 'essence' of this speculation can never appear 'as such' within the 'economic' sphere, in the limited sense, since the transcendental subject-object, capital, is never visible per se and cannot simply be identified with the class that possesses it. It is only outside the spheres of commodity-production and circulation that this subject can appear, mimed by the *antiquaire*, by the demon in the gambling casino, or by the 'dissipator':

Le dissipateur, lui, s'amuse à vivre, à faire courir ses chevaux. Si par hasard il perd ses capitaux, il a la chance d'être attaché à un ministre, à un ambassadeur. Il a encore des amis, une réputation et toujours d'argent. Connaissant les ressorts du monde, il les manoeuvre à son profit. Ce système est-il logique ... ? (99)

The boundless expense, the total speculation of the dissipator is governed by the aim of *profit*: if, like the *marchand*, he wagers everything, his patrimony and his very father, it is in the service of a logic which is the logic of value and which demonstrates the value of logic. His expense is always a productive and profitable investment. The labourer, and even the investor, like all those who cling to their patrimony, suffer the fate of the gamblers, ruined by the very 'hasard' that the dissipator so cleverly masters:

La vie d'un homme occupé à manger sa fortune devient souvent une spéculation; il place ses capitaux en amis, en plaisirs, en protecteurs, en connaissances. Un négociant risque-t-il un million? pendant vingt ans, il ne dort, ni ne boit, ni ne s'amuse; il couve son million, il le fait trotter par toute l'Europe; il s'ennuie, se donne à tous les démons que l'homme a inventés;

puis une liquidation, comme j'en ai vu faire, le laisse souvent sans un sou,
sans un nom, sans un ami (99).

'Sans un nom' – it is also Raphael's patrimony that Rastignac thus describes, and yet this patrimony here emerges not as that of an individual subject, but of a certain subjectivity itself: the subject of self-production, matrix
of all fetishism, that of the phallus no less than that of the commodity. Commodity-production is fetishistic, not simply because it effaces the process (and
relations) of production in the product – the commodity – but because production itself, inasmuch as it is *production of the self*, is commanded by the
chimera (*Gespenst*) of a living presence (the fulfilment of need) which is inherently *imaginary*, an image repressing the circulation and exchange which,
in capitalist production more than elsewhere, is its condition and its limit.
Fetishism – of money, of the phallus, and of the imaginary as such – defines
the innermost origin and end of a subject-producing-its-Self. This subject can
only constitute itself as the possibility of being-present to itself by repressing
castration, the text in which it is inscribed, and determining it as a real absence, a loss (of the penis), a need to be satisfied, a potentiality to be realized.
And yet, the remarkable trait of a society dominated by commodity-production is that this repression turns upon itself, re-turns, since it is no longer the
living human individual that can appear as the subject, but rather capital itself,
which emerges as a 'living monstrosity (*beseeltes Ungeheuer*'),[1] in the trinitarian
figure of value producing surplus value and reuniting in the unity of its movement: investment, speculation, 'Selbstverwertung des Werts.'

Capital itself thus becomes the real subject of (effective) need and its fulfilment, while the vital energies of the individuals are consumed in the process.[2] Consequently, the essential expression of the individual – the name, and
in particular, the paternal name – undergoes a double fate: it becomes the
name of the *dead father*, inasmuch as the law of circulation and exchange
which it reflects entails the consumption of the paternity of the individual
producer, while at the same time circulation and speculation have as their
'end' the production of value, manifested in the fetish, capital: a bodyless
head (*caput*). If capitalist circulation devours all determinate entities, all determinate names, it also preserves and conserves them in the process of production. In the terminology of Georges Bataille, it is a form of 'limited economy'
('économie restreinte') as opposed to 'universal economy' ('économie générale') which is determining.[3] This limited economy of fetishism requires the
production of a name that cannot be that of the father but rather of the
mother, since it must designate the plenitude and presence of self-production,
as production of the Self. Thus, the speculation and 'dissipation' which subverts the paternal law, the emergence of an ineluctable *jeu*, is already inscribed

in that law itself, in the production of the name. However, since what is named is not a determinate entity, a being-present, but the process of production as a whole, this name is necessarily maternal, re-presenting and re-producing a life present-to-itself. Such a life *appears* as the redemption of the paternal death and as an antidote to the castrative wound. The name, *Raphael*, designating the painter of the Redeemer of man, and signifying divine healing, can only be realized by a Divinity which gives and does not take; one which redeems the paternal debt through an absolutely original gift. The name of this 'gift of God,' which must be a feminine (maternal) name, can only be: *Foedora* (from Theo-dore: gift of God).

This name, which breaks the paternal 'law' while conserving it, is precisely the name that comes first to comfort Raphael, and then to captivate him:

> *Comment expliquer la fascination d'un nom? Foedora me poursuivit comme une mauvaise pensée avec laquelle on cherche à transiger (100).*

'Foedora' is the name in its full phenomenality: not that of a dead father, signifying debt, difference, and poverty, but the living expression of a living woman, symbol of desire and theme of (a) life:

> *Mais ce nom, cette femme, n'étaient-ils pas le symbole de tous mes désirs et le thème de ma vie? Le nom réveillait les poésies artificielles du monde. ... La comtesse Foedora, riche et sans amant, n'était-ce pas l'incarnation de mes espérances, de mes visions? Je me créai une femme, je la dessinai dans ma pensée, je la rêvai (100, my emphasis).*

This name is the incarnation of a woman – Raphael is captivated by the name and by the woman even before he sees her. She evokes unlimited 'creation': representations of revery, of art, and of poetry. The woman who bears the name invites possession because she is rich and has no lover: she promises the plenitude of a dual and exclusive relationship, *tertium non datur*.

This name lures Raphael from his 'tomb' because it incarnates the hopes that led him there in the first place. Yet the very presence, reality, and power of this name is inseparable from its phenomenality, its *sound*, which contrasts with and accompanies the silence of his reading:

> *Pendant ma lecture, le nom de Foedora retentissait en moi comme un son que l'on entend dans le lointain, qui ne vous trouble pas, mais qui se fait écouter (100).*

It is this sound that enables the name to traverse and to conserve a secure distance ('que l'on entend dans le lointain, qui ne vous trouble pas') while making itself heard *all the same* ('mais qui se fait écouter'). The power of this name, the wealth that it promises, is thus inseparable from the voice which embodies it. First, there is the irresistible solicitation of an inner voice:

> *Une voix me disait: 'Tu iras chez Foedora.' J'avais beau me débattre avec cette voix et lui crier qu'elle mentait, elle écrasait tous mes raisonnements avec ce nom: Foedora (100).*

And then, at their first meeting, there is the 'outer' voice of Foedora herself: 'Sa voix me causait un délire que j'avais peine à comprimer' (108). If the voice of Foedora produces such ecstasy in Raphael, it is because it presents her to him as a phenomenon – 'Vous êtes un phénomène' he will tell her – which is the expression of an essence, a sign which is inseparable from its referent, inviting the penetration and possession of a perception which traverses (per-) and seizes (-ception). The ecstasy of hearing Foedora is only matched by that of seeing her: 'Combien.d'heures ne suis-je pas resté plongé dans une extase ineffable occupé à *la voir*!' (107-8) This ineffable ecstasy of perception is one into which Raphael can plunge without losing himself, in which distance and difference efface themselves before the presence and plenitude they represent, by virtue of a certain transitoriness:

> *ces teintes transitoires du sentiment, ces riens qui ont tant de prix, ces mots dont l'accent épuise les trésors du langage, ces regards plus féconds que les plus riches poèmes (107).*

Difference and distance become the space in which plenitude and presence unfold, the condition of wealth and fecundity (of language, looks, and poetry): they become these 'riens qui ont tant de prix,' the nothings that produce everything, the movement of *value*. And Raphael's own voice, narrating this 'mystical scene,' rises to reproduce the impossible, to transform and transfigure the abyss that has opened into a mystery.and become the sign of a living soul (the *Wertseele*):

> *Dans chacune des scènes mystiques par lesquelles nous nous éprenons insensiblement d'une femme, s'ouvre un abîme à engloutir toutes les poésies humaines. Eh! comment pourrions-nous reproduire par des gloses les vives et mystérieuses agitations de l'âme ... (107, my emphasis).*

Raphael's own voice, his narration, is only secure in its presence by announcing the difference that separates (and binds) the echo from the original sound, the narration from the narrative, the discourse from communication in which two souls are fused and confused:

> *Je voulais lire un sentiment, un espoir, dans toutes ces phases du visage. Ces discours muets, pénétraient d'âme à âme comme un son dans l'echo ... (108).*

The 'text' which Raphael 'reads' is the embodiment of a voice, presenting and reserving the presence of the speaker, a text in which he finds passion 'empreinte en tout ... écrit sur les paupières italiennes de cette femme.' Yet Foedora is not only a woman: her text, in its fullness and harmony, in its totality, is that of a *novel*:

> *C'était plus qu'une femme, c'était un roman. Oui, ces richesses féminines, l'ensemble harmonieux des lignes, les promesses que cette riche structure faisant à la passion, étaient tempérés par une réserve constante, par une modestie extraordinaire, qui contrastaient avec l'expression de toute la personne. Il fallait une observation aussi sagace que la mienne ... (105).*

'C'était un roman': as a novel Raphael's infinite and dangerous expense seems to find a way of being recovered and reappropriated in and as the meaningful presence of a whole. The 'abyss' into which his desire seems to lead him can perhaps be filled with such meaning; the holes of the text might then become significant signs of a whole, soliciting 'une observation aussi sagace' as that of Raphael. It is this hope, in any case, that draws him from the penury of production into the adventure of a certain speculation.

14

Speculation

The 'theory of fortune' is the fortune of theory. In order to see and hear, to *know* the phenomenon of his desire, Raphael himself must be seen and heard. And this inaugurates a new phase in his struggle against the patrimony of poverty and against nature itself. In order to be seen and heard, he must first 'invest' himself, covering his debts and purifying himself of the stigmata of nature itself:

> *Mon bonheur, mon amour, dépendaient d'une moucheture de fange sur mon gilet blanc! Renoncer à la voir si je me crottais, si je me mouillais! Ne pas posséder cinq sous pour faire effacer par un décrotteur la plus légère tache de boue sur ma botte (114).*

Nature itself becomes the enemy of property and *propriété*, it soils the whiteness of a waistcoat no less than it ruins the form of a hat ('la pluie déformait mon chapeau'), which comes to mirror the state of its wearer:

> *Son existence artificielle arrivait à son dernier période, il était blessé, déjeté, fini, véritable haillon, digne représentant de son maître (113-14).*

Torn, tattered, wounded – this is the 'nature' that Raphael must cover at all costs:

> *Naguère insouciant en fait de toilette, je respectais maintenant mon habit comme un autre moi-même. Entre une blessure à recevoir et la déchirure de mon frac, je n'aurais pas hésité (114).*

The clothes veil and deny a wound whose existence is far from certain: the conditional ('je n'aurais pas') as well as the 'wounded' hat ('digne représentant de son maître' indicates why, at all costs Raphael must cover himself with the clothes of luxury. And yet his desire seems inextricably bound to the wound he seeks to cover and yet incessantly affirms:

> Oh! mon cher ami, quand certaines femmes trouvent du plaisir à nous déchirer le cœur, quand elles se sont promis d'y enfoncer un poignard et de le retourner dans la plaie, ces femmes-là sont adorables, elles aiment ou veulent être aimées (111).

This wound, inflicted by nature, by the woman he loves, or by himself, transforms his desire into a fatality:

> Sa voix me causait un délire que j'avais peine à comprimer. Imitant je ne me rappelle plus quel prince de Lorraine, j'aurais pu ne pas sentir un charbon ardent au creux de ma main pendant qu'elle aurait passé dans ma chevelure des doigts chatouilleux. Ce n'était plus une admiration, un désir, mais un charme, une fatalité (108).

The ambivalence of the wound is that of penetration itself: inflicting a laceration and healing it, filling the hole which it makes whole.

Yet if clothes are the second, supplementary nature of Raphel's speculation, its instrument and medium, the supreme spot remover and veil of vales, is money:

> Si l'amour doit plaider sa cause par des grands sacrifices, il doit les couvrir délicatement d'un voile, les ensevelir dans le silence ... pour eux (les hommes riches) le silence parle et le voile est une grâce, tandis que mon affreuse détresse me condamnait à d'épouvantables souffrances sans qu'il me fût permis de dire: 'J'aime!' ou 'Je meurs' (114).

Money covers, and it talks, making silence itself eloquent: the greater the 'sacrifice,' the greater the reserves. Its own disappearance into circulation is only the sign of its power and presence; it is a veil which expresses what it conceals, a voice which makes itself heard without wasting its breath. Money thus emerges as the medium of a phenomenality which effaces itself, not to be worn away by 'usure,' but rather to produce a translucency that permits a presence and plenitude to shine through, expressing and reserving itself in the infinite circulation of productive investment, the circle of self-production which is always new and always the same. It is the fortune of *theory* by producing the fortune, the light which permits a certain insight to take place. The incarnation of this fortune is Foedora: 'Ce cœur de femme était un dernier billet de loterie chargé de ma fortune' (106). Her 'essence' is a mystery: 'Ce mystère femelle vêtu de cachemire et de broderies' (129), conceals a 'heart' or a 'soul' behind the spectacle of self-effacement and self-production:

> J'aimais cette femme froide dont le cœur voulait être conquis à tout moment, et qui, en effaçant toujours les promesses de la veille, se produisait le lendemain comme une maîtresse nouvelle (113).

Fœdora is a 'novel' in all senses: producing herself always new by effacing what she was, inviting and eluding possession, calling Raphael's desire 'à pénétrer plus avant dans l'impénétrable caractère de Fœdora' (126-7). If she incarnates Raphael's desires, it is not as a creature of flesh and blood, but as a statue: her smile is 'le détestable sourire d'une statue de marbre, paraissant exprimer l'amour, mais froid' (113). This coldness, that of the statue, is that of the perfect speculation, producing itself without ever losing itself. Observing Fœdora at the theatre, Raphael recalls that 'Fœdora se produisait là comme un spectacle dans le spectacle' (128). Like the objects (commodities) of the *magasin d'antiquités*, she can be possessed only speculatively. Yet for Raphael, this possession involves a fatal expense, consuming his meagre resources while augmenting only his debt. His speculation even transforms his family name into a commodity. To get money, he allows Rastignac to 'sell' the life story of his aunt, thus profiting by her name: 'Il (Rastignac) avait vendu ma respectable tante, la marquise de Montbauron' (120). The sale of this 'dead soul' recalls to Raphael the threat of exile which his father had reserved for him were he to stray from the *via recta* of the paternal law: 'J'aime mieux m'embarquer pour le Brésil, et y enseigner aux Indiens l'algèbre, dont je ne sais pas un mot, que de salir le nom de ma famille' (120). And as with his father, his approaching ruin contrasts with the modest, yet profound resources of that other, 'matriarchal' family, the Gaudins. Unknown to him, Pauline supplies him with money from her own savings, watching over him in his distress with 'un regard presque maternel' (116). But the true wealth of the Gaudin household is adumbrated by a dream of Pauline's mother, in which a key that turns in a lock – that of Raphael's room – foretells a future that will put an end to all poverty:

> Ce soir, j'ai lu l'Evangile de saint Jean pendant que Pauline tenait suspendue entre ses doigts notre clef attaché dans une Bible, la clef a tourné. Ce présage annonce que Gaudin se porte bien et prospère. Pauline a recommencé pour vous et pour le jeune homme du numéro sept; mais la clef n'a tourné que pour vous. Nous serons tous riches. Gaudin reviendra millionnaire: je l'ai vu en rêve sur un vaisseau plein de serpents; heureusement l'eau était troublé, ce qui signifie or et pierreries d'outre-mer (117).

The dream bears the promise of the phallus, of a key which turns only for Raphael, of a vessel full of serpents and of the end of a long adventure: the father returning home as millionaire. It is the vision of a fulfilled paternity, announced by the voice of a mother, promising the end of speculation in a future which will finally be present.

15

Going (for) Broke

Once again, Raphael finds himself on the verge of ruin. His speculation, consisting of conspicuous consumption and deficit spending – prophetically named the 'English system' by Rastignac, a century before Keynes – fails to pay off. According to Rastignac, 'l'avenir était de tous les capitaux du monde le plus considérable et le plus solide' (126), and yet it is this very 'solidity' which bars the possession of the woman who embodies the essence of capital, its very 'heart':

> *Vous rencontrez souvent des gens de colossale apparence de qui le cœur est tendre et délicat sous un corps de bronze; mais elle cachait un cœur de bronze sous sa frêle et gracieuse enveloppe. Ma fatale science me déchirait bien des voiles (128).*

Raphael's science is 'fatal' precisely because it tears, and tears away, so many veils; the closer he progresses to this mysterious 'cœur de bronze,' to the 'belle âme' of the countess – 'dont les sentiments et les émanations communiquaient à sa physionomie ce charme qui nous subjugue et nous fascine' (125) – the closer, in short, that his *theory* comes to penetrating and possessing the truth it seeks, the more totally it finds itself engaged in a theatrical spectacle, in a play of mirrors in which there is only duplication and duplicity, the impenetrability of bronze reflecting the rays of a 'second' view; or the claws of a tiger ready to reverse the *déchirement* of that vision:

Je la regardais avec douleur ... elle me paraissait jouer un rôle en actrice consommée ... si mon amour ranimé se peignait alors dans mes yeux, elle en soutenait les rayons sans que la clarté des siens altérât, car ils semblaient, comme ceux des tigres, être doublés par une feuille de métal. En ces moments-là, je la détestais (124).

Fœdora, always the same in her dubious duplicity, produces herself ever anew, spectacle in a spectacle, always different, all the same. If she eludes the possession she invites, it is by virtue of a rhythm that is irregular and eccentric, the secret of her vitality:

Quand je cherchais à m'associer en quelque sorte à l'action de sa vie, je rencontrais en elle une intime et secrète vivacité, je ne sais quoi de saccadé, d'excentrique (123).

This woman, proferring and witholding, a vital centre but irreducibly excentric, a woman who, personnifying the fetishist vision par excellence, is 'toute la femme et point de femme' (132), might, Raphael reflects, have been 'dominée par un homme sec et glacé,' by a 'froid calculateur' (129); by a paternal figure such as the *antiquaire* ('il aurait fallu ne pas l'aimer pour l'obtenir' (128), or even by Raphael's father himself, 'sec et glacé,' cold and calculating, although certainly too 'juste,' 'au fond.' But such calculation, and its laws, are alien to the son ('je l'aimais en homme, en amant, en artiste ... ' (128), who soon finds himself overtaken by the bankruptcy which is his patrimony:

J'étais dans le néant ... j'étais alors sans idées, sans force, comme une jeune fille tombée à genoux devant un tigre. Un homme sans passion et sans argent reste maître de sa personne; mais un malheureux qui aime ne s'appartient plus et ne peut pas se tuer (117).

His *jeu* has led him to a nothingness which repeats (and anticipates) that of the *salon de jeu* where there is not even a nail to hang oneself; where the dispossession of the subject by passion is so total that the very 'end' of life – death – is lost; where the future, that most solid and considerable of capitals, is an image evaporating incessantly into the emptiness of the present.

Yet, if Raphael's debt dispossesses him of his property, power, and of his very sex, it only repeats the past, reproducing the matrimony of life with father, except that his partner is no longer the figure of death-in-life, the skeleton, but the (logically anterior) instrument of that death: a tigress, ready to devour its prey. Raphael has become what he always was, the object of his own game: 'Enfin, elle m'avait joué' (127). His 'theory' has been captivated by the spectacle it sought to capture, by Mallarmé's 'false appearance of the present'[1] reproducing itself ever anew and always the same in a future which is the space of its speculation, of a theatre which consumes all living presence in the spectacle of its presentation.

For Raphael, the fatality of this theatrical present leaves his 'theory' only one possible recourse: to turn back to the past in search of that origin which perhaps will be able to explain the mystery of the present, finally allowing it to be possessed and dominated, to be *known*. As he tells Foedora:

> *Relativement aux autres objects de votre espèce, vous êtes un phénomène. Eh bien, cherchons ensemble, de bonne foi, la cause de cette anomalie psychologique (1·12).*

Raphael therefore devises a plan, a final attempt to lift the veil of Foedora's singular phenomenality, to accede to the heart of the enigma that she represents, a plan which will take him back to the place where that enigma first appeared to him, to Foedora's bedroom. It was there that he was conducted by Rastignac, on the evening of his first encounter with the Countess:

> *Tout à coup il (Rastignac) se leva, me prit par la main, se conduisit à la chambre à coucher, et me montra, sous un dais de mousseline et de moire blanche, un lit voluptueux doucement éclairé, le vrai lit d'une jeune fée fiancée à un génie. N'y a-t-il pas, s'écria-t-il à voix basse, de l'impudeur, de l'insolence et de la coquetterie outre mesure à nous laisser contempler ce trône de l'amour? Ne se donner à personne, et permettre à tout le monde de mettre là sa carte? ... Les plus audacieux de nos maîtres, et même les plus habiles, avouent avoir échoué près d'elle, l'aiment encore et sont des amis dévoués. Cette femme n'est-elle pas une énigme?*
> *– Ces paroles excitèrent en moi une sorte d'ivresse ... (103).*

Now, after all other attempts to penetrate and to seize this enigma have failed, Raphael decides to return to this scene, 'doucement éclairé,' this time not to contemplate the mere veils, the bed under 'un dais de mousseline et de moire blanche,' but to penetrate to the forbidden mystery which they conceal. A singular suspicion provokes Raphael to frame his plan:

> *Peut-être, semblable à lady Delacour, est-elle dévorée par un cancer? Sa vie est sans doute une vie artificielle (133).*

The mystery which has devoured his energies and consumed his vital substance is perhaps itself not unlike a cancer; that of a life devoured by excess, by a certain overproduction, a surplus of vitality fatal to itself: a tumescence, fetishistic nightmare of organic life consuming itself through its very growth, quintessential antithesis and confusion of life and death, 'aus Gegensätzen doppelt geknüpft.'

The intimation of a fatal intimacy of life to itself provokes Raphael to devise a plan which itself repeats and prefigures the very consumption it hopes to unveil ('cette entreprise, qui me *dévorait* l'âme ... ,' 133). The enigma that Raphael seeks to penetrate, however spiritual the 'belle âme' may be, is also ineluctably corporeal, the mystery of a body:

> *Pour examiner cette femme corporellement comme je l'avais étudiée intel-*
> *lectuellement, pour la connaître enfin tout entière, je résolus de passer une*
> *nuit chez elle, dans sa chambre, à son insu (133).*

To 'know' Foedora 'tout entière,' to *grasp* the mystery that hovers about her, can only be to 'know' her body and the secret it conceals. To *conceive* the paradox of her 'vie artificielle,' all artifice must be removed and a certain untainted nature revealed. Foedora's bedroom thus becomes the setting of the most archaic of all scenes.

Raphael 'enters' (re-enters) the room armed with 'un petit canif anglais, à défaut de poignard' (the knife, it should be noted, *takes the place* of a dagger that is missing: the supplement is already deficient) and conceals himself behind a curtain. In order not to be seen, he must suspend himself behind the curtain, 'comme une araignée dans sa toile.' He then describes the measures he takes to assure himself a clear view of the scene:

> *La moire blanche et la mousseline des rideaux formaient devant moi de*
> *gros plis semblables à des tuyaux d'orgue, où je pratiquai des trous avec*
> *mon canif afin de tout voir par ces espèces de meurtrières (134, my emphasis).*

The scene is not merely set: the scenario has already begun before the star arrives. Raphael is hidden behind curtains which embody luxury itself, and which furnish his protection: indeed, they become, by metaphor, his innermost product, the web which he spins out of his entrails, culmination of that fruitless labour in his attic tomb, 'ce travail de ver à soie inconnu au monde ... ' (92). The slashes of his dagger – small as it is – penetrate the veil, rendering it transparent for him while preserving its opacity for others. The holes he cuts, 'espèces de meurtrières,' will enable him to take possession of the scene visually while he himself can remain secure behind the curtain, out of sight and seeing all. His 'murders' are confined to the curtain (for the moment). The spider can and need do no further harm: he has spun and cut his web; in it he hangs listening. When the Countess is finally alone, she rewards his patience; she begins to sing and Raphael breathes in the sounds:

> *Je tendis les forces de mon âme pour aspirer les sons. De note en note, la*
> *voix s'éleva; Foedora sembla s'animer, les richesses de son gosier se déploy-*
> *èrent, et cette mélodie prit alors quelque chose de divin. ... Celle qui chan-*
> *tait ainsi devait savoir bien aimer. La beauté de cette voix fut donc un*

> mystère de plus dans une femme déjà si mystérieuse. ... *Je la voyais alors comme je te vois,* elle paraissait s'écouter elle-même et ressentir une volupté qui lui fût particulière; *elle éprouvait comme une jouissance d'amour (136, my emphasis).*

The mysterious beauty of her voice, of Foedora singing to herself, becomes an image of 'jouissance' precisely by virtue of the narcissistic self-sufficiency that it represents. Nothing is lost, nothing is needed. The image of Foedora singing to herself unites two prototypical gestures, each of which confirms the presence of a certain 'phonocentrism': the song, denying the non-identity of sound and sense; and the *s'écouter elle-même*, which – as Derrida has shown in his analysis of Husserl [2] – has construed the voice to be the exemplary medium of Western metaphysics.

It is the image of this presence that is *repeated* in the narrative situation of Raphael recounting his life – 'je la voyais alors comme je te vois' – and he literally drinks in the sounds in order to take part in the *volupté* of a perfection which, by its very nature, eludes all immediate appropriation. It is solely by the medium and means of Foedora's voice that this penetration and participation is possible:

> *La comtesse avait dans l'organe une clarté vive, une justesse de ton, je ne sais quoi d'harmonique et de vibrant* qui pénétrait, remuait et chatouillait le cœur *(136, my emphasis).*

And when Raphael goes on to stress the erotic aspect of that penetration – 'les musiciennes sont presque toujours amoureuses. Celle qui chantait ainsi devait savoir bien aimer' – it is clear that the organ which 'pénétrait, remuait et chatouillait' is the voice fulfilling a phallic function, maintaining the distance and the mystery necessary to support the illusion of the fetishist, his denial of maternal castration. It is this image of the voice, present to itself in its song, that supports the chimera of an economy of life in which nothing is lost, in which the 'richesses de son gosier se déployèrent,' but without the danger of being wasted or lost: the expense of a breath (of life) which simultaneously reappropriates itself. The narcissistic circle of self-production finds its voice in the *rondo* of Foedora. Yet as in the antique shop, this image, by virtue of its very perfection, excludes the penetration, the possession, and the desire it evokes. All the same, this desire cannot renounce possession; thus, more veils must be lifted:

> *Elle vint devant la cheminée en achevant le principal motif de ce* rondo; *mais, quand elle se tut, sa physionomie changea, ses traits se décomposèrent et sa figure exprima la fatigue. Elle venait d'ôter un masque; actrice, son rôle était fini. ... La voilà vraie! me dis-je (136, my emphasis).*

For Raphael, the *true* Fœdora can only begin where the *spectacle* ends, where the mask is cast off and a certain decomposition sets in. Yet as the veils fall and the lineaments of luxury are laid aside one by one – a process which Raphael observes with 'un plaisir indicible' – the enigma grows:

> *Il n'y avait rien que de très naturel dans tous ses mouvements, et nul symp-*
> *tome ne me révéla ni les souffrances secrètes ni les passions que j'avais*
> *supposées (137).*

The passions, secret sufferings, the monstrosity which Raphael seeks, fail to appear. And then, the 'last' veil is lifted, and falls:

> *Justine la délaça. Je la contemplai curieusement au moment où le dernier*
> *voile s'enleva. Elle avait un corsage de vierge qui m'éblouit; à travers sa*
> *chemise et à la lueur des bougies, son corps blanc et rose étincela comme*
> *une statue d'argent qui brille sous son enveloppe de gaze (137).*

Once again, at the crucial instant of discovery Raphael is 'blinded,' this time by the very *perfection* of Fœdora ('nulle imperfection ne devait lui faire re-douter les yeux furtifs de l'amour') which defies all appropriation just as her 'corsage de vierge' excludes all corruption. The body of Fœdora, by virtue of its very perfection, mocks all attempts at possession. Like a 'statue d'argent' it is impenetrable in her splendour, blinding through its veil (*'qui brille sous son enveloppe de gaze'*); but even *after* the last veil has fallen, there is still a veil, veil within the veil, image behind the image, *'spectacle dans le spectacle.'* And still, the last word has not been said:

> *La comtesse se retourna plusieurs fois; elle était agitée, elle soupirait; ses*
> *lèvres laissaient échapper un léger bruit* perceptible *à l'ouie et qui indiquait*
> *des mouvements d'impatience, elle avança la main vers la table, y prit une*
> *fiole, versa dans son lait avant de le boire quatre ou cinq gouttes d'une liq-*
> *ueur brune; enfin, après quelques soupirs pénibles, elle s'écria: – Mon Dieu!*
> *(138, my emphasis)*

After the brown fluid has been used to alleviate an invisible ailment in what *seems* to be the epitome of perfection, Fœdora's exclamation offers a last handle for Raphael's desire to seize upon:

> *Ce mot, insignifiant ou profond, sans substance ou plein de réalités,* pou-
> vait s'interpréter également *par le bonheur ou par la souffrance, par une*
> *douleur de corps ou par de peines. Etait-ce imprécation ou prière, souvenir*
> *ou avenir, regret ou crainte?* Il y avait toute une vie dans cette parole, vie
> d'indigence ou de richesse; *il y tenait même un crime! L'énigme cachée*
> *dans ce beau semblant de femme renaissait, Fœdora pouvait être*

expliquée de tant de manières, qu'elle devenait inexplicable (138, my emphasis).

Foedora's exclamation is a sign, and the sleep which follows appears to Raphael to confirm the language of his desire, the space of the penetration he desires: it offers him the inexhaustible pursuit of *meaning*, of an ambiguity which allows him to participate in the enigma without the peril of resolving it.

Raphael's 'interpretation' directly prefigures an entire tradition of Balzac criticism:

Les fantaisies du souffle qui passait entre ses dents, tantôt faible, tantôt accentué, grave ou léger, formaient une sorte de langage auquel j'attachais des pensées et des sentiments. Je rêvais avec elle, j'espérais m'initier à ses secrets en pénétrant dans son sommeil, je flottais entre mille partis contraires, entre mille jugements (ibid.).

Foedora's words thus constitute an ambiguity that invites an interpretative discourse to penetrate and to appropriate what her visible image offers and withholds. And this invitation is inseparable from her voice; for it is not merely the articulation of language, of its ambiguous significance, that solicits Raphael's desire, but the accents in which the words are clad. If there is 'toute une vie dans cette parole' it is by virtue of its vocal accent: 'Cette exclamation et surtout l'accent qu'elle y mit me brisèrent le cœur' (*ibid.*). Standing before the bed of the sleeping Foedora, Raphael is seized by the temptation of another 'glissement,' and by another image:

Il y eut un moment où je me représentai Foedora se réveillant dans mes bras. Je pouvais me mettre tout doucement à ses côtés, m'y glisser et l'étreindre (139).

At the prospect of direct possession, however, Raphael flees in confusion, yet not before he has reawakened the 'énigme cachée dans ce beau semblant de femme.' His observation has taken him to the end point of his desire: to the total translucence of Foedora's body, radiating its untainted freshness and vitality, 'un corsage de vierge' blinding Raphael 'à travers sa chemise,' to the solidity and brilliance of a silver statue, shining 'sous son enveloppe de gaze.' Yet above all, the translucence is that of a voice singing and hearing itself, allowing itself to be heard. This is the supreme expression of the indeterminable, unresolvable enigma of a woman who is more (and less) than a woman: 'ce beau semblant de femme,' deploying its enigmatic charms in the text of a novel that seems inexhaustible in the richness of the meanings it contains and the *explications* it invites, but also absorbs and transcends. When Raphael concludes that 'Foedora pouvait être expliquée de tant de manières, qu'elle devenait inexplicable' (138), he expresses the desire of infinite interpretation and appropriation which, there should be no mistake, prevails no less for modern critics, for whom Balzac exemplifies a 'tradition' alleged to be safely overcome.

All the more important, therefore, to remark that the result of this night of forbidden observation is Raphael's decision to try once again to win Foedora. This time he will wager all he has left to penetrate to her innermost secret:

> *En lui racontant ma vie, mon amour, mes sacrifices, peut-être pourrais-je éveiller en elle la pitié ... (139).*

All that he has left, however, is the story of his life, an act of autobiographical narration, presenting his past in all of its meaning. This, then, is his ultimate resort:

> *Je lui racontai mes sacrifices, je lui peignis ma vie, non pas comme je te la raconte aujourd'hui, dans l'ivresse du vin, mais dans la noble ivresse du cœur. ... Mon accent fut celui des dernières prières faites par un mourant sur le champ de bataille. Elle pleura. Je m'arrêtai. Grand Dieu! ses larmes étaient le fruit de cette émotion factice acheté cent sous à la porte d'un théâtre, j'avais eu le succès d'un bon acteur (141-2).*

His voice, narrating his life as the expression of a single desire, producing himself in its accents, is not the pale, reproductive voice of his 'present' narration: it is the summary of himself and his history, its *presentation*. But Foedora, listening, moved to tears, reflects it as a representation, making Raphael no longer a mere spectator but an actor. An unwilling actor in a drama he can no longer dream of mastering, gambler in a game which has no end, entry, or exit.

Confronted by the irreducibility of Foedora's *jeu*, Raphael desperately plays his last card, a final attempt to trump. As she is about to retire he exclaims: 'Et dans deux heures, vous vous écrierez: Mon Dieu!' The Countess replies:

> *Avant-hier! Oui ... je pensais à mon agent de change, j'avais oublié de lui faire convertir mes rentes de cinq en trois, et, dans la journée, le trois avait baissé (143).*

The heart of Foedora, her beautiful soul, the centre of her life and vitality, her 'Dieu,' is the *schöne Wertseele*, nothing more or less than an irreducible exchange, yet one which demands to be reduced since its ultimate *value* is living presence, the fulfilment of desire and the satisfaction of needs. It is the solution of fetishism, the 'dialectic' of a castration that is where it is not and is not where it is, manifest in the double knot of the antithesis. Foedora has no 'heart,' her eccentricity is irreducible, and yet her 'heart' is precisely her 'heartlessness,' her centre 'is' her eccentricity. She transforms a determinate absence – as such she is never to be 'had' – into the sign and veil of a transcendent presence, the production of her Self in a never-ending circle of speculation. And the centre of this circle, her most intimate 'referent,' is the numbers game, a financial transaction – 'convertir mes rentes de cinq en trois' – in which she cannot lose, any more than money itself (and the value it manifests) can lose ('et dans la journée, le trois avait baissé').

Fœdora is the very movement of productive investment, of speculation. She represents herself as the pure possibility of a certain possession, not direct (she 'is' never present), but indirect, to be had speculatively or intuitively, through interpretation or imagination:

> *Nous restâmes dix minutes environ plongés dans un profond silence. Je l'admirais, lui prétant des charmes auxquels elle mentait. En ce moment, elle était à moi, à moi seul. ... Je possédais cette ravissante créature, comme il était permis de la posséder, intuitivement; je l'enveloppai dans mon désir, la tins, la serrai, mon imagination l'épousa ... en ce moment, je n'en voulais pas à son corps, je souhaitais une âme, une vie, ce bonheur idéal et complet (140-1).*

The compromise which is thus reached – desire enveloping and possessing its object speculatively – is enforced by the fate that his desire knows to await itself should it ever lift the 'last' veil – the veil it itself throws over its object ('je l'enveloppai dans mon désir') – for behind the veil lurk the claws of castration:

> *Fœdora se laissa flatter, caresser avec un incroyable abandon. Mais ne m'accuse pas de niaiserie: si j'avais voulu faire un pas de plus au-delà de cette câlinerie fraternelle, j'eusse senti les griffes de la chatte (140).*

Raphael's denial – 'mais ne m'accuse pas ... ' – confirms the castration he cannot escape, and which is confounded with the object of his desire. This denial, it should be remarked, is already traced, and displaced, in his self-portrayal, as a spider hanging in its web. This metaphor articulates the antithetical desire and dread that characterizes the fetishistic denial, the negation of a knowledge that produces not a dialectical *Aufhebung* but an antithesis and an alternative. If, in the code of fetishism, the spider in its web can represent 'the penis attributed to the mother, as being embedded in the female genitals' (Karl Abraham),[3] then the fact that Raphael *depicts himself* as this spider, again the image of his image, articulates his anguished effort to retain what he knows to be 'lost' – a loss he cannot accept – by becoming the maternal phallus. Yet the identification thus implicit in the metaphor of the spider, hanging in the web it has spun, only re-enacts – or 'acts out' – what it seeks to deny: the 'petites meurtrières' performed with the small knife, perforating the curtain and making it resemble the spider web, indicate the murderous origin of the spider and of the web in which it hangs, in order, above all, to hide its *feet* from fatal exposure. The web, product of a murder, hides the murderer.

Thus, if Raphael is able to postpone his discovery of the fatal non-secret of castration by investing and enveloping Foedora with the veil of his desire, it is his self-image that completes the scene by providing the *key* to the enigma: the murder which is the origin and end, life and death, of his desire to perceive, to know.

Yet it is in the form of the figure itself – the metaphor based on visible resemblance – that the fetishist imagination finds its strongest resource and greatest peril. The non-being of the ultimate referent, castration, is metonymically displaced and can thus be recovered, imaginatively, in the spider web enveloping the spider, as black as Foedora is white, as dark as she is brilliant. The interstice which 'is' only as difference and articulation, is transformed into the black-white antithesis of absence and presence. Yet it is no accident that the 'spider' only *is* as long as it hangs in its web, invisible, and does not fall. This *fall*, and the exposure it would entail, become the very condition of the spider's metaphorical existence. The metaphor, as visible resemblance, thus veils that which, were it to be seen, would 'cease' to be and yet which can only 'be' by being seen: value, the maternal phallus, and the divine gift which is Foedora, 'la femme sans cœur.'

16

The 'Dissipational System'

Tu as le présent, m'écriai-je, et moi l'avenir! Je ne perds qu'une femme, et tu perds un nom, une famille. Le temps est gros de ma vengeance: il t'apportera la laideur et une mort solitaire; à moi la gloire! (144)

With these words, Raphael takes leave of Foedora. In the face of his failure to grasp the living presence she embodies, Raphael can only affirm the dubious heritage of his patrimony: 'name' and 'family,' the name of his (paternal) family. He invokes the name of his (dead) father as his guarantee against 'laideur et une mort solitaire,' which await Foedora; but, lacking the *present* which is the property of Foedora – 'tu as le présent' – the future of this name and its promises are threadbare indeed. For in failing to possess this female being, the phenomenon of a certain living presence, Raphael himself has been stripped of his own presence of mind; Foedora has turned his self back upon itself as that of an actor, playing a role, and yet unlike the countess, being consumed in the spectacle. The inability to possess Foedora threatens to detach all of Raphael's representations – that is, the self-image which is his identity – from their referents, inserting them into a circulation, into a 'dance' that defies all comprehension, and threatens reason itself:

Je suis fou! [he cries to Rastignac] Je sens la folie rugir par moments dans mon cerveau. Mes idées sont comme des fantômes, elles dansent devant moi sans que je puisse les saisir (145).

The presence of Foedora was the guarantee of a certain 'reality,' and of the sanity it founds; her narcissistic self-sufficiency, with its dialectic of absence and presence, appearance and disappearance, seemed to suggest an original and transcendent cause, a plenitude which would found and fill the enigma. If the notion of 'reality' is inseparable from and constituted by a certain self-sufficiency, by a presence that can only be 'given' as a product (factum) and process of production (factor), then the enigma of Foedora – 'spectacle dans le spectacle' – strikes at the 'heart' of 'reality' even while seemingly embodying it. Like the fetishism of commodities and of the maternal phallus, she denies the *jeu* of castration and yet confirms it all the same, pointing towards a 'past' that never was or will be present, towards a production of self whose origin is an irreducible (numerical: ie, differential) exchange. Her 'reality' is that of the *phantasm*, representation of a representation, reflection of a reflection, *speculation* in the most emphatic sense.

And yet as in fetishism (whether social or psychic), exchange and circulation are only mimed: they are comprehended as a totality, the hole is fixed as a whole, the economy is limited and determined by the *telos* of production, which never ceases to direct all circulation and substitution, to give them their meaning and their truth. The economy of expense is that of Veblen's 'conspicuous consumption,' not that of Bataille's 'économie générale.'

Through Foedora, Raphael has seen that the presence he desires, the very life of his desire, cannot be *had*, it cannot be possessed ('Je n'appartiendrai à personne' Foedora tells him [142]). What he cannot *have*, however, he may *become*; this is the ultimate resort and resource of fetishism: not so much to possess what by definition, 'aus Gegensätzen doppelt verknüpft,' cannot be possessed because it is constantly divesting and investing itself, re-covering by dis-covering, because its value is to be where it is not, and not to be where it is; but rather to become this very movement of *dérobement*, and thus to master the ambivalence of castration as negativity, determining difference as absence. The 'ontological difference' is put to work to produce the enigma of an absent and yet ubiquitous Presence which can only be Being itself. Had Raphael endeavoured to produce himself by associating, participating, and identifying his life with the phantasmagorical apparition of Foedora, with the elusive and yet irreducible corporeal substance of a woman, 'toute la femme et point de femme,' only to discover that what awaited him were the claws of the cat, then his next step is inevitably to associate himself not with the illusory and fatal *product*, but with the *process*: to be (-come) what could not be *had*: the 'dissipational system' itself.

At the start of his 'labours,' Raphael had pledged to 'mourir pour vivre'; now he simply inverts the terms, and decides to live in order to die. He will not build a tomb in order to rise, triumphant, out of its ashes, but rather as

Rastignac puts it, 'créer un nouveau genre de mort en ... débattant ainsi contre la vie.' Following Rastignac's counsel, he will take a new *plunge*, in the hope of discovering a new Queen:

> *Plonge-toi dans une dissolution profonde, ta passion ou toi, vous y périrez. L'intempérance, mon cher, est la reine de toutes les morts (145-6).*

The 'système dissipationnel,' the 'débauche' begins, necessarily, with yet another transgression of the patrimony that it nonetheless faithfully serves. For in its antithetical nature, this patrimony always proscribes what it prescribes: its law is directed towards the salvation of the paternal name, while prohibiting the very means of this salvation: the *jeu*.

To replenish his exhausted reserves, the only means available to Raphael is: 'aller au jeu.' But the weight of the paternal interdiction prevents him from himself going to the casino: instead, after forsaking the security of the Gaudin household – not forgetting to put his 'clef à sa place habituelle' before leaving – he awaits Rastignac's return:

> *La vie de dissipation à laquelle je me vouais apparut devant moi bizarrement exprimée par la chambre où j'attendais ... (147).*

The scene he then describes bears all the marks of the scenario of fetishism. It begins with a clock and a woman, which occupy the ex-centric centre of the room:

> *Au milieu de la cheminée s'élevait une pendule surmontée d'une Vénus accroupie sur sa tortue, et qui tenait entre ses bras un cigare à demi consumé (147).*

On the mantelpiece, above the fireplace, source of warmth and light in the room, stands a clock, surmounted by a Venus squatting on her 'turtle': the passage of time, which the fetishist must incessantly seek to reverse or at least to neutralize, inasmuch as it has deprived him of the illusion he cannot renounce, is 'surmounted' by the Goddess of love, who, however, is not erect but squats on the turtle of time, on the very transience she surmounts. Without pursuing the evident 'genital' and 'anal' implications of the figure, we need only remark the incongruous object she holds in – 'entre' – her arms: a half-consumed cigar, visible image of the compromise that fetishism concludes with the phallus.

Raphael continues his description of this amorous scene:

> *Des meubles élégants, présents de l'amour, étaient épars. De vieilles chaussettes traînaient sur un voluptueux divan. Le confortable fauteuil à ressorts dans lequel j'étais plongé portait des cicatrices comme un vieux soldat, il*

*offrait aux regards ses bras déchirés, et montrait incrustées sur son dossier
la pommade et l'huile antique apportées par toutes les têtes d'amis. L'opulence et la misère s'accouplaient naïvement dans le lit, sur les murs, partout
(147-8).*

Inscribed in the amorous scene is the scenario of a certain 'accouplement':
the naïve union of an antithesis, of 'opulence' and 'poverty'; aged socks strewn
over a voluptuous couch; the very armchair in which Raphael is 'plunged'
bears the 'scars,' 'rents,' and stains of former struggles. Yet the confusion of
the antithesis serves also as a reassuring fusion, uniting the opposing terms in
the stability of a *tableau*, determining the holes as the space of a whole, which
is the reflection and reflexion – the reflexive movement – of life itself:

> *Ce tableau ne manquait pas d'ailleurs de poésie. La vie s'y dressait avec ses
> paillettes et ses haillons, soudaine, incomplète comme elle est réellement,
> mais vive, mais fantasque ... (148).*

The incompleteness of life becomes the source of its very vivacity, its phantasmagorical aspect the essence of its reality. Its absence and *usure* are recovered
and recuperated in the infinite movement of its self-preservation, deploying
itself within the stable symmetry of an homogeneous space. A final detail exemplifies this reappropriation, and yet also indicates – once reread – its essential instability:

> *Ici, la bougie était fichée dans le fourreau vert d'un briquet phosphorique;
> là, gisait un portrait de femme dépouillé de sa monture d'or ciselé (148).*

The Easter candle, image of paternal rectitude, is resurrected as the profane
'bougie,' securely implanted in a stable foundation ('fichée dans le fourreau
vert d'un briquet phosphorique'). Yet the softness of the green felt recalls,
not without accident, Raphael's terror 'd'un tapis vert' which has kept him
waiting for Rastignac in this room. For the implantation of the paternal phallus in its (maternal) base is haunted by the incendiary power of that 'briquet
phosphorique': beneath the green felt, the possibility of the ultimate conflagration is hidden (a possibility that will emerge unmistakably towards the end
of the novel). And the second detail, 'un portrait de femme dépouillé de sa
monture d'or ciselé,' is no less menacing. It inserts itself in the text as the
omen of a 'dépouillement' which is not merely metaphorical but literal. During his courtship of Foedora, Raphael had considered a desperate measure:

> *Pour pouvoir y conduire la comtesse (aux Funambules), je pensai à mettre
> en gage le cercle d'or qui entourait le portrait de ma mère (130).*

For the fetishist, clinging to the imaginary-perceptive sphere, the importance of the maternal portrait can hardly be surpassed. To sell the gold frame which surrounds and protects that portrait is to expose it to the deadly *usure* of the commodity-world; to strip the tableau of its frame is to abandon the possibility of confining and comprehending the infinite circulation in a circle. Raphael is 'saved' from this fatal transaction by the generosity of Pauline, supplementing the maternal role. Yet now the portrait of an unnamed woman has been stripped of its gold setting, deprived of its base, confirming the ambivalent 'surmounting' of time by the Venus in the loss of its mount (*monture*). Of a mount which already bears the marks of *incision*, which is 'ciselé.' Thus, the antithetical symmetry of the tableau – of the 'ici/là' – is shaken by the scenario of a scene in which 'là' is already 'ici' and 'ici,' 'là.' And when Rastignac finally returns from the *jeu*, with 'son chapeau plein d'or' containing 'les plaisirs du monde,' the scenario can 'begin' again, this time as the *débauche*. Yet with each repetition of this scene, the circle grows smaller, concentrates into a centre which is its origin and end, its life and death.

Like everything else, the 'dissipational system' thus begins with a *jeu*. And it continues as a perpetual game and gamble, one which Raphael plays while still respecting the letter of the paternal law:

> *Je me lançai dans un tourbillon de plaisirs creux et réels tout à la fois. Je jouais, gagnais et perdais tour à tour d'énormes sommes, mais au bal, chez nos amis; jamais dans les maisons de jeu, pour lesquelles je conservai ma sainte et primitive horreur (149).*

The confusion of reality and unreality – 'plaisirs creux et réels tout à la fois' – is total, except for the one unshaken point of reference: that sacred and archaic horror, not simply of gambling, but of its lieu and milieu, the nameless 'tripot' regulated by another law, and designated by numbers.

The 'débauche' to which he abandons himself is Raphael's effort to *produce* what in Foedora he vainly tried to *possess*. Like Foedora, debauchery is the theory and essence of a certain life – 'la théorie de cette large vie' – and like her, it is essentially dramatic, and the drama of an essence, or of a system which is not limited to particular pleasures,

> *ses jouissances de détail, mais ... qui ... les résument, les lui fertilisent en lui créant une vie dramatique dans sa vie, en nécessitant une exorbitante, une prompte dissipation de ses forces (150).*

Gone is the reserve of Foedora, that eccentricity which eludes all possession, and in its place is the exorbitance of a total expense – 'une prompte dissipation de ses forces' – directed at 'créant une vie dramatique dans sa vie.' The purpose of this system, theory, 'science,' is the creation of a living drama which is both a part of life and yet which 'resumes' and 'comprehends' it, from within:

> *Pour l'homme privé ... la débauche comprend tout, elle est une perpétuelle étreinte de toute la vie, ou mieux, un duel avec une puissance inconnue, avec un monstre ... (151).*

Here, the 'second act' of the *débauche* begins: from a science and system, creating and disposing over its object, it becomes a struggle, a 'duel,' and *dual*. It is the struggle of a certain productive consumption, the struggle with 'nature' to recreate oneself, to be one's own origin and to eliminate all difference. It is the total fusion and confusion of need and desire:

> *La nature vous a donné je ne sais quel estomac étroit ou paresseux; vous le domptez, vous l'élargissez, vous apprenez à porter le vin, vous apprivoisez l'ivresse, vous passez les nuits sans sommeil, vous vous faites enfin un tempérament de colonel de cuirassiers, en vous créant vous-même une seconde fois, comme pour fronder Dieu! (151, my emphasis).*

If, therefore, 'la débauche est certainement un art comme la poésie' (150), it is because it is the reproduction of the self, by a self consuming its own difference, its 'first nature,' to create a second in which the son is his own father and the father his own son, heretical model of the Trinity and of the trinitarian movement of capital.[1] And if fetishism is the struggle to deny and master the difference of castration, the next (third) act of the *débauche* clearly describes the struggle for sexual mastery – for the mastery of sex (of its difference) – and its culmination in a sphere of imagination and reverie:

> *Quand l'homme s'est ainsi métamorphosé, quand, vieux soldat, le néophyte a façonné son âme à l'artillerie, ses jambes à la marche, sans encore appartenir au monstre, mais sans savoir entre eux quel est le maître, ils se roulent l'un sur l'autre, tantôt vainqueurs, tantôt vaincus, dans une sphère où tout est merveilleux, où s'endorment les douleurs de l'âme, où revivent seulement des fantômes d'idées (151, my emphasis).*

The classic model of 'alienation' and disappropriation is here *mise-en-scène* set into the scene which is its 'original' context, that of fetishism. The effort to reduce the ineluctable third – the 'law' of difference, whose place is occupied by the father and designated by the metaphor of 'castration' – the effort for the subject to 'copulate' with its own *copula*, to reappropriate its predicates, its presence as predication, leads to a struggle for 'mastery' that can only be imaginary – 'dans une sphère où tout est merveilleux' – and which denies the very corporeality it affirms: 'Enfin, la débauche est sans doute au corps ce que sont à l'âme les plaisirs mystiques' (151). It is the mysterium and mystery of a body which is its own spirit, striving for a *union* in which all relation to the other is surpassed. Closely related to Rousseau's 'dangereux supplément,'[2] its medium is not the exteriority of 'ecstasy' (*ekstase*), but the interiority of *inebriation*: 'L'ivresse vous plonge en des rêves dont les fantasmagories sont aussi curieuses que peuvent l'être celles de l'extase (151). And above all, this inner appropriation and sufficiency is that of a *young girl*: 'Vous avez des heures ravissantes comme les caprices d'une jeune fille,' and of a sovereign, the king of kings, investing the world he has created:

> *Pendant ces heures avinées, les hommes et les choses comparaissent devant vous, vêtus de vos livrées. Roi de la création, vous la transformez à vos souhaits (152).*

But at this very moment of apparent triumph and complete appropriation, in accordance with a classic and by now familiar gesture the appropriation is abruptly expropriated (act four):

> *A travers ce délire perpétuel, le jeu vous verse, à votre gré, son plomb fondu dans les veines. Un jour, vous appartenez au monstre; vous avez alors, comme je l'eus, un réveil, enragé: l'impuissance est assise à votre chevet. Vieux guerrier, une phtisie vous dévore ... moi, peut-être une pulmonie va me dire: 'Partons!' comme elle a mit jadis à Raphael d'Urbin, tué par un excès d'amour. Voilà comment j'ai vécu! (152)*

This fourth act of the drama which is the *débauche* seems the last: the producer is expropriated, consumed by his own expense, like that other Raphael, 'tué par un excès d'amour.' And yet the mention of this name marks (and remarks) the place of the invisible fifth act: the *narration* itself, reappropriating the meaning of a life which is the destruction of meaning, presenting a self whose narrated existence consists in ineluctable self-consumption. The sudden return of the 'moi' re-establishes the unity of narration and narrated, the representation of the subject through its 'own' voice, present-to-itself in the narration that revives the 'life' that is past: 'Voilà comment j'ai vécu!' Nor is the context of that 'moi' indifferent: for it is a 'moi' whose life is menaced by a very particular consumption ('une pulmonie') the exhaustion of its very breath, the disappearance of its voice, the same voice which animates the narration itself. The voice of Raphael, a name which now assumes a third meaning: the name of the painter of the Saviour, the name promising the divine healing of all wounds, now names the man who is dead of 'un excès d'amour,' whose very desire for a certain life will be his death. If, therefore, the menace of castration marked by the desire implied in the name Raphael converges with the exhaustion of a breath and the disappearance of a voice, it is because this voice can only speak and make itself heard in a silence and a space that it can never master, and through an expense, a *dissipation* which can never be reappropriated as a system: in short, in and through a text that no imagination, be it that of reverie itself, can ever fully comprehend.

17

The Signature and the Voice

But the dissipational system does not produce only an imaginary world: its *chef d'oeuvre* is the reality of debt. The reality of Raphael's patrimony reappears when he is forced to sign away the name he once sought to make, on a bill of exchange. With this signature his name enters fully into the circulation of value, irreversibly separated from the person it continues to express but to whom it no longer belongs. The new life of this name, as signature, continues the process of dying: 'Pour continuer de mourir, je signai des lettres de change ... '[1] and continues it as a work of the imagination:

> *Mon imagination me montrait mon nom voyageant, de ville en ville, dans les places de l'Europe. Notre nom, c'est nous-mêmes, a dit Eusèbe Salverte. Après des courses vagabondes, j'allais, comme le double d'un Allemand, revenir à mon logis d'où je n'étais pas sorti, pour me réveiller moi-même en sursaut (153, Balzac's emphasis).*

This doubling of his Self in his signature, returning after a world tour to reawaken Raphael with a start, is also the expression of a *value* that is not that of Raphael's property but of his debt: 'Ma signature valait trois mille francs, je ne les valais pas moi-même!' (153) His signature thus becomes the fatal expression and exposure of his identity, the stigma of a Self that is no longer its own:

> *Leurs clercs (des huissiers) avaient le droit de s'emparer de moi, de griffoner*

*mon nom, de le salir, de s'en moquer. JE DEVAIS! Devoir, est-ce donc
s'appartenir? (153)*

This indebtedness is the return of a certain paternity, of an economy that
demands a strict accounting for each expense:

*D'autres hommes ne pouvaient-ils pas me demander compte de ma vie? ...
pourquoi je dormais, marchais, pensais, m'amusais sans les payer? Au
milieu d'une poésie, au sein d'une idée, ou à déjeuner, entouré d'amis, de
joie, de douces railleries, je pouvais voir entrer un monsieur en habit marron, tenant à la main un chapeau rapé. Ce monsieur sera ma dette, ce sera
ma lettre de change, un spectre qui flétrira ma joie, me forcera de quitter
la table pour lui parler; il m'enlèvera ma gaieté, ma maîtresse, tout, jusqu'à
mon lit (153-4).*

The tyranny of the debt no less than its very *habit* – 'en habit marron' – recall
the figure of Raphael's father, returning at the 'end' of the *jeu* to reclaim the
illicit debt that founded it. The creditors, like M. de Valentin, have no under-
standing for the debt as a work of art, an expression of the imagination: 'Une
dette est une œuvre d'imagination qu'ils ne comprennent pas' (154), nor do
they allow for the grandeur and generosity of an expense:

*Des élans de l'âme entraînent, subjuguent souvent un emprunteur, tandis
que rien de grand ne subjugue, rien de généreux ne guide ceux qui vivent
dans l'argent et ne connaissent que l'argent (154).*

For the debtor, however, the debt, 'œuvre d'imagination,' is a living creature,
his child, incarnation of himself: the father fails to acknowledge that he is son
of his son ('Ce monsieur sera *ma* dette, ce sera *ma* lettre de change ... '); the
huissiers ('Ces dettes à deux pattes ... ces dettes incarnés') forget that they
owe their very existence to the creditor they seek to devour.

But the debt can return to its creator in another, no less menacing form:

*Enfin la lettre de change peut se métamorphoser en vieillard chargé de
famille, flanqué de vertus. Je devrais peut-être à un vivant tableau de
Greuze, à un paralytique environné d'enfants, à la veuve d'un soldat, qui
tous me tendront des mains suppliantes (154).*

The remorse of these 'metamorphoses' only thinly veils a more direct menace:
the old man flanked by virtues becomes the *paralytic* surrounded by his *children*, and finally – again a scenario – the widow of a soldier. The hands which
supplicate Raphael trace the destruction of the father and the heritage of the
son. As his patrimony and his product, even the debt that strips him of his
property is still his own, the skin of his self:

> *Devenus la proie des harpies du Châtelet, ces doux esclaves matériels al-*
> *laient donc être enlevés par des recors et brutalement jetés sur la place.*
> *Ah! ma dépouille était encore moi-même (155).*

The life of these debts, their value, is that of representations consuming the
presence which is their origin: *their* life is *its* death, and yet it is a life-in-death,
since the very figures of dispossession affirm the property of the debtor whom
they consume; they are 'his own' debts, the skin of his life, the exclamation of
a living being: 'Ah! ma dépouille était encore moi-même.'

The movement of this negative production and speculation – debt affirming the 'property,' the selfhood, of the debtor – is inherently endless, a closed
circle of circulation. Yet for the debtor as individual 'subject,' the circle
shrinks into its centre. The 'imaginary' capitalization of debt decapitates the
debtor it reflects:

> *La sonnette de mon appartement retentissait dans mon cœur, elle me frap-*
> *pait où l'on doit frapper les rois, à la tête. C'était un martyre, sans le ciel*
> *pour récompense (155).*

The destitution of the King – his decapitalization and decapitation – leaves
Raphael a single resort: denied 'le ciel pour récompense,' he must seek redemption on earth, in a certain *cave*:

> *Mes lettres de change furent protestées. Trois jours après, je les payai;*
> *voici comment. Un spéculateur vint me proposer de lui vendre l'île que je*
> *possédais dans la Loire et où était le tombeau de ma mère. J'acceptai. En*
> *signant le contrat chez le notaire de mon acquéreur, je sentis au fond de*
> *l'étude obscure une fraîcheur semblable à celle d'une cave. Je frissonnai en*
> *reconnaissant le même froid humide qui m'avait saisi sur le bord de la fosse*
> *où gisait mon père. J'accueillis ce hasard comme un funeste présage. Il me*
> *semblait entendre la voix de ma mère et voir son ombre; je ne sais quelle*
> *puissance faisait sentir vaguement mon propre nom dans mon oreille, au*
> *milieu d'un bruit de cloches (155).*

The signature, with which Raphael divests himself of his last possession, of
the property which is the site of the maternal tomb, brings him to the verge
of the abyss, 'où gisait mon père,' a fact that Raphael immediately senses to
be 'un funeste présage.' In divesting himself of the maternal tomb, the most
powerful *Denkmal* of fetishism is abandoned to commodity circulation and
the indispensable barrier protecting desire from fatal fulfilment dissolves. The
cool breeze he feels upon signing the contract is the breath of this death-in-
life, situating him already in a 'cave' which can only be the tomb of castration.

Yet the fascination of this deadly cave is only fully revealed in the singular phenomenon which follows, as though responding to his gesture and his desire: the appearance of his mother, of her voice and her shadow, calling him – by his *proper name*. The fatality of his family (ie, paternal) name disappears in this hallucination, through which his mother solicits and confirms the presence of the son, calling him by name. This hallucination is perhaps the exemplary representation, preserving the presence of son and mother precisely in and through death: it is perfectly, maternally porous;[2] the speaker is absent, dead, and yet the voice is alive, affirming the presence and property of the son, called by his *proper* name. The voice of the dead mother replaces and excludes all *griffonnage*: that of the signature (of the paternal name) no less than that of the deadly tiger. All fatal exposure is banned, just as the maternal voice itself resounds 'au milieu d'un bruit de cloches,' wrapped up in the protective garment of bells, the sound of which is significant without being divided by the circulation of articulation; framed in these bells, its centre, the voice becomes a distant and yet audible appeal, mastering all separation in the secure space of its resonance, promising the presence of a life beyond death.

Here in this scene, where a maternal voice masters death to call the son by his proper name, a promise and desire become legible which have shaped perhaps not merely the text of *La Peau de chagrin*, but the very context of Western thought: the desire of a certain translucence or porosity. In the commentary solicited by another 'bruit de cloches' – those in Trakl's *Ein Winterabend* – Martin Heidegger writes as the *porte-parole* of this desire:

> *What does the first stanza call? It calls things, bids them come. Where? Not to be present among things present. ... The place of arrival which is also called in the calling is a presence sheltered in absence [ein ins Abwesen geborgenes Anwesen]. The naming call bids things to come into such an arrival. Bidding [Das Heißen: also naming, calling – SW.] is inviting. ... The tolling of the evening bell brings them, as mortals, before the divine.*[3]

To call by name, 'der nennende Ruf,' is to announce a 'coming' (*heißt kommen*) which leads mortals to the divine. Named, such mortals are reborn, no longer exposed to the fatality of a *present* that necessarily exhausts itself, but named in an absence that preserves the transcendence of their presence. The desire of the (proper) name is the desire of a life made secure in its presence by determining difference as absence ('a presence sheltered in absence').

Thus, Heidegger's text can explicate Balzac's. And yet the more interesting explication may well work the other way round. For what Balzac's story suggests is that the Divinity that solicits such Presence may itself not be exempt from difference – in this case, from the sexual difference. Instead of *'das' Göttliche* we would therefore have to read: *die Göttliche*. Is it an accident

that the proper, Christian name is pronounced by the voice of the (dead)
mother, denying – and confirming – death as the origin and end of life? Of a
life seeking to engender itself in the plenitude of its presence, and to redeem
the property of a name from the debt in which it is inscribed?

18

Antiphrasis

Raphael's narrative comes full circle and draws to a close:

> *Riche à millions, j'aurais toujours joué, mangé, couru. Je ne voulais plus rester seul avec moi-même. ... Les liens qui attachent un homme à la famille étaient brisés en moi pour toujours. Galérien du plaisir, je devais accomplir ma destinée de suicide. Pendant les derniers jours de ma fortune [following the sale of his island and the liquidation of his debts], je fis chaque soir des excès incroyables; mais chaque matin, la mort me rejetait dans la vie. Semblable à un rentier viager, j'aurais pu passer tranquillement dans un incendie. Enfin je me trouvai seul avec un pièce de vingt francs, je me souvins alors du bonheur de Rastignac ... (156).*

All of his efforts to appropriate a certain vital presence – labour, speculation, dissipation – have led only to that fatal signature, to a debt which even the spectral voice of his mother cannot redeem but only defer. The vicious circle of life in search of itself is resumed and reassumed in the voice which represents it as narration. This voice is Raphael's last resort and resource: it alone can redeem the caducity of a life constantly exhausting and expending itself in its representations. And yet having arrived at the 'conclusion' of his narrative, the very same destiny seems to afflict that narration itself: as representation it seems to detach itself from the living presence it is intended to revive. Raphael is 'exaspéré par l'image de sa vie ... insensiblement enivré par le torrent de ses paroles,' and again, a certain intoxication and madness results:

'Raphael s'anima, s'exalta comme un homme complètement privé de raison' (156). What haunts him now, at the end of his narration, is the nightmare of his life: a life which can only produce itself in representations and yet which is barred from reappropriating itself in its products. The obstacle is identical to the one which separates two voices: the one expressing and presenting the life of its speaker, from the other seeking to reproduce and to reappropriate this presence; the voice of memory from that of narration. Between these two voices, the very essence and presence of life – its *property* – is consumed, the fatal debt of the paternal law.

Suddenly, as though in response to this dilemma, Raphael remembers the talisman:

> Eh! eh! ... s'écria Raphael en pensant tout à coup à son talisman, qu'il tira de sa poche ... .
> Vous m'appartenez, fameuse propriété! (156)

The talisman offers itself as the possibility of uniting those two voices, that of expense (expression) and that of reappropriation (narration). In it Raphael recognizes a unique power that might put an end to the silence that has haunted his life:

> Ma vie à été un trop long silence. Maintenant je vais me venger du monde entier. Je ne m'amuserai pas à dissiper de vils écus, j'imiterai, je résumerai mon époque en consomment des vies humaines, et des intelligences, des âmes. Voilà un luxe qui n'est pas mesquin, n'est-ce pas? l'opulence de la peste! (157)

The *peau de chagrin* is the means of production, the organ by which life can begin to speak for itself, to expose itself without being divested of its property. It is the sign of a testament which seems no longer that of his patrimony of debt, but of total possession and mastery, the symbol of a new King:

> Vois-tu cette peau? c'est le testament de Salomon. Il est à moi, Salomon, ce petit cuistre de roi! J'ai l'Arabie, Pétrée encore. L'univers est à moi. Tu es à moi, si je veux ... tu seras mon valet (157).

And yet the opulence of the skin is that of 'la peste' (antecedent of Artaud's magic wand), and the power it contains is again not without its cost. The skin is no simple natural phenomenon, but the bearer of a pact; its productivity is the 'product' of an exchange. And the name of this exchange is 'antiphrasis':

> Cette peau se rétrécit quand j'ai un désir ... c'est une antiphrase. Le brahmane, – il se trouve un brahmane là-dessous! – le brahmane donc était un goguenard, parce que les désirs, vois-tu, doivent étendre ... (158).

The skin, surface of a certain life and instrument, medium and organ of its

presentation, conceals a sinister figure – a brahman, who exacts his due. Like
the paternal purse and keys, like the *jeu* itself, the talisman is not a gift but a
loan: it defers Raphael's debt but does not efface it. Its power is that of the
breath of life, yet joined to the breath of death. It is in the most literal sense
an *antiphrase*: it redeems the word of desire, incarnates it, fulfils it – *la parole
pleine* – yet only at the cost of its own existence. And this existence is identical to that of its owner, the spokesman of desire. If, as Derrida has written, it
is the essence of the representation to efface itself, to disappear:

> *La représentation parfaite devrait re-présenter parfaitement. Elle restaure
> la présence et s'efface comme représentation absolue. Ce mouvement est
> nécessaire. Le telos de l'image est sa propre imperceptibilité.*[1]

– then the *peau de chagrin* is the consummation, and crisis, of representation.
And it is therefore entirely necessary that it be inseparable from the exemplary medium of representation (expression and reappropriation of an original
presence) which is the voice.

What is clearly marked in the text of Balzac and what merits remarking is
this: contrary to the *statement* of Raphael himself – 'cette peau se rétrécit
quand j'ai un désir' – it is not the mere 'having' of a desire that is crucial, but
its *enunciation*, its *utterance by a voice*. If this small detail has been over-
looked by most readers of this text, it is nonetheless unmistakably described
in the incident which opens the novel's third and final section, 'L'Agonie.'
Raphael, 'ensevelie' once again, in a new and more luxurious tomb, his mansion,
is visited by a former teacher, M. Porriquet. The latter's garrulousness, suggested
by his name, contrasts sharply with the 'silence claustral' of the house. M.
Porriquet has come to ask financial assistance of his former and now wealthy
pupil Raphael, 'sans savoir précisément à quelle interrogation il répondait,'
and seeking only to get rid of the old man – another old man with a claim to
make – replies: 'Je n'y puis rien, rien du tout. *Je souhaite bien vivement que
vous réussissiez*' (author's italics). This mechanical phrase, expressing a desire
quite different from its literal meaning, nevertheless exacts its toll:

> *En ce moment, sans apercevoir l'effet que produisirent sur le front jaune et
> ridé du vieillard ces banales paroles, pleines d'égoisme et d'insouciance,
> Raphael se dressa comme un jeune chevreuil effrayé. Il vit une légère ligne
> blanche entre le bord de la peau noire et le dessin rouge ... (173, my emphasis).*

Raphael's voice as such, *à la lettre*, and not his intention, is decisive. And yet
that intention – to get rid of the old man – confirms, in its oedipal context,
the debt that he himself must pay. M. Porriquet takes, as it were, a piece of
the *peau de chagrin* with him, and with it, a piece of Raphael's life. Raphael's
life shrinks once again, this time not through the voice which represents, but
through the voice which presents and vivifies. Yet the *peau de chagrin* does

not simply disappear: for Raphael has taken precautions to control and to master the talisman. He has mounted it

> *sur une étoffe blanche où ses contours fatidiques étaient soigneusement dessinés par une ligne rouge qui l'encadrait exactement (172).*

It is his attempt to control the menace he struggled against in Foedora: the menace of the tiger:

> *La peau de chagrin était comme un tigre avec lequel il lui fallait vivre, sans en réveiller la férocité (*ibid.*).*

And yet, since it is the very power of the talisman to efface all distance separating the word of desire from its fulfilment, the consumption of life, of its very breath, is no longer situated in the pursuit of a woman (tiger) who cannot be caught, but rather in the very fulfilment, the enunciation of desire itself.

Against this fatal destiny, Raphael summons up precisely what he had hitherto fled: the power of the pen. With the pen he traces the contours of the *peau* upon the white cloth which he has given it as its *base*. And thus, the disappearance of the skin is also the production of a certain inscription: 'Il vit une légère ligne blanche entre le bord de la peau noire et le dessin rouge ... ' (173). The red line, recalling the reddish pamphlet in which his father was wrapped, and the coral lips of Foedora ('le corail intelligent de ses lèvres s'animait, se dépliait, se repliait,' 108), marks the disappearance of the skin by producing a new 'ligne blanche.' The hide, already bearer of an inscription, produces, through its self-consumption, the consumption of (a) desire, a new space of inscription, which is the base and frame of the disappearing image, representation of Raphael's life.

The power of the talisman, thus fulfilling the words of desire and consuming them at once, is thus the power and fatality of a certain consumption. In the most literal sense: consummation and consumption of the voice and of the breath which is its very life. This is inscribed in Raphael's first wish, during the evening of the orgy. He wishes to be rich, and the desire is fulfilled by a legacy: that of his maternal uncle, Major O'Flaherty. For the first time, it is the maternal name that Raphael must name and which brings him wealth:

> *Monsieur ... madame votre mère n'était-elle pas une demoiselle O'Flaherty?*
> *Oui, répondit Raphael assez machinalement;* Barbe-Marie *(162, my emphasis).*

Upon learning that he is the heir to a great fortune, 'liquide et palpable,' and hearing the full name of his mother spoken,

Raphael se leva soudain en laissant échapper le mouvement brusque d'un homme qui reçoit une blessure. Il se fit comme une acclamation silencieuse ... (162).

The wound he 'receives' is no longer that of his patrimony, but rather, in its usual and unusual (but literal) sense, that of his *matrimony:* of his maternal legacy and the union it now offers. Raphael's agony thus only begins in earnest when it is no longer the paternal debt, the pursuit for fulfilment, that determines his existence but rather that fulfilment itself, embodied in the plenitude and resources of the maternal name, and whose figure is the *peau de chagrin.* This name, his mother's proper name, which Raphael states 'assez machinalement,' is caught up in the double knot of fetishism: Barbe-Marie, the bearded Marie, the barbed Marie, recalling and resuming the spider in its web, and its 'petites meurtrières,' the ominous darkness of the cavern where the maternal shadow appeared. This name, which is also an image, denies and confirms the non-image of castration in the barbs of its beard.

Yet the name is also linked, in the text, to another formula which haunts Raphael as the very figure of the undecidable antithesis, the matrix of his malady:

Le oui *et* non *humain me poursuit partout! Toujours le* Carymary, Carymara *de Rabelais: je suis spirituellement malade, carymary! ou matériellement malade, carymara! (216, Balzac's emphasis).*

This formula - which will return when Raphael seeks the answer to his malady, to the *peau de chagrin,* in the knowledge of the *savants* - becomes itself fully legible only when reinserted into the Rabelaisian context from which it is taken. There, the enigmatic terms are part of an exorcism:

Otez ces gens moirs! Marmara
Carimari, carimara .... [2]

The formula seeks to remove 'ces gens noirs,' a certain shadow. And the sequence of 'meaningless' phonemes reveals a not so meaningless nucleus: *mama.* Marmara - mama, carimari - cara Marie, carimara - cara mama. The fetishist, who lives from the yes-and-no of his denial, is pursued by the 'yes and know' of his desire: the desire to know what lies behind the veil, and the terror of that discovery.

His malady is spiritual and material at once, because he confronts castration as a material and spiritual fact, as a real absence and an imaginary presence. But his effort to strip away the darkness in order to see - for the fetishist, *voir* and *savoir* are one - reveals a blank space, the whiteness which blinds, or the blackness of a cave which devours.

Here, then, for the first time, Raphael's life is menaced not by deprivation but by plenitude; not by paternal indebtedness but by the wealth and consumption of his maternal heritage:

> *Raphael regarda trois fois le talisman, qui jouait à l'aise dans les impitoyables lignes imprimées sur la serviette. ... Le monde lui appartenait, il pouvait tout, ne voulait plus rien. ... Puis il croyait à la peau de chagrin, il s'écoutait respirer, il se sentit malade, il se demandait:*
>
> *Ne suis-je pas pulmonique? Ma mère n'est-elle pas morte de la poitrine? (163)*

The resources of the maternal legacy are present in the *peau de chagrin*; yet it is no longer a voice reviving the dead, but rather the dying *of* the voice, the opening of a space which is that of inscription and of *jeu*: 'le talisman, qui jouait à l'aise dans les impitoyables lignes imprimées ... ' (163). It is therefore no accident that the radical violation of the paternal law which opens the novel – Raphael's entry into the *salon de jeu* – marks the turn from patrimony to matrimony. For paradoxically it is not so much his poverty that drives Raphael to the casino: rather it is the compulsion to divest himself of a property which is the fusion and confusion of poverty and wealth, a property which is as inalienable as the *peau de chagrin*: a skin which cannot be shed. Raphael's entry into the casino, where everything can be lost and yet where death is banned, is his (final) attempt to throw away all he has in order to learn the secret of his destiny. He goes to the casino in order to lose, and yet, hours later, he takes possession of the *peau de chagrin*. If he breaks the paternal interdiction in entering the site of 'une passion essentiellement imposable' it is in order to gain access to another law, which would enable him to 'pay' the castrative debt:

> *Disons que le joueur, contrairement aux apparences, ne veut plus être hors la loi, qu'il tente de rentrer dans l'ordre symbolique, légal, celui du signifiant phallique et, la dette castrative payée, la maintenir pour avoir accès à son désir et à la problématique de la transgression.*[3]

In the casino, Raphael divests himself of his last possession in order to recover his property, the selfhood his patrimony denies. R. Tostain, whose essay on 'Le Joueur' I here follow, traces the origin of this form of fetishism to a deficient patrimony:

> *C'est bien parce que son père a manqué de quelconque façon à sa fonction de législateur et d'interdicteur, qu'il n'a jamais pu le concevoir comme transcendant, comme une donnée irréductible du signifiant, que son fils, s'il est joueur, cherchera dans le jeu la Loi qui lui permettra la transgression.*[4]

Yet this paternal deficiency, which prevents the son from renouncing 'à son avoir pour pouvoir donner,' is dictated by the general movement of self-production in capitalist society: M. de Valentin's refusal of the *jeu*, of the ineluctable exchange and circulation of value in the commodity-world, abandons his son all the more totally to that world and to its aporias. Raphael throws away all he has: through his pursuit of Foedora, through dissipation, through the *jeu*, but these 'throws' are always *directed* by a desire of reappropriation, the desire of property and of the proper name. It is this that leads him to accept the pact with the *peau de chagrin*, which is nothing but the most radical expression of this desire. It is a desire as inalienable as his very skin; when later, at the height of his idyllic life with Pauline, he will try to throw away the talisman – down a deep well – it will return to him ineluctably, smaller than ever. No well, cave, or hole is deep enough to swallow up what cannot be consumed from without – the (oral) phantasm of desire – because its consumption is inscribed in it.

This consumption, which ends Raphael's narration and begins his 'agony,' is 'consumption' *tout court*: of his breath, and of the voice. It 'begins' the 'end' of his narration – a narration that intervenes between his initial use of the talisman and the emergence of its consequences: a narration that postpones those consequences while it unfolds. The narration is literally enveloped, together with the orgy itself, by the night:

> *La nuit enveloppa d'un crêpe cette longue orgie dans laquelle le récit de Raphael avait été comme une orgie de paroles, de mots sans idées, et d'idées auxquelles les expressions avaient souvent manqué (159).*

Like all expressions of his life, Raphael's narrative – once his *narration* has ceased – is cut off from its referent: 'mots sans idées,' ideas lacking expressions, an orgy of words that suffers the same fate as the orgy which evokes it. This 'crisis' – the separation of representation from what it represents – solicits, once again, the intervention of another voice, another narration to give it meaning and direction, a voice appropriating the scene as tableau and invoking its readers as observers to sanction the authenticity of this new and transcendant narrative discourse:

> *Le tableau fut complet. C'était la vie fangeuse au sein du luxe, un horrible mélange des pompes et des misères humaines, le réveil de la débauche. ... Vous eussiez dit la Mort souriant au milieu d'une famille pestiférée ... (160).*

The self-consumption of the *débauche* – of the orgy of words and the orgy itself – produces a new discourse, and a new *word*: 'Vous eussiez dit *la Mort* ... .' Mallarmé's 'absente de tous bouquets' manifests itself in the allegorical figure which is not so much an image as a word: *la Mort*. As Raphael's voice – the voice of a living being, present, representing its history and its life – dies down and away, it relapses into the language of action, becomes the immediate expression of a life which cannot but be that of self-consumption. Its absence solicits, once again, the advent of another narration, expression of another life and another subject. The narrative which consumes itself, figured in the *peau de chagrin*, is re-covered, its malady recuperated in the discourse of a voice that seeks to master the menace of an 'antiphrase.'

19

A Remark on Reading

For a first reading, the novel's final section, 'L'Agonie' confirms Poulet's observation, already cited, that the Balzacian protagonist is more decisive as an expression of a past than as the possibility of a future. And this is perhaps even more true for a second reading, no longer naïvely participating in the suspense of the story, but rather critically reviewing the laws of its movement. For this reading, which could be designated as that of literary criticism in its traditional sense, the narrative has *divided itself*, its end is determined by its beginning, and even more, its beginning by its end; its structure is archeo-teleological, consisting of functions that constitute the novel as a meaningful work and a coherent whole. This second, properly *critical* reading – and it goes without saying that such 'numerical' designations mark phases in the process of reading, not empirical facts – will have identified a sphere of *determinance*, to employ Poulet's term, which acts as the principle and power of totalization. The analytical work of such criticism is guided inevitably by a synthetic goal: its reading is regressive-progressive, aimed at elaborating and making *explicit* the implicit reserves of meaning in a work that, in its totality and meaningful stability, can properly be called a *book*. Such a critical reading would, for example, point to the repetitive nature of the text in order to identify the essence of that repetition as inherently self-identical, as a transcendental referent. It would (and does!) identify the 'problem' of *La Peau de chagrin* as that of intensity versus duration, of the Self and the Other, leaving the supposed coherence of such categories unquestioned. Thus, this second, critical reading renders itself, inexorably and more or less voluntarily, the *porte-parole* of the *work* (if not of the author 'himself'): it literally *bears out* the words of the novel, bearing them to gestation, repeating their gesture, as the son faithfully repeats that of the father. In so doing, such a critical reading is consummately faithful to the work, the book, to the product as the expression of a producer: in short, to the process of production itself (of the Self). But in so doing it must ignore whatever calls all these categories into question by bringing their *context* to light: it overlooks the textuality of the text.

This is only accessible to a *third reading*, which is neither naïve and immediate, nor regressive-progressive, which reads neither from beginning to end, nor simply from end to beginning. The third reading 'discovers' its text not as an object to be perceived and comprehended in the presence of an intuition or through the mediation of reflection but rather as the context of a desire which has already (always) inscribed the *reader* in the very text he is reading; a text which therefore defines and delimits the reader by putting the latter's desire into play, in the interplay of desire and text, of reading and writing; a reading which is inexorably always a rereading and a writing which is rewriting. This *textual reader* reads his 'own' desire, yet not merely expressed, represented in a work waiting to be repossessed by an interpretation that strives to fix its price and to define its value; the textual reader discovers his own desire as reader inscribed in the text, in a repetition which is irreducible because it precedes what it seems (only) to repeat. The reading, rereading, and rewriting of a text necessarily disarticulate and dislocate the position of the 'reader,' disrupting the *founding* categories of his 'subjectivity,' repeating this subjectivity as the subjection to a 'text' which 'covers'and protects, and yet 'in'which it is inscribed.

Thus, if the repetitiveness of the Balzacian text is perceived by traditional criticism as signifying the blows of a fate, of a destiny and destination that transcend the text – be it through that of the volume, of the *Comédie humaine* itself as a whole – in a process of totalization which, if open-ended, is nonetheless interminable and inexhaustible, such criticism has succumbed to the seduction of a desire which the *text* of the novel – the novel read *as* text – has placed on the scene. This criticism takes desire *at its word*, instead of reading it *literally, à la lettre: in its stead.* To read desire *literally*, in its stead, in figures and metaphors which cannot be reduced to a name or an expression, is to re-mark the difference: not between desire and its other, but rather 'within' desire itself, *instead* of 'itself,' in a disaggregation which precedes and founds all synthesis and projection. It is within the perspective of this textual, literal reading, which is always an incitement of desire, that Raphael's 'Agonie'must be reread; within the movement of a text which is not that of infinite totalization but of a certain, mortal interminability. If the fulfilment of Raphael's desire is his passion and agony, if its life is its death, it is in this desire itself that we must seek its torment.

20

Origen, or the Automat

The struggle that marks Raphael's 'agony' is not that of desire and its other: it is a struggle of a certain desire with itself. This desire, capable of fulfilling itself in its very utterance, of producing itself as a living presence through its mere word, finds the life it seeks consumed in its very consummation. At the moment when its virtuality is actualized, this actuality reveals itself to be the confusion of death and life. Or the confusion of a name: Raphael. To combat this confusion, Raphael returns to the strict economies of the paternal regime; only this time, it is to master the menace not of debt or of poverty, but of an opulence and power which are even more deadly. What he now seeks to ward off is not simply the threat of his patrimony but also the malady of his mother:

> Le lendemain du jour où, soudainement enrichi par un testament, il avait vu décroître la peau de chagrin, il s'était trouvé chez son notaire. Là, un médecin assez en vogue avait raconté sérieusement, au dessert, la manière dont un Suisse attaqué de pulmonie s'en était guéri. Cet homme n'avait pas dit un mot pendant dix ans, et s'était soumis à ne respirer que six fois par minute dans l'air épais d'une vacherie en suivant un régime alimentaire extrêmement doux. 'Je serai cet homme!' se dit en lui-même Raphael, qui voulait vivre à tout prix. Au sein de luxe, il mena la vie d'une machine à vapeur (171).

The problem that Raphael now faces is that of a certain surplus value: his name, previously worth nothing, and his person worth less, are now worth too much: they fuse and confuse meanings which logically should exclude each other or at least be structured as an antithesis: God hath healed, the painter of the Saviour, the man who died from an excess of love – the promise of a life beyond death becomes the reality, the actuality of a death-in-life, of a living which is absolutely inseparable from dying, from death as the 'end' of life and as its entelechy. The breath of life is no longer the sign of a living presence but of its expiration.

Therefore, Raphael seeks to return to the prescriptions of the paternal law. As with the *peau de chagrin* itself – which he seeks to measure and control by means of mounting it on a cloth, and then tracing its contours, fixing it within a frame – it is to a certain form of writing that he turns as an antidote to the threat of asphyxiation. He thus returns to the paternal *via recta*, and its taciturn economy by means of an inscription intended to abolish all chance in advance. In short, Raphael seeks to program his life and his desires in a book:

> *Le menu est dressé pour l'année entière, jour par jour. M. le marquis n'a rien à souhaiter. ... Le programme est imprimé, il sait le matin son dîner par cœur. Pour lors, il s'habille à la même heure, avec les mêmes habits, le même linge posés toujours par moi ... sur le même fauteuil. ... Il m'a donné, Monsieur, un petit livre à apprendre par cœur, et où sont écrits tous mes devoirs, un vrai catéchisme! ... il est bon comme le bon pain,* jamais il ne dit mot, *mais, par exemple, silence complet à l'hôtel et dans le jardin! Enfin, mon maître n'a pas un seul désir à former, tout marche au doigt et à l'œil, et recta! (168, my emphasis)*

It is a book that can be learned by heart and then thrown away, for its contents define the pattern of an eternal repetition, a routine which is always the same. Raphael's desire for a life of total self-expense returns as that of self-regulating, self-repeating, self-preserving automatism:

> *Presque joyeux de devenir une sorte d'automate, il abdiquait la vie pour vivre et dépouillait son âme de toutes les poésies du désir ... il s'était fait chaste à la manière d'Origène, en châtrant son imagination (171).*

Raphael's 'joy' in becoming 'a sort of automat' represents, even more than the *jeu* itself perhaps, the effort of the fetishistic desire to avoid the consequences of its denial: it is the effort of that desire to renounce itself, to re-enact the very movement of excoriation that divests it of its self-presence ('il abdiquait la vie pour vivre et dépouillait son âme de toutes les poésies du désir'). Ultimately it is the effort of a desire which only *is* in its denial of castration, to recover itself through the repetition and reappropriation of a castration which for it can only be *imaginary*: 'en châtrant son imagination.' The imagination, faculty of producing representations, and the voice, organ of imaginary reproduction, must both be 'chastised' if the desire for a certain living presence, for the maternal phallus as its embodiment is to survive its own fulfilment. The self-regulating machine which is the result of this self-castration, repeats and reintegrates the animation of the Self in the inanimate 'life' of the machine: a machine which regulates itself (automat), producing and conserving human life in its absence, as pure duration.

This pattern recapitulates that of a history of production as the maintenance and development of the Self, and which culminates in the self-regulating productivity of dead human labour, in and through highly *automated* means of production in which 'living labour' is no longer the primary productive factor (although still the only producer of 'value'). However, as long as the complicity of subjectivity and productivity – the domination of value as *production for the sake of production* – prevails; as long as the production of value is not regulated, programmed, *and reduced*, thus liberating the space and time of non-productive *play*, the scene of life fulfilling and maintaining itself in the denial of its impossible desire – the life of the automat assumed by Raphael de Valentin – will remain its exemplary allegory and articulation.

21

Revue 1:
The Perils of Pauline

Raphael's program is demolished by the very contingency it, as book, had sought to exclude and to master: the theatre. If Raphael is drawn to forsake his tomb by a compulsion which eludes all (psychological) verisimilitude, it is because the name, 'Raphael,' designates not a person but the *locus of a desire*; this desire, the only real protagonist of the novel, must play itself out to its end, if only because it is, ultimately, nothing but a desire of the end. The name, Raphael, circumscribes this play of desire, which is no less a play of names: paternal, maternal, filial; family and proper; proper and improper – all of which mark and remark their 'property.' 'Raphael's' fascination with the *jeu*: as gambling, spectacle, and theatre, is the playground – the play of a non-'ground' – where a certain desire displays the denial that founds and confounds it at once.

Thus, if 'Raphael's' appearance at the theatre violates the verisimilitude of a certain 'reality,' it conforms to the only necessity that is decisive for this text: that of fetishistic desire, denying and affirming the *jeu* it thus seeks to master and to which it is subjected. The spectacle which confronts him is that of his own life. His entry recalls the dramatic pathos of the *salon de jeu*, except that this time the enigma is no longer fresh: it seems to have suffered the very same *usure* that afflicts all phenomena in the commodity-world, and which even the voice of the narrator can neither efface nor redeem:

Voyez-vous cette fastueuse voiture, ce coupé simple en dehors, de couleur brune, mais sur les panneaux duquel brille l'écusson d'une antique et noble famille? Quand ce coupé passe rapidement, les grisettes l'admirent, en convoitent le satin jaune. ... Deux laquais en livrée se tiennent derrière cette voiture aristocratique; mais au fond, sur la soie, gît une tête brûlante aux yeux cernés, la tête de Raphael, triste et pensif. Fatale image de la richesse!

Qu'a-t-il fait, celui-là, pour être si riche? dit un pauvre étudiant en droit qui, faute d'un écu, ne pouvait entendre les magiques accords de Rossini (175).

It is as though the very production of Raphael: the (self)-narration that has filled his name with meaning and given it *value* (the enigmatic value of a luxury) has consumed him in the process. Although for the first time in the novel he is called *Valentin*, his stature and value are *inflated* rather than increased. Like Lucien de Rubempré in *Splendeurs et misères des courtisanes*, he has become a *schöner Schein:* but it is the glitter of the commodity, of an enigma that hides nothing but its own end, the semblance of a secret which is not. This debasement of the enigma by the inflation of a certain discourse is reflected in the wonder of the poor student, echoing that of the gamblers in the casino. This young student repeats and reflects the position once occupied by Raphael, the desire of a certain luxury. And yet the unfolding of this desire reveals its non-essence to be that of an imaginary denial, that of an ego captivated by its narcissistic projections, projected towards the mystery of a future which is only the reflection of its past: a review which becomes a revue.

The narrative structure of this final section is that of the revue: a series of disconnected images or scenes, spaced around an imaginary centre: the fatal malady of Raphael. The review as revue begins at the theatre itself, where the scenes and stations of Raphael's past pass before his eyes in rapid and summary succession: the journalists and speculators, the *antiquaire*, who has now become the lover of Euphrasie, Foedora, Taillefer, Emile, and finally, inevitably, Pauline:

Non plus la Pauline de l'hôtel Saint-Quentin, mais ... cette maîtresse accomplie, si souvent rêvées ... et vivant au sein du luxe, en un mot, Foedora douée d'une belle âme, ou Pauline comtesse et deux fois millionnaire comme l'était Foedora (181-2).

The essence of the revue is the imaginary satisfaction of a desire which, because what it wants is its death, must be constantly displaced and replaced in a series of images which are always new and always the same, allowing fetishist denial the illusion of producing and reappropriating itself in the presence of its movement. Thus, instead of condemning the 'schematism' of this return of Pauline and of its predictably fatal consequences, a textual reading will seek to interrogate the necessity of this 'scheme' and to retrace the desire it not merely expresses but articulates.

The trait of Pauline's return to be noted is the manner in which it fulfils and exceeds the prophetic dream of her mother: 'Tu ne sais pas? mon père est revenu. Je suis une riche héritière' (183). The dream has come true and for the first time it is the father who is source of an affluence two times greater than that of Fœdora. But alas, the rich old man is 'bien malade':

> *Tu ne sais pas, pauvre chéri! mon père est bien malade. Il est revenu des Indes, bien souffrant ... je dois me trouver à son réveil ... je suis la maîtresse au logis ... (186).*

'*Bien* malade,' and '*bien* souffrant' – gravely ill, to be sure, yet in our revue also happily ill and suffering. The reunion of Raphael and Pauline appears as a play which, evidently, exceeds the intent of the narration, subverting a certain seriousness. Raphael, 'ivre de bonheur,' embraces Pauline, who cries 'Mon père ... mon père,' castigating herself as 'une fille dénaturée ... je ne pense plus ni à père, ni à mère, ni à rien dans le monde' (186).

The *bien malade* is *bientôt: bien mort*, and the two children retreat into the second tableau of the revue, an idyllic herbarium, a second nature purified of the poverty of the first, a *Closerie de lilas*:

> *Quand tout Paris se chauffait encore devant les tristes foyers, les deux jeunes époux riaient sous un berceau de caméllias, de lilas, des bruyères. Leurs têtes joyeuses s'élevaient au-dessus des narcisses, des muguets et des roses du Bengale (189).*

In this floral scene, all of Raphael's desires are represented without lack, it is the inversion, and 'reversion' of the matutinal scene in the casino:

> *Il abondait dans cette scène matinale un bonheur inexprimable, comme tout ce qui est naturel et vrai. Raphael feignait toujours de lire sa feuille, et contemplait à la dérobée Pauline aux prises avec le chat, sa Pauline enveloppé d'un long peignoir qui la lui voilait imparfaitement, sa Pauline les cheveux en désordre et montrant un petit pied blanc veiné de bleu dans une pantoufle de velours noir (189).*

Down to Pauline's foot, these are the images of a desire which can 'feast its eyes' without end or surfeit, hidden by a 'feuille,' which evokes the wrath of Pauline – 'Je suis jalouse du journal' – who surreptitiously throws it away, into the garden. Yet the throw-away of a throwaway – which will become a theme in Joyce's *Ulysses* – opens the way for the fatal return, borne by the gardener, of a 'singulière plante marine' in which Raphael recognizes the 'inexorable peau de chagrin, qui n'avait pas six pouces carrés du superficies (190). The glance which is no longer protected by a *feuille* is exposed to the view of its image from which nothing separates it but an *empty space*. And this image, which in turn is nothing but the reflection of the desiring glance itself – 'ta vie est ma vie' (191) Pauline tells Raphael – reveals itself, behind the veil, to be the image of an empty space, but of one which 'grows' on the white cloth, between the red inscription and the black edge of the mounted skin: the space of a margin becoming the (w)hole.

22

Revue 2: Diagnosis

If the novel of fetishism assumes the form of a revue, it is because its founding desire is the desire to *review* the 'original' non-perception which it denies (and confirms). The series of images that pretend to a novelty which is, in fact, repetition of the same, reflects the desire to deny the non-mystery of castration by making it visible. The search to discover the mystery of this non-mystery can only be a review of what never was seen and yet – for the desire which denies castration – must appear, be it only as absence or enigma. The fetishist is thus the *savant malgré lui*: he knows what he refuses to know, and refuses what he knows. He seeks in the outside world of perception what he will not recognize as the very possibility and impossibility of his being. He dissociates his life from his death, in order to reunite them as terms of a simple exteriority, of an antithesis: ultimately, that of desire and fulfilment. He refuses to recognize fulfilment as the projection of his desire, and desire as the rejection of fulfilment. He repudiates this fusion and confusion, determining it to be a malady which must be healed. Raphael's malady is this confusion of the paternal and the maternal: the illness of his mother, and that of his father (-in-law):

> *Tu as pendant ton sommeil une petite toux sèche, absolument semblable à celle de mon père, qui meurt d'une phtisie. J'ai reconnue dans le bruit de tes poumons quelques-uns des effets bizarres de cette maladie (210).*

It is as though the fatality of his patrimony returns, here through the law of matrimony, to confirm the mortal heritage of Raphael's maternal line: yet the inversion is symptomatic of the disease itself. For the disease of consumption afflicts not the poor – here, at least – but the rich; it is the result of affluence and luxury, of the dream of self-production, and ultimately, of the desire of the maternal phallus, of a life which engenders itself. But which also consumes itself – this makes the dream into a nightmare, and projects the dreamer into the search for a knowledge he refuses to know. Raphael flees the perils of Pauline and seeks out the *savants*.

First on his list is the eminent zoologist, M. Lavrille. He is greeted there by *les canards*:

> *Tous les canards du monde étaient là, criant, barbotant, grouillant et formant une espèce de chambre canarde ... (192).*

Inserted in the context of the revue we are reading, the *canards* – 'vivant sans rencontrer de chasseurs, sous l'œil des naturalistes qui les regardaient par hasard' – represent, humorously, both the refuge Raphael is seeking, that of a certain nature, and the menace that he is fleeing: a representation cut off from what it represents, an orgy of sounds without sense, words without meaning, and above all a story (narrative) lacking its point(e): the *canard*.

But the *canards* are not only in front of M. Lavrille's house: they are inside it, in his etymological investigation of the history of the *peau de chagrin:*

> *La peau que vous me présentez ... est la peau d'un onagre. Nous varions sur l'origine du nom. Les uns prétendent que* Chagri *est un mot turc, d'autres veulent que* Chagri *soit la ville où cette dépouille zoologique subit une préparation chimique assez bien décrite par Pallas, et qui lui donne le grain particulier que nous admirons;* Martellens *m'a écrit que* Châagri *est un ruisseau ... (195).*

The etymology of the name cannot reach its origin, the information it presents is ambiguous, the secret of the talisman is as difficult to grasp as the *onagre* itself and as mysterious: 'Il est plein de mystères ... il est presque impossible de le saisir dans les montagnes ... ' (195). And if Raphael leaves empty-handed, with a mere nomenclature, the naturalist nevertheless furnishes him more information than he perhaps wants to know. The *onagre*, he relates, has a remarkable history:

> *Moïse avait défendu de l'accoupler avec ses congénères. Mais l'onagre est encore plus fameux par les prostitutions dont il a été l'objet ... (194).*[1]

The origin of the animal is thus linked with the prohibition of incest and with prostitution, with the law and its transgression; as the embodiment of a radical *impropriety* the *onagre* reveals its complicity with the phallus and money, and its vestigial surface, the *peau de chagrin*, fulfils this destination. Yet paradoxically enough this object of prostitution, capable of reproducing its *genus* only by transgressing the ban of Moses – reproduction as transgression – is also considered to be a king, 'le roi zoologique de l'Orient' (195), but one whose survival can only be illicit and illegitimate. Small wonder, then, that the value of such an animal is as immeasurable as the talisman itself: 'Enfin, un onagre apprivoisé vaut des sommes immenses' (195).

Oriental sovereign of a life permitted to reproduce itself only through transgression, the *onagre* is both the origin of chagrin and the chagrin of the origin. This chagrin is prescribed in the proscription of the law forbidding the onagre to reproduce itself with its own kind, thus defining its property as improper and preparing the way for the 'prostitutions dont il a été l'objet.' For the *onagre* emerges here as the figure of value itself, of a creature which can only reproduce itself through its other, thus adulterating that self; or, in coupling with its congenerates, preserving its purity at the cost of transgressing the biblical ban. And since its self is thus prescribed to be the self of another, it is inevitably the self of a certain prostitution, placing itself in place of another, prostituting its self. If the *onagre* is 'presque impossible de ... saisir,' it is because it is all too easy to have, just as Raphael has the skin, but cannot control it, as his next visit to the mechanical engineer, M. Planchette, proves: the terrible machine which tries to stretch the skin – *res extensa* par excellence – is destroyed. Raphael concludes: 'Faute de pouvoir inventer des choses ... il parait que vous en êtes réduits à inventer des noms' (204). Finally, the line dividing the name from the thing, matter from spirit, representation from presence, is confirmed by the conflicting and yet complementary diagnoses given Raphael by the three doctors he visits: Brisset, the materialist, observes that 'il n'existe plus d'estomac: l'homme a disparu. L'intellect est atrophé, parce que l'homme ne digère plus' (214), and thus confirms the progress of a certain 'consumption' – self-consumption of a body no longer able to consume its other and forced thereby to feed upon itself, to deplete its inner reserves. Caméristus, the vitalist, finds the cause of the malady not in the stomach but in the mind:

> Messieurs, le principe vital, l'archée de Van Helmont, est atteint en lui, la vitalité même est attaquée dans son essence ... de là proviennent les désordres ... le mouvement n'est pas venu de l'épigastre au cerveau, mais du cerveau vers l'épigastre (215).

Yet it is Maugredie, the eclectic pragmatist, 'pyrrhonien et moqueur,' who gives the most pertinent diagnosis, in a joke which consummates the *revue*:

> En effet, répliqua Maugredie en affectant un air grave et rendant à Raphael sa peau de chagrin, la racorcissement du cuir est un fait inexplicable et cependant naturel, qui, depuis l'origine du monde, fait le désespoir de la médecine et des jolies femmes (212-15).

'The despair of medicine and of beautiful women' is a skin which inexorably
shrinks, a leather which protects but also exposes a certain flesh, or non-flesh,
a membrane covering and discovering the surface of a life whose purity is that
of prostitution, the impropriety of property itself, the irreducibility of value,
transgression, substitution: that is, of 'castration.' The *peau de chagrin* is the
veil and vestige of a life which can never be present to itself, a life which can
only live through its other, whose legality and legitimacy is that of (self-)
transgression, of a pre- and proscription. And since it veils nothing but the
value of a *vale* – itself a reflection of the desire figured in the paternal name
of Raphael de *Valentin* – it is the despair of a desire that seeks to heal its
wounds while representing itself in the image which confronts Raphael as he
returns home after his futile search and research:

> *Voir votre maîtresse endormie, rieuse dans un songe paisible sous votre
> protection, vous aimant même en rêve, au moment où la créature semble
> cesser d'être ... voir une femme confiante,* demi-nue, mais enveloppé dans
> son amour comme dans un manteau, *et chaste au sein du désordre; admirer
> ses vêtements épars, un bas de soie rapidement quitté la veille pour vous
> plaire,* une ceinture dénouée qui vous accuse une foi infinie, *n'est-ce pas
> une joie sans nom? Cette ceinture est un poème entier; la femme qu'elle
> protégait n'existe plus, elle vous appartient, elle est devenue vous ... (209,
> my emphasis).*

His mistress, 'une femme confiante, demi-nue, mais enveloppée dans son
amour comme dans un manteau,' secure in the mantle of love which seems to
transcend death itself, be it only a dream, embodies the purity of a property
which is all and nothing, the fulness of a representation which effaces itself to
present its owner: 'la femme qu'elle protégait n'existe plus, elle vous appartient, elle est devenue vous ... .' Here, the veil binds indissolubly the representation to the desire it re-presents and fulfils, it is the 'ceinture dénouée qui vous
accuse une foi infinie,' the 'double knot' of credit and credibility required to
deny the non-secret of castration and thus to make it the object of a diagnosis.

23

Homecoming

Raphael's destiny seems to repeat that of the *onagre*: he is compelled to flee the society of his fellows, first Pauline, then his fellow patients in a sanatorium (after killing one in a duel). Yet the further he runs from the menace of the Same, in search of the healing force of an Other, the more ineluctably he is confronted with that Other as the reflection of the Same: the projection and expression of a desire seeking in vain to flee from itself: all the same.

His last refuge is in the Auvergne:

> *Aux eaux du mont Dore, il retrouva ce monde qui toujours s'éloignait de lui avec l'empressement que les animaux mettent à fuir un des leurs, étendu mort, après l'avoir flairé de loin (231).*

The *onagre* was forbidden to copulate with its congenerates: Raphael pursues a world which flees him as though he had already violated that taboo, and upon whom the verdict of capital punishment had already been pronounced. Raphael flees his fellows; but the world he seeks out is the site, not of his salvation, of his healing, but of his execution.

> *Son premier soin fut-il de chercher un asile écarté aux environs des eaux. Il sentait instinctivement le besoin de se rapprocher de la nature, des émotions vraies et de cette vie végétative à laquelle nous nous laissons si complaisamment aller au milieu des champs. ... A peu près à une demi-lieu du village, Raphael se trouva dans un endroit où, coquette et joyeuse comme*

un enfant, la nature semblait avoir pris plaisir à cacher des trésors; en voy-
ant cette retraite pittoresque et naïve, il résout d'y vivre. La vie devait y
être tranquille, spontanée, frugiforme comme celle d'une plante (231,
my emphasis).

The nature into which Raphael flees as his final refuge is 'picturesque and
naïve,' marked by a childlike playfulness, seemingly devoid of the ravages
of desire, life in its most secure form, that of the plant; nature, playing a game
of hide-and-seek with inexhaustible reserves. In a deep valley, framed and
protected from the outside world by high cliffs, Raphael discovers what he
had vainly sought in the *automaton* of the *Jeu*:

Le monde paraissait finir là ... c'était une nature naïve et bonne, une rusti-
cité vraie ... (qui) n'avait d'analogie avec aucune idée, ne procédait que
d'elle-même, vrai triomphe du hasard *(233, my emphasis).*

The self-generating self-sufficiency of inexhaustible nature is free of malady,
usure, and of the ravages of age. Its timeless repetition knows no end:

La santé débordait dans cette nature plantureuse, la vieillesse et l'enfance
y étaient belles; enfin il y avait dans tous ces types d'existence un laisser-
aller primordial, une routine de bonheur ... (234).

Nothing seems lacking in 'ce tableau délicieux' where 'tout avait son lustre ...
tout y était harmonieux à voir,' and where 'un silence majestueux ... régnait'
(233). This 'luster' is not that of luxury but of a more perfect exchange in
which nothing is lost and everything retained, as in 'la nappe d'eau claire où
se réfléchissaient fidèlement les cimes granitiques, les arbres, la maison et le
ciel.' And yet this 'tableau délicieux' which reflects Raphael's desire for an
inexhaustible, self-sufficient life without loss or death is more than a tableau
or an image, safely framed and where 'tout y était harmonieux à *voir*' - it is a
scene, synopsis, and figure of the desire it captivates; and, even more, it is a
scenario, describing a certain origin. This description must be read as the allegory of a desire which, in returning to the site of a certain infancy, discovers
in the very arcanum it seeks the traces of a fatality that is its original destiny.

The valley where the world seems to end, and to begin, is described as
follows:

Figurez-vous un cône renversé, mais un cône de granit largement évasé,
espèce de cuvette dont les bords étaient morcelés par des anfractuosités
bizarres: ici des tables droites sans végétation, unies, bleuâtres, et sur les-
quelles les rayons solaires glissaient comme sur un miroir; là, des rochers
entamés par des cassures, ridés par des ravins, d'où pendaient des quartiers
de lave dont la chute était lentement préparée par les eaux pluviales, et

souvent couronnés de quelques arbres rabougris que torturaient les vents;
puis, çà et là, des redans obscurs et frais d'où s'élevaient un bouquet de
châtaigniers hauts comme des cèdres, ou des grottes jaunâtres qui ouvrai-
ent une bouche noire et profonde, palissée de ronces, de fleurs, et garnie
d'une langue de verdure. Au fond de cette coupe, peut-être l'ancien cratère
d'un volcan, se trouvait un étang, dont l'eau pure avait l'éclat du diamant.
Autour de ce bassin profond, bordé de granit, de saules, de glaieuls, de
frênes et de mille plantes aromatiques alors en fleur, régnait une prairie
verte comme un boulingrin anglais; son herbe fine et jolie était arrosée par
les infiltrations qui ruisselaient entre les fentes des rochers, et engraissé par
les dépouilles végétales que les orages entraînaient sans cesse des hautes
cimes vers le fond.

Irrégulièrement taillé en dents de loup comme le bas d'une robe, l'étang
pouvait avoir trois arpents d'étendue; selon les rapprochements des rochers
et de l'eau, la prairie avait un arpent ou deux de largeur, en quelques en-
droits, à peine restait-il assez de place pour le passage des vaches. A une
certaine hauteur, la végétation cessait. Le granit affectait dans les airs les
formes les plus bizarres, et contractait ces teintes vaporeuses qui donnent
aux montagnes élevées de vagues ressemblances avec les nuages du ciel. Au
doux aspect du vallon, ces rochers nus et pelés opposaient les sauvages et
stériles images de la désolation, des éboulements à craindre, des formes si
capricieuses que l'une de ces roches est nommé le Capucin, tant elle res-
semble à un moine. Parfois ces aiguilles pointues, ces piles audacieuses, ces
cavernes aeriennes s'illuminaient tour à tour, suivant le cours du soleil ou
les fantaisies de l'atmosphère, et prenaient les nuances de l'or, se teignaient
de pourpre, devenaient d'un rose vif, ou ternes ou grises. Ces hauteurs of-
fraient un spectacle continuel et changeant commes les reflets irisés de la
gorge des pigeons (231-2).[1]

If I have taken the liberty of citing this passage *in extenso*, it is because the
description is nothing less than the *mise-en-scène* of the desire indicated by
the name Raphael de Valentin, and which shapes the novel: the desire to return to and to recover the origin of life itself. The descent into the valley is
that into a certain image: that of a 'bassin profond bordé de granit.' The sur-
rounding cliffs frame and protect the fertile valley, and if the barren, inanimate nature of the rocks contrasts with the lush vegetation below, there appears
to be a profound harmony between the two, that of a reflection: the rocks
mirror the rays of the sun, which 'glissaient' on the smooth surfaces, while
'l'eau pure' of the pond below shines with 'l'éclat du diamant.' The second
paragraph, describing the same scene, but this time ascending, extends this
complicity of reflection – the harmony of a protective inanimate and a

protected animate nature – to the very heavens themselves; the tips of the mountains shrouded in mist display 'vagues ressemblances avec les nuages du ciel.' The image is of an harmonious, analogical nature, offering the aspect of 'un spectacle continuel et changeant comme les reflets irisés de la gorge des pigeons.' But this spectacle has its own scenario and a distinctive climax:

> *Souvent, entre deux lames de lave que vous eussiez dit séparées par un coup de hache, un beau rayon de lumière pénétrait, à l'aurore ou au coucher du soleil, jusqu'au fond de cette riante corbeille où il se jouait dans les eaux du bassin, semblable à la raie d'or qui perce la fente d'un volet et traverse une chambre espagnole, soigneusement close pour la siestre. Quand le soleil planait au-dessus du vieux cratère, rempli d'eau par quelque révolution antédeluvienne, les flancs rocailleux s'échauffaient, l'ancien volcan s'allumait, et sa rapide chaleur réveillait les germes, fécondait la végétation, colorait les fleurs et mûrissait les fruits de ce petit coin de terre ignoré (232).*

The penetration of the solar rays engenders life within the valley – but only by awakening the dormant heat of the ancient volcano hidden beneath the water. The penetration is gentle, 'semblable à la raie d'or qui perce la fente d'un volet et traverse une chambre espagnole, soigneusement close pour la siestre,' and the life-giving response it awakens – 'les flancs rocailleux s'échauffaient, l'ancien volcan s'allumait ... sa rapide chaleur' – seems devoid of that original volcanic violence. And yet this eruptive, archaic force, apparently domesticated in the protective rocks and the fertile basin, 'remplie d'eau par quelque révolution antédeluvienne,' has left its trace: the rocks, formed by the crystallization of molten lava, are riven with fissures, 'évasé,' 'morcelés par des anfractuosités bizarres,' 'entamés par des cassures, ridés par des ravins,' making the protection they afford appear not merely bizarre, but precarious. If the cliffs domesticate 'les orages,' if the fertile basin is 'arrosé par les infiltrations qui ruisselaient entre les fentes des rochers' and 'engraissé par les dépouilles végétales' fed by the storms, there is also the menace of 'éboulements à craindre.' The gentle penetration of the rays of the sun enters 'entre deux lames de lave que vous eussiez dit *séparées par un coup de hache*' (my italics). Finally, the bottom and centre of the scene, the pond, is described as 'irrégulièrement taillé *en dents de loup comme le bas d'une robe*'; at certain places it barely leaves 'assez de place pour le passage des vaches.' The association of the tooth-shaped contours of the lake with the bottom of a dress suggests the danger that lurks beneath the lake and under the dress:

> *Thus the foot or shoe owes its attraction as a fetish, or part of it, to the circumstance that the inquisitive boy used to peer up the woman's legs towards her genitals.*[2]

Muted, metaphorically – and even more: metonymically – the menace of a deadly consumption haunts this idyllic scene, and the *dents de loup* are enmeshed in an entire network of glyphic traces: the rocks are, as we have seen, *eaten away – morcelés, entamés, ridés* – by the very forces which nourish the vegetation below, the waters of the storm. Yet this destiny is not accidental, for it is already present in the very origins of the rocks themselves: the eruption of deadly, molten lava, crystallizing into those bizarre and irregular shapes whose fissures, between and within them, appear to have been the work of 'un coup de hache'; yet it is a 'coup de hache' that is their very origin.

The same pattern is to be found in the vegetation growing on the cliffs: 'quelques arbres rabougris que torturaient les vents,' mutilated by their exposure; and yet the more fortunate 'châtaigniers hauts comme des cèdres' rise out of 'redans [from: *re-dents*] obscurs et frais,' reminiscent of the 'étude obscure' of the notaire where Raphael felt 'le même froid humide qui m'avait saisit sur le bord de la fosse où gisait mon père' (155). The 'fosse' itself is recalled by 'des grottes jaunâtres qui ouvraient *une bouche noire et profonde, palissée de ronces, de fleurs, et garnée d'une langue de verdure*' (my emphasis), and again it is the vegetation which serves as garnish and as instrument of destruction, the tongue which draws and plunges its prey into a 'bouche noire et profonde.' The origin of this scenery is indicated by the *mouth which devours* – what psychoanalysts have termed the 'vagina dentata.'[3] The eruption of fatal fluid, molten lava, becomes life-giving only through petrification in the bizarre and riven rocks, bearing the marks of an origin, inscribed in their fissures and crevices, which never ceases to threaten the life it engenders and protects. Here, as in the *salon de jeu*, the very solidity of reality is menaced by an *usure* which is ineluctable because it is the very origin of this reality; and this condemns Raphael's search for a durable, permanent existence beyond the ravages of such *usure*: inscribed in the rocks he finds the scenario of his own destiny and the scene of his desire.

This scenery is a phantasm, in the sense given the term by Laplanche and Pontalis:

> *Le fantasme n'est pas l'objet du désir, il est scène. Dans le fantasme, en effet, le sujet ne vise pas l'objet ou son signe, il figure lui-même pris dans la séquence d'images. Il ne se représente pas l'objet désiré mais il est représenté participant à la scène, sans que, dans les formes les plus proches de fantasme originaire, une place puisse lui être assigné ... .*[4]

If this scene is, as I have suggested, very close to what Freud termed the 'primal scene' (*Urszene*), then there is all the more reason to search, with prudence, for Raphael's place 'in' it. This place, it seems at first, is essentially that of the spectator, separated from and yet participating in the 'spectacle continuel et changeant,' from the security of an irreducible distance. When however he foresakes this rôle to enter the scene, under a compulsion which is as irresistible as it is fatal, the tableau – 'ce tableau délicieux' – becomes his tomb. The antithesis resists dialectical synthesis: it is only as an object, over against and yet present to the observer, that the tableau can conserve the life it represents, resisting the *usure* that dooms all immediate presence to exhaustion in the instant of its being there, consummation as (self-) consumption.

The tableau 'tables' time in the fixture of its frame. Yet this frame is riven with fissures: 'un cône de granit largement évasé.' Another framework is required, one which is immune to the decay of the objects it gathers in its space. Laplanche and Pontalis indicate what it might be:

> *Tout en étant toujours présent dans le fantasme, le sujet peut y être* sous une forme désubjectivée, *c'est-à-dire dans* la syntaxe même de la séquence en question.[5]

And indeed, if we observe the syntax of the description, we will find that it is here that the tableau has its ultimate support and resource. The initial appeal to the reader – 'figurez-vous' – inaugurates the space of an imaginary dialogue which the following description then organizes in terms of a certain *symmetry*: that of descent and ascent, deploying the representation in an homogeneous space, with a precise *centre* and *base*:

> ici *des tables droites sans végétation* ... là, *des rochers entamés par des cassures* ... puis, ça et là, *des redans obscurs et frais* ... Au fond de *cette coupe* ... autour de *ce bassin profond* ... *(231-2).*

The 'inverted cone' configures the imaginary form – an inverted triangle – of Raphael's translation of the pact inscribed in the skin, as well as reflecting the 'V' and 'val' contained in his name, 'Valentin.' It also reflects the dwindling of the skin itself, its 'contractive power' ('sa force contractile'). At the same time, this inverted cone frames and protects a homogeneous space in which bizarre forms accumulate without ever seeming to threaten the basic stability. Yet the organization of this space, its support and its structure, is effected by means of the descriptive discourse of a narration which feigns a dialogue with the reader – 'figurez-vous ... ' – in order to present a tableau harmoniously and symmetrically ordered around a centre, and erected upon a base.

The source of this narration, off-stage, is nonetheless the absent point from which a line extends to that other point, the reader, in order that a third point – the tableau itself – take (its) place, fixed by the glance of speaker and listener, 'author' and 'reader.' The 'ici – là' of the tableau – its objective stability – is a reflection of the 'je-vous' of speaker and listener, founding the space of representation in the complicity of a narration which makes itself heard.

The tableau can thus appear to master the danger of a certain consumption through the reassuring form of reflection. The 'spectacle continuel et changeant' it comprehends appears within its frame 'comme les reflets irisés de la gorge des pigeons.' This 'gorge' does not swallow, it only reflects. Like the reader whom the narration seeks to define and to dominate as listener, Raphael participates in the scene, yet seemingly without having to enter into it, remaining outside, a spectator, and still in contact with it, through the transparency of a certain distance, by means of odours, which correspond exactly, in this visual relationship, to the resonance of the narrative voice: 'Les tièdes senteurs des eaux, des fleurs et des grottes qui parfumaient ce réduit solitaire causèrent à Raphael une sensation presque voluptueuse' (234). Yet such participation cannot still the desire it engages any more than in the *magasin d'antiquités.* The aporia of this desire is that it must always strive to lift the veil, to abolish the distance separating it from its object, even when that distance is filled with a sound or an odour. For this desire, constituted by its duplicitous denial of castration, to be left alone with 'itself' is for it to be condemned to death.

If, as has often been observed, the essence of the 'Balzacian' desire is its movement of *projection*, it is because of this compulsion to reject the castration which, paradoxically, constitutes and deconstitutes its 'self.' This is why this desire is ultimately a desire for an impossible identification, the desire *to be, to be-come*, to come-to-be what it cannot simply *have*, since its *possession* is inextricably interwoven with its *loss*: the (maternal) phallus. This desire can only *be* by becoming this other, be it through the symbolic fling of the *jeu* – throwing away what it has in order to become one with the *autómaton*, or demon of the *jeu* – or through the imaginary projection by which Raphael seeks 'à m'associer en quelque sorte à l'action de [Foedora's] vie' (123). And if Raphael's flight from Pauline is determined by the fact that this identification has been consummated – 'elle est devenue vous' – by his recognition of the truth of Pauline's words: 'La femme que vous aimerez vous tuera!' (131) – it is only to succumb to the temptation of another *glissement*:

> *Il tenta de s'associer au mouvement intime de cette nature et de s'identifier assez complètement à sa passive obéissance* pour tomber sous la loi despotique et conservatrice qui régit les existences instinctives. *Il ne voulait plus être chargé de lui-même.* Semblable à ces criminels d'autrefois, qui, poursuivis par la justice, étaient sauvés s'ils atteignaient l'ombre d'un autel, il essayait de se glisser *dans le sanctuaire de la vie. Il réussit à devenir partie intégrante de cette large et puissante fructification: il avait épousé les intempéries de l'air*, habité tous les creux de rochers ... enfin, *il s'était si parfaitement uni à cette terre animée qu'*il en avait en quelque sorte saisi l'âme et pénétré les secrets *(237, my emphasis).*

The 'despotic and conservative law' to which Raphael seeks to subjugate himself is a maternal law, that of 'cette large et puissante fructification'; and the law whose justice pursues him, from which he 'essayait de se glisser dans le sanctuaire de la vie,' is the law of a certain 'death' or mortality: the paternal law, the castrative debt, which he seeks to deny in his very gesture of flight, in that *glissement*, and yet which he cannot but affirm, even in the very 'creux de rochers' which he imaginatively inhabits; 'creux' embedded in 'rocks' which can only be, ultimately, volcanic, which transform the apparent solidity of the tomb into a fatal liquidity, substance into value, the phallic image into the phallic trace, trace of a 'phallus' that never was present.

This is the non-soul and non-secret that his desire vainly seeks to 'seize' and to 'penetrate'; the living substance into which he seeks – 'fantastically' and phantasmatically – to 'implant' himself:

> *Pour lui, les formes infinies de tous les règnes étaient les développements d'une même substance, les combinaisons d'un même mouvement, vaste respiration d'un être immense qui agissait, pensait, marchait, grandissait, et avec lequel il voulait grandir, marcher, penser, agir. Il avait fantastiquement mêlé sa vie à la vie de ce rocher, il s'y était implanté (237).*

The living substance, the 'être immense' into which he thus seeks to penetrate and to implant himself is that of a 'vaste respiration,' the essential expression and manifestation of a life which 'agissait, pensait, marchait, grandissait' and whose apparent self-presence creates the space of all possible identification and appropriation. For Raphael's self-projection, his identification with the Other, is always a moment in a movement of self-appropriation, in which the image absorbs the self only to be finally devoured by it: 'il n'y eut plus d'univers, l'univers passa tout en lui' (236). And with this final fusion, the ineluctable malady of a self which 'is' only as self-consumption, is reaffirmed. The self comes home in a nature which is the site of its birth and of its death, its *bed*:

> *Pour les malades, le monde commence au chevet et finit au pied de leur lit. Ce paysage fut le lit de Raphael (236).*

The 'respiration' of this immense Being is no longer the sign of life, but of death: its 'creux' are no longer a solid habitation but a devouring orifice:

> *Qui n'a pas, une fois dans sa vie, espionné les pas et démarches d'une fourmi, glissé des pailles dans l'unique orifice par lequel respire une limace blonde ... (236).*

The blackness of this orifice and the brightness of the 'limace blonde' is the fatal fusion and confusion of that other vital play of light and shadow, the translucence of the veil, the light of Fœdora, 'plus vive que la lumière même'

(108), or the harmonious reflection of the rays of the sun. It is the same confusion of light and dark that is reflected in the light of the *peau de chagrin* itself, in the onagre, 'sillonnée de bandes plus ou moins fauves et ressembl(ant) beaucoup à la peau du zèbre' (194), and this fatal phenomenon – the fatality of the phenomenon – reappears here. Raphael has sought refuge with a family living in this valley, by situating himself between two males, father and son:

> *Aussitôt, Valentin se résolut à vivre entre ce vieillard et cet enfant, à respirer dans leur atmosphère, à manger de leur pain, à boire de leur eau, à dormir de leur sommeil, à se faire de leur sang dans les veines (236).*

But his refuge, between father and son, is threatened and then destroyed by the mother: a mother who sees the signs of death, a martyrdom whose redemption is anything but certain, the bankruptcy of a certain life and its economy. Raphael hears as she complains to her family:

> *Et (Raphael) est vraiment pâle comme un Jésus de cire! ... Et il ne sent déjà pas bon, tout de même! Ça lui est égal, il se consume à courir comme s'il avait de la santé à vendre ... je payerions bien un cierge pour sauver une si douce créature, si bonne un agneau pascal ... (238).*

The pallor of the father, the 'cierge pascal,' returns as the fatality of the son, 'agneau pascal,' sacrifice of a certain paternity, sacrificed to, and by a certain maternity. This pallor appears as the fusion and confusion of phenomenality itself: the brilliance and transparency of a manifestation, consuming itself in a fatal self-exposure.

Yet it is another apparition, another shadow, that complements and completes Raphael's pallor:

> *Tout à coup, l'Auvergnate elle-même se dressa soudain devant lui comme une ombre dans l'ombre du soir; par une bizarrerie de poète, il voulut trouver, dans son jupon rayé de noir et de blanc, une vague ressemblance avec les côtes desséchées d'un spectre (239).*

It is the return of the maternal shadow and of the paternal skeleton, united in 'les côtes désséchées d'un spectre,' in this shadow in the shadows ('une ombre dans l'ombre du soir'), and her apron, 'rayé de noir et de blanc,' confirms the legacy of the onagre, of its skin, 'striped like that of a zebra.'

Raphael's death is thus inseparable from the death, the disappearance of a certain phenomenality, the emergence of a certain non-phenomenality, the confusion of light and dark, of a light which is dark and of a dark which is light, no longer to be mastered by any perception: the apparition of the phallus, as a veil which is not to be lifted. The 'carymary-caramara,' 'ôtez ces gens noirs,' returns in figures who are not to be wished away:

Un matin, il vit deux hommes vêtus de noir qui rôdèrent dèrent autour de lui, le flairèrent et l'étudièrent à la dérobée. ... Il reconnut en eux le médecin et le curé des eaux ... attirés par l'odeur d'une mort prochaine. Il entrevit alors son propre convoi, il entendit le chant des prêtres, il compta les cierges, et ne vit plus qu'à travers un crêpe les beautés de cette riche nature, au sein de laquelle il croyait avoir rencontré la vie. ... Le lendemain, il partit pour Paris ... (240).

Raphael's approaching death is the death of the image, and yet it too is 'recovered' by the 'crêpe' which conceals and yet reveals the 'beautés de cette riche nature.' These beauties display themselves before his eyes as Raphael makes his final journey home, to Paris:

La nature s'étalait à ses yeux avec une cruelle coquetterie ... séductions sans fin! La nature, agitée, vivace comme un enfant, contenant à peine l'amour et la sève du mois de juin, attirait fatalement les regards éteints du malade (241).

The spectacle that unfolds before him closes the circle of his wanderings, enclosing him within it. It is the return of the country fair, which had marked the beginning of his adventure, in the dead-end street where the Hôtel Saint-Quentin was situated:

Vers le soir ... il fut réveillé par une joyeuse musique et se trouva devant une fête de village ... les petits enfants se rigolaient, les vieilles femmes parlaient en riant: tout avait une voix, et le plaisir enjolivait même les habits et les tables dressés ... (241).

The richness of an image in which 'tout avait une voix,' overwhelms the dying Raphael, whose own voice is practically gone, drawing from him a fatal desire:

(Il) ne put réprimer une sinistre interjection ni le désir d'imposer silence à ces violons, d'anéantir ce mouvement, d'assourdir ces clameurs, de dissiper cette fête insolente. (ibid.).

His desire to put an end to the sounds of the fair, to 'impose silence,' is, of course, immediately realized: the spectacle vanishes in a sudden thunderstorm, vanishes that is, except for a single figure:

Sur l'échafaud de l'orchestre, un ménétrier aveugle continuait à jouer sur sa clarinette une ronde criarde. Cette musique sans danseurs, ce vieillard solitaire au profil grimaud, en haillons, les cheveux épars, et caché dans l'ombre d'un tilleul, étaient comme une image fantastique du souhait de Raphael (ibid., *my emphasis).*

The solitary ministrel, playing the clarinet and hidden in the shadow of a linden tree, is indeed the 'image fantastique du souhait de Raphael,' the fatal compromise of his denial, blind in order not to see what cannot be seen, yet itself barely visible, seen by Raphael; the allegory of *usure*, yet emitting a sound which accompanies an absent dance, a sound which is unaware of its own solitude, another 'round' ('une ronde criarde'), whose cry will have never been answered. And finally, not simply on a stage, but on a scaffold as well ('echafaud'): the scene and the death of a desire.

For the 'life' of this desire thrives on nothing but the mortality it denies; in repudiating the 'difference' of castration, it produces the fantasy of a life which is without difference, and hence indistinguishable from death. The bed of life becomes the bed of death, the radiance of life dreaming the dream of its presence, the reverie and apparition of a certain infancy – all this appears during the final moments of Raphael's life:

> *Raphael ... resplendissait de beauté pendant son sommeil. Un rose vif colorait ses joues blanches. Son front, gracieux comme celui d'une jeune fille, exprimait le génie. La vie était en fleur sur ce visage tranquille et reposé. Vous eussiez dit un jeune enfant endormi sous la protection de sa mère. Son sommeil était un bon sommeil, sa bouche vermeille laissait passer un souffle égal et pur, il souriait, transporté sans doute par un rêve dans une belle vie (245).*

The dreams of this 'belle vie' are legible in the metaphors in which Raphael is described: the return 'home' to a state of infancy, protected by an all-powerful, all-giving mother – 'vous eussiez dit un jeune enfant endormi sous la protection de sa mère' – a time before the fatal discovery of the phallic difference, of castration and the difference between the sexes, when the young boy was 'gracieux comme ... une jeune fille,' when the perfect presence of an undifferentiated sex could be perfectly expressed ('son front ... exprimait le génie'), and when a 'bouche vermeille' opened only to emit 'un souffle égal et pur.' In this image, that of a bed which is the scene of a desire, of its birth and death, is expressed the desire which 'animates' the textuality and texture of so many figures of the *Comédie humaine*, the desire of a certain confusion and fusion of the sexes, exemplified in Seraphita, since that fusion must be essentially feminine. It is the desire of a primary narcissism which, as I have suggested throughout, is not the trait of a particular abnormal, 'neurotic' subject but *the tendency of subjectivity itself*, inasmuch as it has been constituted by an epoch of self-production governed by the desire for a life of self-presence, and hence for the purity of an origin which is its phantasmatic condition. This desire, in the words of André Green, is

Désir de l'Un, aspiration à une totalité auto-suffisante et immortelle dont l'auto-engendrement est la condition, mort et négation de la mort à la fois.[6]

It is, therefore, the desire for a dream which will replace and complete reality: the dream of a 'belle vie' which will be more real than 'reality' itself. It is the dream of Raphael de Valentin, of the *Comédie humaine*, and of the critics it has never ceased to seduce and to command. Critics for whom the death that follows can be 'forgotten' since it is only the sign of the immortal life of a self-totalizing totality, the presence of a work, the production of a voice.

24

Finale:
Projection

- *Te voilà donc?*
Ces mots, prononcés d'une voix argentine, dissipèrent les figures nuageuses
de son sommeil. A la lueur de la lampe, il vit assise sur son lit sa Pauline ...
(245).

Raphael's last reverie, 'les figures nuageuses de son sommeil,' are *dissipated* by
the figure of dissipation itself, seated at the foot of his bed. It is as the fulfilment of the *débauche* - 'un réveil enragé: l'impuissance est assise à votre che-
vet ... une phtisie vous dévore ... ' (152) - that Pauline appears before him,
the image of all his desires, and yet an image that a breath can blow away:

> Raphael resta stupéfait à l'aspect de cette figure blanche comme les pétales
> d'une fleur des eaux, et qui, accompagnée de longs cheveux noirs, semblait
> encore plus blanche dans l'ombre. ... Vétus de blanc, la tête penchée et
> foulant à peine le lit, elle était là comme un ange descendu des cieux,
> comme une apparition qu'un souffle pouvait faire disparaître (245).

This apparition, 'belle image de ma belle vie,' is the fulfilment of the medium
of the imaginary; of a certain whiteness, the effort to tame, to domesticate
the stripes of the *onagre*; of the spectral figure of living death, or of a life-in-
death. The effort, product of a desire, to master the hole ('la maille rompue')
as the whole is what A. Green has called a 'negative hallucination,' which characterizes primary narcissism.[1] The apparition which confronts Raphael is that

of a living, natural whiteness ('cette figure blanche comme les pétales d'une fleur des eaux'), framed and fixed within a certain darkness, a whiteness which lives in the contrast of an antithesis, of an external contiguity to the blackness it excludes, and which includes it: 'et qui, accompagnée de longs cheveux noirs, semblait encore plus blanche dans l'ombre.' The purity and intensity of this whiteness, framed in the darkness of hair and of the shadow, expresses the desire and the dilemma of a life which will never have been (present-to-itself): it is the image of the matrix of that life, generating and producing itself, the phallic mother, the representation, visual or acoustic, which truly represents because it effaces itself before the 'truth' of what it discovers and recovers; yet this discovery exceeds all truth, whose space it opens: the non-secret of castration.

This is why this image, an apparition, opens on a non-reality which can only be the death of the desire it expresses. The apparition which captivates his desire is its life and its death at once, for its own transparency reflects and exposes the non-secret that confuses his life and death: 'Si tu me regardes encore, je vais mourir' (246). The image of life, the maternal phallus, is discovered to be the image of death, of her 'castration,' and the castration of the mother can only be that of the son as well. The fatal apparition, the fatality which haunts the entire realm of phenomenality for the fetishist, can only be overcome by the immediate (re-)union with what cannot appear as such but only as an apparition: by becoming one, by fusing with the (maternal) phallus, by breaking down all barriers and lifting all veils, by the throw which overcomes all distance, which comes home.

It is Raphael's last *entry*, breaking down the translucent walls of representation in the desperate effort to seize the 'life' that has never ceased to elude his possession and to torment his desire. Raphael, with his dwindling forces – 'à mesure que grandissait ce désir, la peau, en se contractant, lui chatouillait la main' – breaks down the door behind which Pauline has locked herself in, and is confronted by the spectacle of the final struggle of life against *itself*; against a *Self* which is its *Death*:

> *(Raphael) vit sa maîtresse à demi nue se roulant sur un canapé. Pauline avait tenté vainement de se déchirer le sein, et pour se donner une prompte mort, elle cherchait à s'étrangler avec son châle. ... Ses cheveux étaient épars, ses epaules nues, ses vêtements en désordre, et, dans cette lutte avec la mort, les yeux en pleurs, le visage enflammé, se tordant sous un horrible désespoir, elle présentait à Raphael, ivre d'amour, mille beautées qui augmentèrent son délire; il se jeta sur elle avec la légèreté d'un oiseau de proie, brisa le châle et voulut la prendre dans ses bras (274).*

Raphael's final, violent entry carries fetishism to its end and to its origin; the denial of castration as the 'original' separation from the maternal presence. This denial, no less than the presence it seeks to recover, assumes this separation, but only as a totalizing force, as a process of reappropriation: the image of the (lost) mother becomes the 'structure encadrante pour le sujet lui-même' (Green);[2] Raphael's entry is always the effort to re-enter this frame, to reinsert himself within it in order to reinsert it within himself.[3]

This separation, which fetishism denies, making it the framework of the subject itself, determining it as totality, is linked to a particular object, which subsequently will (have) become the substitute of the lost phallus: the maternal *breast*, 'lost' to the child at precisely the moment where he can perceive the mother as an other, *as a totality*, distinct from himself, providing him with the model for his own narcissistic identification. (Green: 'Freud donne comme contemporain de la perte du sein le moment où peut être appréhendé la personne totale de la mère.'[4] The spectacle which confronts Raphael is the final – because original – antithesis: life unwrapping itself in a fatal, orgasmic convulsion, the mortal ambiguity of a desire which can only be called autoerotic. It is precisely this 'struggle with death' that Raphael has always sought, and, in his fashion, always fought; and when he makes his final throw – casting *himself* upon Pauline, hurling himself into the scene, 'avec la légèreté d'un oiseau de proie' – his 'prey' is himself, his 'Self.' The shawl he 'breaks' is the final veil, the 'maille rompue' of a certain net, the 'small murders' punctured in a curtain. Yet without this veil, there can be no investment, and the expense must be mortal.

As the skin vanishes into its centre, Raphael's life retreats into his body, into the vulnerability of his innermost point:

> *Le moribond chercha des paroles pour exprimer le désir qui dévorait toutes ses forces; mais il ne trouva que les sons étranglés du râle dans sa poitrine, dont chaque respiration, creusée plus avant, semblait partir des ses entrailles (247).*

But this 'point' or centre only devours, reflecting the lost object, the presence that Raphael seeks, with his dying breath, to regain:

> *Enfin, ne pouvant bientôt plus former de sons, il mordit Pauline au sein (247).*

The breath of his life expires for lack of the presence that it might express. His mouth seeks finally to escape the interstices of articulation, of differences which devour all presence, by recovering and ingesting the object, which, in the history and the economy of the 'subject,' marks the point at which a certain representation constituted itself speculatively, as the re-presentation of a lost presence. But the ambivalence of the fetishist denial can only result in the confusion of love and hate, appropriation and destruction: in the 'bird of prey' 'saving' its victim, and destroying it ('mordit'), all the same: destroying the image and reflection, the spectacle of its own destruction, the destruction of its 'own.'

If Raphael dies, we may conclude, it is because he has nothing more to say, and yet, cannot stay silent. Another discourse, however, the narration, reserves for itself the final word.

25

Epilogue

'Et que devint Pauline?' (274) For the modern 'critical' reader, the 'Epilogue' which this question ushers in is the undeniable confirmation of the distance which separates him from the Balzacian text. He immediately recognizes the question and the reader who asks it as irreducibly alien, and historically obsolete. If not earlier, then at least here, he indignantly abrogates the contract which has bound him to the text. The naïveté of the question, the idleness of the curiosity it expresses, reflects a desire which cannot possibly be his own. A desire he can comprehend, but not one he can share. And yet, as the reproach of naïveté indicates, this desire is not simply indifferent: it is, however slightly, the cause of an embarrassment which the comprehending smile of the modern critic can veil, but not wholly conceal; which his 'comprehension' can sublimate, but not efface. Both the critic, and the 'naïve' reader who abruptly enters the scene with this question, are moved by *the desire to know*, by the fascination of a certain *meaning*, and it is precisely this desire which the 'Epilogue' seeks to satisfy. After the 'end' of the novel, however.

And this is what so violates modern literary sensibility, for it calls into question the immanence of the narrative. Instead of the meaningful finality of a concluded work, there is the implicit acknowledgement that the question of meaning is still open, and can only be resolved by a dialogue which appears to violate the very laws of the modern novel. What are those 'laws'?

In his already cited essay on 'The Storyteller,' Walter Benjamin indicated their origin. 'The meaning of life is really the center around which the novel turns.'[1] But the 'meaning of life' only becomes problematic when the 'end' of life is no longer simply its self-evident goal, but its unsettling limitation; when death, in other words, has ceased to be an integrative factor, marking the place of life in an ordered cosmos, but instead calls that place into question. This is why Benjamin – here following Lukács' *Theory of the Novel* – points to 'the solitary individual' as the 'birthplace of the novel.'[2] The novel, he argues, seeks to provide a response to the 'profound perplexity of the living' confronted – as isolated individuals – with the enigmatic finality of death. And the 'meaning of life' is, in this perspective, 'nothing but the initial expression of the perplexity with which its reader sees himself transposed into this particular written life.'[3] The search for the 'meaning of life' thus inscribes the novel reader in the text to be read. And it is here that the distinctive quality of the novel as opposed to all other form of epic literature emerges for Benjamin. In his view the novel is uniquely and irreducibly textual:

> *What distinguishes the novel from the story (and from the epic in the narrower sense) is its essential dependence on the book. The dissemination of the novel became possible only with the invention of printing. What can be handed on orally, the wealth of the epic, is structured differently from what constitutes the stock in trade of the novel. What distinguishes the novel from all other forms of prose literature – the fairy tale, the legend, even the novella – is that it neither derives from the oral tradition nor leads to it. This is particularly true of storytelling. The storyteller [der Erzähler] takes what he tells from experience, either his own or as reported by others. And he in turn makes it into the experience of those listening to his story.*

The novelist has already taken leave (*hat sich abgeschieden*).[4] Between the novel and the story there is a radical discontinuity, the novel 'neither derives from the oral tradition nor leads to it' ('noch in sie eingeht'). The *Erzähler* – and it is here that we should note that the word means not merely storyteller, but also narrator – and his listeners are bound by a common experience, which is present to both and which is origin and end of the narration. It is this experience which is expressed in the 'living speech' of a narrator who is heard and understood at the moment he speaks.[5] As opposed to this living presence of narration (embracing the narrator and his listeners), the novelist is 'abgeschieden': departed, absent, but also deceased. The death of the novelist thus appears as the condition of the novel: as text it is constituted by the absence of the author.

The novel, then, as Benjamin describes it, assumes the form of an aporia: summoned to affirm the meaning of a life that is limited and delimited by the finality of death, its mode of existence, as a text, repeats that finality in the absence of its author. The immanence of the novel arises from this absence:

the novel must produce itself. And this means: it must *write its own end*. The novel responds to the finality of death with the finitude of its form:

> *Indeed, there is no story for which the question, 'what happened then?' would not be justified. The novel, by contrast, cannot hope to take the smallest step beyond that border where it has inscribed 'The End' at the bottom of the page, and thereby invited the reader to present his presentiment of the meaning of life.*[6]

The novel invites the reader to present his sense of the meaning of life by writing its end, by endorsing its finality as inscribed in the novel. The novel that writes its own end, however, and closes itself only by transcending that closure, by pointing to itself as a work that will never cease to mean – its own end. This, at least, is doubtless what led Poulet, in the passage quoted at the beginning, to seek to describe Balzac in terms of a final figure, one of 'séparation' and 'attente.'

If, however, the 'Epilogue' violates the laws of the novel, according to a certain modern sensibility at least, is it not precisely because its very existence *defers the end* – and thus, prevents that presentiment of the reader from fully presenting itself, in his endorsement of that end?

Raphael's 'final' gesture, in which he *literally* 'projects himself beyond (*au delà de*) his being' – his *death* – does not secure the meaning of his life; it does not suffice to end, or to close the novel. For the first and only time, the reader, hitherto a willing and silent partner, *protests*: 'Et que devint Pauline?' And he insists: the question will be repeated three times. As though the text of the novel had not sufficed, in itself, to give the meaning of a life – or the life of a meaning. It is as though the disappearance of Raphael is afflicted with the same *usure* that characterizes all the phenomena of the novel: if they become transparent, it is not through a process of revelation or the confirmation of an enigma, but as part of a process of disintegration. And it is this disintegration that the curious reader of the novel cannot accept, for it threatens his own life as well. *De tua res agitur*:

> *The novel is significant, therefore, not because it presents someone else's fate to us, somewhat didactically, but because this other fate, by virtue of the flame that consumes it, gives us the warmth that we never get from our own. What draws the reader to the novel is the hope of being able to warm his shivering life on the death about which he reads.*[7]

Raphael's death lacks the warmth which he himself sought in vain in the 'novel' that was Foedora. It has not fulfilled its promise. Or perhaps it has fulfilled it all too well. If from the very first the figure of Raphael de Valentin commanded attention by the death that he bore aloft as his destiny; if he imposed his own narration upon his listener, Emile, as the 'compte de mon suicide qui gronde qui se dresse, qui m'appelle et que je salue' (84), has that account been paid, in the end? The question, 'Et que devint Pauline?' invites us to suspect that the *compte*, if not the *conte*, is still open. And that perhaps it can only be closed, concluded, by the voice of the Narrator himself, as opposed to anything that voice can say. In this context, the following observation of Benjamin seems pertinent:

> Whoever listens to a story is in the company of the storyteller; even some-one who reads partakes of this society. The reader of a novel, however, is solitary. He is more alone than any other reader. (Even the reader of a poem is prepared to lend his voice to the words for the benefit of a listen-er.) In this solitude of his, the reader of the novel seizes upon his material more jealously than any other reader. He is ready to appropriate it entirely, to devour it, as it were. Indeed, he destroys and devours the material like logs in the fireplace. The suspense that runs through the novel is very much like the draft that stimulates the flame in the fireplace and enlivens its play.[8]

The intervention of a narrative voice, then, would alleviate the solitude of the reader and create at least the illusion of his participation in what Benjamin aptly terms 'the community of listeners.'[9] The presence of such a voice in the text would seem to reassert the transcendence of life over death, meaning over non-meaning, of the voice over writing ('even someone who reads partakes of this society'). The suggested dialogue would thus warm the reader at his hearth:

> Ah Pauline? bien. Etes-vous quelquefois resté, par une douce soirée d'hiver, devant votre foyer domestique, voluptueusement livré à des souvenirs d'amour ou de jeunesse en contemplant les rayures produites par le feu sur un morceau de chêne? Ici, la combustion dessine les cases rouges d'un dam-ier; là, elle miroite des velours; de petites flammes bleues courent, bondis-sent et jouent sur le fond ardent du brasier. Vient un peintre inconnu qui se sert de cette flamme; par un artifice unique, il trace au sein de ces flam-boyantes teintes violettes ou empourprées une figure supernaturelle et d'une delicatesse inouïe, phénomène fugitif que le hasard ne recommencera jamais: c'est une femme aux cheveux emportés par le vent, et dont le profil respire une passion délicieuse: du feu dans le feu! Elle sourit, elle expire, vous ne la reverrez plus. Adieu, fleur de la flamme! adieu, principle incomplet, in-attendu, venu trop tôt ou trop tard pour être quelque beau diamant! (247-8)

'Mais Pauline?' The question, repeated, solicits a response which now recounts the second section of the novel, 'La femme sans cœur':

Vous n'y êtes pas? Je recommence. Place! place! Elle arrive, la voici, la reine des illusions, la femme qui passe comme un baiser, la femme vive comme un éclair, comme lui jaillie brûlante du ciel, l'être incrée, tout esprit, tout amour! Elle a revêtu je ne sais quel corps de flamme, ou pour elle la flamme s'est un moment animée! Les lignes de ses formes sont d'une pureté qui vous dit qu'elle vient du ciel. Ne resplendit-elle pas comme un ange? n'entendez-vous pas le frémissement aérien de ses ailes? Plus légère que l'oiseau, elle s'abat près de vous et ses terribles yeux fascinent; sa douce mais puissante haleine attire vos lèvres par une force magique; elle fuit et vous entraîne, vous ne sentez plus la terre. Vous voulez passer une seule fois votre main chatouillée, votre main fanatisée sur ce corps de neige, froisser ses cheveux d'or, baiser ses yeux étincelants. Une vapeur vous en- ivre, une musique enchanteresse vous charme. Vous tressaillez de tous vos nerfs, vous êtes tout désir, tout souffrance. O bonheur sans nom! vous avez touché les lèvres de cette femme; mais tout à coup une atroce douleur vous réveille. Ah! ah! votre tête a porté sur l'angle de votre lit, vous en avez em- brassé l'acajou brun, les dorures froides, quelque bronze, un Amour en cuivre (248).

The scenario here sketched repeats and resumes 'la femme sans cœur,' from the reveries of Raphael and the appearance of Foedora ('la reine des illusions') to the rude awakening after the *débauche* ('mais tout à coup une atroce dou- leur vous réveille'). The phenomenality of Foedora is that of 'l'être incrée,' whose origin is obscure and who seems to engender herself, ever anew and al- ways the same; a heavenly creature ('elle vient du ciel') who fascinates with her splendour and with her glance ('ses terribles yeux fascinent'), who captiv- ates with her song ('une musique enchanteresse ... vous tressaillez de tous vos nerfs, vous êtes tout désir, tout souffrance'), who invites possession and eludes it ('elle fuit et vous entraîne, vous ne sentez plus la terre'), whose 'heart' is of bronze ('quelque bronze, un Amour en cuivre') or is not at all: a representa- tion which represents a 'presence' that is itself nothing but representation, 'spectacle dans le spectacle.' A phenomenon without a cause or essence, she is phenomenality itself, producing its own medium, radiating its own light as a garment ('elle a revêtu je ne sais quel corps de flamme'), *portemanteau* whose mantle no one else can have because it is not to be had: the dream of a desire bound to the veil it seeks to lift. A *glance* and a *Glanz*.[10]

'Mais, monsieur, Pauline?' Repeating his question a third time, the reader seems not so much in search of information, or even of the warmth of an end- ing: rather, he seems reluctant to let that end come. If, as Benjamin writes, the origin of the novel is to be traced to a certain *perplexity (Ratlosigkeit),* the counsel *(Rat)* that it offers is less a *response* than a refusal to let the end come: 'Counsel is less an answer to a question than a proposal concerning the continuation of a story in the process of unfolding.'[11] The question of the reader, and the response of the narration, aim precisely at this proposed continuation: recounting the narrative and indicating its continuation.

Such a continuation can only have the form of a circle; and indeed, the third response returns to another matutinal scene, resuming and completing that with which the novel began:

> Encore! écoutez. Par une belle matinée, en partant de Tours, un jeune homme embarqué sur la ville-d'Angers tenait dans sa main la main d'une jolie femme. Unis, ainsi, tous deux admirèrent longtemps, au-dessus des larges eaux de la Loire, une blanche figure, artificiellement éclose au sein du brouillard comme un fruit des eaux et du soleil, ou comme un caprice des nuées et de l'air (248).

When the end comes, the reader will not be left empty-handed, or with a 'main chatouillé' by a dwindling peau de chagrin, the expiration of desire: instead, like the young man, holding 'dans sa main la main d'une jolie femme,' he will be secure in the contemplation of a certain image: a 'blanche figure, artificiellement éclose au sein du brouillard.' The conclusion is excluded, the close is disclosed in this image, that of an artificial birth of a life perfectly inclosed in a milieu of translucency, 'au sein du brouillard,' the spectacular recovery of that 'sein.'

> Elle se promenait entre les îles, elle agitait sa tête à travers les hauts peupliers; puis devenue gigantesque, elle faisait ou resplendir les milles plis de sa robe, ou briller l'auréole décrite par le soleil autour de son visage; elle planait sur les hameaux, sur les collines, et semblait défendre au bateau à vapeur de passer devant le château d'Ussé. Vous eussiez dit le fantôme de la Dame des Belles Cousines qui voulait protéger son pays contre les invasions modernes (248-9).

This 'figure blanche,' who suddenly becomes 'gigantesque,' is the matrix of the novel: she wanders about the islands of the Loire, one of which is the site of a maternal tomb, a phantom who seems ('vous eussiez dit') to protect her country against 'les invasions modernes.' She is, or seems, the fulfilment of a dream, the image of a maternal presence defending against all danger, an image which does not consume itself or flee, but which gives itself to the glance of the lovers, safely enclosed in a garment of life, the origin or reflection of a radiance which is her expression ('elle faisait ou resplendir les mille plis de sa robe, ou briller l'auréole décrite par le soleil autour de son visage'). No longer the 'queen of illusions,' she appears as the phenomenon presenting itself, protecting a certain perception and a certain possession against 'les invasions modernes.'

And yet, the comparison which the narrator places in the mouth of his listeners deserves to be remarked: 'Vous eussiez dit le fantôme de la Dame des belles cousines ... .' This 'phantom,' in the text to which the allusion refers, *Le Petit Jehan de Saintré* of Antoine de la Salle, is a poor protectress. For she betrays and humiliates her lover, 'le *petit* Jehan,' the matrix of a maternal betrayal which makes this final image of security a *phantom*. It is, indeed, the repetition of Pauline, and the fulfilment of her words to Raphael: 'la femme que vous aimerez vous tuera!' For that woman can only be the site of a discovery which is the birth and death of the desire that denies, and affirms it: the discovery of that non-image which is the 'phallus,' the non-secret of 'castration.'

In his essay on 'Fetishism' Freud begins by relating a remarkable and exemplary case:

> *Most extraordinary seems the case of a young man who had elevated a certain 'Glanz auf der Nase' [shine on the nose] to a fetishistic condition. The surprising explanation of this was that the patient had been raised in an English nursery and had later gone to Germany, where he almost completely forgot his mother-tongue. The fetish, which stemmed from his early childhood, had to be read as English rather than German; the 'Glanz auf der Nase' was really a 'glance at the nose'; the nose was thus the fetish, which, by the way, he could endow whenever he wished with that particular luster [Glanzlicht] that others could not perceive.*[12]

This case is also remarkable for two reasons, which Freud does not discuss. First, because the homophonic equation of 'Glanz' and 'glance' describes precisely the two poles of the perceptive-imaginary sphere which the fetishistic denial of castration (the phallus) refuses to articulate. Second, and perhaps more importantly, because that articulation is already present, unconsciously, in the identification of the two signifiers: *glance* and *Glanz*, in the reduction of their difference in the homophony, *Glanz (auf der Nase)*, in *the apparent presence of a single word*. The denial of the non-image of castration, the denial of the irreducible interplay of the deferring difference ('différance') is the production of a representation which pretends to re-present a presence that is identical to itself and yet which only 'is' in its stead, instead of its Self. Hence, the only durable compromise is the fetish, 'aus Gegensätzen doppelt geknüpft,' as the visible image veiling its non-object, the medium of translucency which allows the enigma to take (its) place; and as the audible image, the word which appears secure in the unity of sound and sense – *Glanz* – but which in fact only *signifies* by virtue of a differential disunity, not merely *between* sound and sense, but *within* each sphere: within the signified no less than the signifier.

This is why, in the text we have been reading, the linguistic figures – metaphors, metonymies, and so on – do not simply illustrate and complete the meaning but rather dislocate and subvert it. They reveal it to be not a substance, present to itself and expressed in the univocity of a word, or, in the exemplary case, in a *proper name*, but rather to be a trace of something else, the indomitable movement of transference and substitution which defines and delimits the textuality of the text.

Yet it is this movement that the desire which denies the difference of castration must seek, at all costs, to reduce: ultimately by creating, producing, and determining that distance, by giving it the form of an enigma, secret, or mystery, the *form* of a determinate absence: a blank space *calling* to be filled, an eloquent silence, an elusive, intangible entity. And in a passage of the third response which we have hitherto omitted from our recounting – our 'third' type of textual reading is nothing but a certain recounting of the *conte* – this elusiveness takes what is perhaps its most decisive form, that of a certain anamnesis:

> *Tout à tour, ondine ou sylphide, cette fluide créature voltigeait dans les airs comme un mot vainement cherché qui court dans la mémoire sans se laisser saisir ... (248).*

This is the *Wunschbild* that structures the Balzacian text, a text *malgré lui*: the representation of a meaning, present to itself and expressed in a word, yet in a word 'vainement cherché qui court dans la mémoire sans se laisser saisir': which cannot be grasped and yet whose existence, whose presence-to-itself is confirmed precisely by the *hole* it leaves in one's memory, by the blankness and whiteness of a space which is determinate and defined, *by the very narrative voice which enunciates it.* It is the absence of this word, an oblivion – not of repression but of that denial which leaves a visible trace – that opens the space of the sign, the space within which 'tout se tient,' the space of discursivity, the flow and flight of speech, the unfolding and production of the voice. The absence of the word, of the name, is the fire in the fire, the negativity that enables reappropriation to take place, the virtuality of a self which can produce itself, the need which calls for satisfaction, installing the language of labour as the labour of language. This absent, forgotten word, which is yet remembered *as a word*, circumscribes 'the hidden place of production.' It is the absent centre and matrix of a novel which disappears into its centre as irresistibly as the *peau de chagrin*: death and life of the work, *all the same*.

It is to redeem this fatal indifference and confusion that the narration raises its voice, once again, after the end, in the 'Epilogue,' deferring an 'end' which is both fulfilment and undoing, in which all is the same. Yet this voice, seeking to recover and to reappropriate the dwindling substance of its product in a posthumous frame – end of the end – is itself inscribed in a text that it no longer commands. Repeating the gesture of its author – 'La mort est inévitable – oublions-la!' – it seeks to save the essence of its discourse by forgetting the pale white words of its text. But we have seen and heard, we have read it all before: the gesture itself is caught up and marked by the very *usure* it has sought to designate, depict, and display. The reading that catches up with this discourse unwraps the text of 'Balzac' only to discover that there is no (-thing) inside.

Postface:
Et que devint *S/Z*?

Un étudiant américain (ou positiviste, ou contestataire: je ne puis démêler)
identifie, comme si cela allait de soi, subjectivité et narcissisme; il pense
sans doute que la subjectivité consiste à parler de soi, et à en dire du bien.
... Cependant, aujourd'hui, le sujet se prend ailleurs. ... Pourquoi ne parlerais-je
pas de 'moi,' puisque 'moi' n'est plus 'soi'? R. Barthes, *Barthes par lui-même*[1]

If *Unwrapping Balzac* pursued its reading of *La Peau de chagrin* with an almost provocative disregard of the circumstances in which the novel was written, and then continually revised,[2] the circumstances of its own writing return
to haunt it. From the very first reader on, the comparison to *S/Z* imposed
itself. Seven years later, however, the fact that Barthes' study was mentioned
in the (otherwise rather scant) bibliography, without being discussed in the
text itself, struck readers as a conspicuous and puzzling omission, and certainly as one that should be remedied for publication.

But the omission is more easily explained than remedied. When *S/Z* first
appeared in print, in 1970, *Unwrapping Balzac* had already been written.
Barthes' 'transcription' thus found its way into the bibliography, but not into
the body of the text. That the latter could have survived such an intrusion in
its existing form seemed to me then no more likely than it does today. But
given the manifest, if somewhat misleading resemblances of the two readings,
there is no doubt that the reader has every right to his (her) curiosity, and
that the question, 'Et que devint *S/Z*?' deserves a response. Whether or not

the remarks that follow can be considered as the beginning of such a response, I shall leave to the reader to decide. All that is certain is that they continue the story.

That *S/Z* and *Unwrapping Balzac* are similar enough to invite comparison is difficult to dispute. Both attempt a detailed reading of a single, Balzacian text, employing concepts and categories developed by French Structuralism and in its aftermath. Both readings, moreover, bear the mark of the intellectual ebullience that characterized and end of the sixties, in Europe at least, and that was soon to yield to a hangover that has proven to be no less intense and perhaps more persistent. 'Participer ... dans l'édification (collective) d'une théorie libératrice du Signifiant' was how Barthes defined his goal on the back cover of *S/Z*, and the tone and spirit of this declaration was by no means entirely alien to *Unwrapping Balzac*. But the latter, if it was at times more obsessively insistent than *S/Z* was also more cautious: in order to construct a theory, liberating or otherwise, one had to have a *site*. Hence, the effort in *Unwrapping Balzac* was directed at clearing the ground, by retracing the manner in which it had been occupied by a certain process of production, circulation, and exchange.

For *S/Z*, by contrast, such scruples seemed superfluous: the ground seemed already clear, the ground rules already established. If *Unwrapping Balzac* begins by questioning the opposition of Old and New, Traditional and Modern as being itself a rather traditional operation, *S/Z* uses that opposition as a springboard to propel itself forward: 'J'ai copié un texte, ancien, très ancien, un texte antérieur, puisqu'il a été écrit avant notre modernité.'[3] *S/Z* was obviously more concerned with where it was headed than with where it was or had been. The latter seemed self-evident. What was of interest, therefore, was the new kind of reading it was attempting, which would delve into the text's play of signification rather than reveal its meaning; which would 'éviter de le structurer *de trop*, de lui donner ce supplément de structure qui lui viendrait d'une dissertation et le fermerait' (20). Unlike such *dissertations*, then, *S/Z* would break down (or break up) its text into its raw 'semantic material' (21), leaving it to criticism and interpretation to do with that material as they saw fit. In short, *S/Z* would give its text a thorough *working over*: 'malmener le text ... lui couper la parole' (22).

And the ease and verve with which it set about accomplishing this aim could only underscore the distance separating it and its site from that other place, where, more or less simultaneously, Balzac was being laboriously unwrapped, some 1400 kilometers to the east. For *S/Z* the problem of beginning existed as little as the problem of place: safely settled in the effervescent Capital, it had only to make itself the echo of the codes and systems of discourse reverberating there.[4] Not that Barthes' Five Codes were simply a repetition of their linguistic or theoretical models: 'Le code est une perspective de citations, un mirage de structures ... autant d'éclats de ce quelque chose qui a toujours été déjà lu, vu, fait, vécu: le code est le sillon de ce déjà' (27-8, author's italics). And yet, the successful application of those codes, whether 'mirages' or not, implied that one was situated precisely at their intersection, where a certain *déjà* ('déjà lu, vu,' etc.) could be taken more or less for granted – even if their familiarity had something cloying to it, slightly *écoeurant* ('Ce vomissement du stéréotype' 104, returns as a leitmotif throughout *S/Z*, apropos the code as '*stereotype*').

With whatever reservations, and despite occasional attacks of nausea, the familiarity of *S/Z* with its text (however 'ancien' and 'antérieur'), with its readers, and its own place, makes the very project of 'unwrapping' suspect, if not indeed superfluous. If texts could speak – and perhaps they can – *S/Z* would surely have told *Unwrapping Balzac*: 'No more unwrapping, if you please; Balzac has already – *déjà* – done enough of that.' For instance:

> *L'artiste sarrasinien veut déshabiller l'apparence, aller toujours plus loin, derrière. ... Même règle pour l'écrivain réaliste (et sa postérité critique): il faut aller derrière le papier ... (mais ce qu'il y a derrière le papier, ce n'est pas le réel, le référent, c'est la Référence, la 'subtile immensité des écritures'). Ce mouvement, qui pousse Sarrasine, l'artiste réaliste et le critique ... conduit à un échec. ... sous la Zambinella ... il y a le rien de la castration. ... on ne peut authentifier l'enveloppe des choses, arrêter le mouvement dilatoire du signifiant (128-9).*

Unwrapping? 'Déjà lu, déjà vu – déjà là.'

But even if texts could talk, that would be no guarantee that they could listen. *Unwrapping Balzac*, for instance, would probably have heard no further than that 'déjà,' or rather, the way in which *S/Z* takes it for granted. For, far from the Capital and its Codes, nothing was more enigmatic for *Unwrapping Balzac* than that 'déjà': whether in Barthes or in Balzac. Indeed, its very unwrapping could be considered an attempt to unravel the enigma of an 'already' that does not speak for itself, unless it is to ask: 'How did it, we, I get *here*? W(here)? T(here)?'

Small wonder, then, that *Unwrapping Balzac* is fascinated with entries, especially those that never quite take place, like Raphael's hesitation-waltz on the threshold of the salon de jeu, a triple-take that is also its own *entrée en matière*. By contrast, what is striking in *S/Z* is the effortlessness of its *entrées*: whether that of the writer, of the reader, or of the text itself. The Narrator is simply – already – *there*, waiting to be read as it were. Where? Ensconced in a corner, on the border of two worlds, just inside enough to see everything going on, and sufficiently outside not to be seen himself. An insider-outsider, not entirely unlike the writer of *S/Z* perhaps. But also not unlike Raphael de Valentin.

The latter, you will recall, came – in the process of being unwrapped – to resemble the Critic-at-Large, just as Sarrasine in *S/Z*, is a model of the realistic critic and artist. And yet, unlike *S/Z*, *Unwrapping Balzac* is not so convinced that there is any simple alternative to that critique, or to that gesture. Least of all, in *S/Z* itself. To suggest that a reader who has come to liberate the play of the Signifier might bear some resemblance to the Balzacian hero, hiding behind a curtain and waiting to see the forbidden, might seem as unfair as uncharitable.

And yet it is neither. One of the unquestionable high points, indeed a climax of *S/Z* is the discovery that the text need not only be *read*, but at a crucial point, at least, can also be *seen* ('déjà lu, vu ... '):

> *Or, par une dernière reversion culturelle – la plus piquante – tout cela, nous pouvons le* voir *(et non plus seulement le lire); l'Endymion qui est dans le texte est ce même Endymion qui est dans un musée (notre musée: le Louvre). ... Nous avons le droit d'arriver chez Bulloz, rue Bonaparte, et de demander que l'on nous ouvre le carton ... où nous découvrirons la photographie du castrat (77).*

Ca pique, sans doute: the chance that *we* have, for once, to leave our desks behind, to descend into the street, to proceed to the rue Bonaparte, and once there, to avail ourselves of our *right* (it is, after all, *our* museum) to have that box opened for us (perhaps even by *un vieillard?*), so that we can make the startling discovery, seeing with our own eyes: 'la photographie du castrat.' We can do all this, providing that we are in the capital, of course. But even as readers, we can, for once, 'voir, et non plus seulement ... lire' – simply by opening the book, *S/Z*.

That this chance is a cause for excitement, not simply for Balzacian heroes such as Sarrasine or Raphael, nor even for their critical posterity, but also for those who consider themselves outsiders, or at least on the fringes of that posterity – all this may come as a surprise, but it is hardly accidental. For that posterity reaches further than one might suspect. For instance, to the 'liberation' of the Signifier itself, inasmuch as it presupposes the Lacanian interpretation of 'castration.' For the latter, situated at the crossroads of the 'symbolic' and the 'imaginary,' is itself inseparable from a certain experience of *perception* which it has been reluctant to reflect. And since the Lacanian version of castration indelibly marks the reading of *S/Z* – however free or heuristic Barthes' use of 'theory' may be – it is no wonder that his reading ultimately aspires *to see*. Or rather, to discover what cannot simply be seen, but what cannot *not* be seen either – all the same. For by determining 'castration' as a category of *absence* (manque, béance, trou, etc.), what the Lacanian 'theory' does is essentially to act out castration, repeating what Freud described as an 'infantile sexual theory.' Here as there 'castration' serves to designate a last-ditch effort to retain an image of the Other (the maternal phallus), and with it, an image of the Self. For if the Self is to be whole, then the object of its desire cannot be any less so: the mother must have the phallus, or at least she must have had it (and *be* it). In this perspective, 'castration' implies the desire to keep the image whole through an image of the hole. 'Today's hole was yesterday's whole,' the child tells himself.

What Freud neglects to mention, while describing it unambiguously, is that this 'infantile sexual theory' is, first and foremost perhaps: a *story*; it is not simply a concept, a term, or a (negative) perception: it only functions as a narrative, with a narrator and also with a listener (the two are almost, but not quite, the same). It is all too easy to get so absorbed in the story that one forgets that one is listening at all. For this story is necessarily illustrated – that is precisely its point. But it is a story, all the same.

And it is a story that inevitably exceeds whatever it can tell. In *S/Z*, for instance, the telling of stories is retraced to desire: 'A l'origine du Récit, le désir' (95) writes Barthes, commenting the manner in which the narrator comes to tell the story of Sarrasine. But the desire at work is identified with what is represented, thematically, in the story (the desire of the narrator to sleep with the young woman). Conclusion: 'Le récit est déterminé non par un désir de raconter mais par un désir d'échanger' (97). 'Non par ... mais par' – as if the one could be opposed to the other. What 'castration' as narration suggests, by contrast, is that the two converge, and at a precise point: in the narcissistic interest of the subject to recognize itself in the image of another.

And, to return to the discovery of the rue Bonaparte, nothing proves to be more difficult than that apparently so simple and so exhilarating excursion, to see (for) oneself. Even an old and venerable text, written long before *our* time, could have told us that. Provided that we were prepared to read it – and not to forget what we read. For if the text tells us that the portrait of Vien 'a servi plus tard pour l'Endymion de Girodet' (257), nowhere is it asserted that the photo of this painting is 'la photographie du castrat.' Indeed, to borrow a word from the code of the Capital, 'rien est moins sûr.' For 'ce grand peintre,' Vien, 'n'a jamais vu l'original' (237), but only the *statue*, itself already a copy of the 'original.' The 'classical text' remains – hélas! – *lisible*: neither more, nor less.

To read it is to retell – and to continue – its story. Which is, in turn, to revise it, more or less faithfully, more or less violently, and thus to invite others to try their hand. A game of chance? Surely, in part. But one we can hardly choose not to play.

Notes

CHAPTER 1: INTRODUCTION

1 G. Genette, *Figures* I (Paris: Editions du Seuil 1966) 243.
2 *Ibid*. 234.
3 *Ibid*. 240.
4 G. Lukács, *Balzac und der französische Realismus* (Berlin: Aufbau Verlag 1951) 5.
5 A. Béguin, *Balzac lu et relu* (Paris: Editions du Seuil 1965) 30.
6 *Ibid*.
7 *Ibid*.
8 *Ibid*. 43.
9 *Ibid*. 155.
10 *Ibid*. 30.
11 A. Allemand, *Unité et structure de l'univers balzacien* (Paris: Plon 1965) 171.
12 *Ibid*. 313.
13 G.W.F. Hegel, *Wissenschaft der Logik*, Vol. I, Bk I (East Berlin: Reclam 1963) 71.
14 G. Poulet, *La Distance intérieure* (Paris: Plon 1952) 193.
15 *Ibid*.
16 *Ibid*. 187.
17 *Ibid*. 193.
18 *Ibid*.
19 Balzac, *La Comédie humaine*, X, Bibliothèque de la Pléiade (Paris 1950) 348.
20 *Ibid*.

21 *Ibid.*
22 *Ibid.* 347.

CHAPTER 2: 'LA TRES SPIRITUELLE EPIGRAPHE DU LIVRE . . . '

1 Cited by M. Allem in his introduction to *La Peau de chagrin* (Paris: Classiques Garnier 1967) xix.
2 L. Sterne, *Tristram Shandy* (London: Everyman's Library 1964) 445.
3 *Ibid.* 444.
4 *Ibid.* 445.
5 For this information, and in countless other cases, I am deeply indebted to Professor A.G. Falconer.
6 H. de Balzac, 'Le Cousin Pons,' Pléiade, VI, 627.

CHAPTER 3: WORK AND PLAY

1 Balzac, *La Comédie humaine*, Bibliothèque de la Pléiade Vol. IX (Paris 1949-59) 11. All future references to this work will be to this edition and will be given in parentheses in the body of the text.
2 Sigmund Engländer, *Geschichte der französischen Arbeiter-Associationen* [History of the French Workers' Associations], cited by Walter Benjamin in *Charles Baudelaire: A Lyric Poet in the Era of High Capitalism* (London: New Left Books 1973) 47 (translation modified).
3 Balzac, *Modeste Mignon*, Oeuvres complètes, Les Bibliophiles de l'originale (Paris 1965) Vol. IV, p. 172 (cited by Benjamin, *Charles Baudelaire* 47).
4 Cited in Allem, *La Peau de Chagrin* 309.
5 *Ibid.*
6 *Ibid.* 312.
7 Baudelaire, Oeuvres complètes, Bibliothèque de la Pléiade (Paris 1961) 692.
8 Karl Marx, *Capital*, Vol. I (New York: International Publishers 1970³) 176.
9 *Ibid.* 35.
10 Karl Marx, *Grundrisse* (New York: Vintage Books 1973), translated by Martin Nicolaus, 233-4.
11 *Ibid.* 154.

CHAPTER 5: POSTPONEMENT

1 Walter Benjamin, *Ursprung des deutschen Trauerspieles* (Frankfurt am Main: Suhrkamp Verlag 1963) 246: 'Produktion der Leiche ist, vom Tode her betrachtet, das Leben.'

2 Karl Marx, *Grundrisse* (New York: Vintage Books 1973), translated by Martin Nicolaus 233 (translation modified).

CHAPTER 7: THE TRUCE OF A TEXT

1 G.W.F. Hegel, *Enzyklopädie* (Hamburg: Meiner 1959) 369.
2 In the first edition of the novel only the French version of the inscription was printed; in later editions it was changed to Arabic, while the mention of Sanscrit, stemming from the first edition, was retained. See M. Allem, introduction to *La Peau de Chagrin* (Paris: Classiques Garnier 1967) 336.
3 In this context reference should be made to Linda Rudich's essay, 'Balzac et Marx,' in A.G. Falconer and H. Mitterand, *La Lecture sociocritique du texte romanesque* (Toronto: Hakkert 1975). See also in the same volume the essay of Jean Paris on *Z. Marcas*.
4 The essence of the 'fetishistic character of the commodity' as described by Marx entails precisely the obfuscation of the *social* process of production that engenders surplus value. See *Capital*, Vol. I. (New York: International Publishers 1970[3]), Chap. 1, Sect. 4: 'The Fetishism of Commodities and the Secret Thereof,' 71ff.

CHAPTER 8: THE CANARD

1 Balzac, *Monographie de la presse parisienne* (Paris: J.J. Pauvert 1965) 27.
2 *Ibid*. 36-7.
3 *Ibid*. 199.
4 *Ibid*. 40.
5 *Ibid*. 210-11.
6 *Ibid*.
7 *Ibid*. 145.
8 *Ibid*. 173.
9 *Ibid*.
10 *Ibid*.
11 *Ibid*. 36.
12 *Ibid*. 160-1.
13 *Ibid*. 41
14 *Ibid*. 160.
15 *Ibid*. 64-5.

CHAPTER 9: A BURST OF LAUGHTER

1 G. Poulet, *La Distance intérieure* (Paris: Plon 1952) 183.

CHAPTER 11: THE BROKEN NET

1 J. Lacan, *Ecrits* (Paris: Editions du Seuil 1966) 690.
2 *Ibid.*
3 J. Derrida, 'La Double Séance,' *La Dissémination* (Paris: Editions du Seuil 1972) 300 n.
4 *Ibid.*, 251 and passim.
5 In one of his last writings, 'Analysis Terminable and Interminable,' Freud refers to the 'rock' (*Fels*) of castration as that which seems to withstand most stubbornly all change.
6 R. Tostain, 'Le Joueur: Essai psychoanalytique,' *L'Inconscient II* (Paris: Presses Universitaires de France 1967) 132.

CHAPTER 12: THE MATRIX

1 Walter Benjamin, 'The Storyteller,' *Illuminations* (New York: Schocken 1969) 94.
2 K. Marx, *Capital*, Vol. I (New York: International Publishers 1970³) 47.
3 It is worth remarking that Balzac appears to have invented this phrase by reversing (and doubling) Coleridge's famous 'Life-in-Death,' from 'The Ancient Mariner.' Cf. the note of Fernand Lotte in Vol. XI of the Pléiade edition of *La Comédie humaine* (Paris 1950) 1290. M. Bardèche, in his *Balzac romancier* (Paris: Plon 1940), uses the relation of life and death to construct a comprehensive typology of the various characters in *La peau de chagrin*, which, although it gets the philological facts of the matter wrong, is not without interest (cf. pp. 335ff.).
4 S. Freud, 'Fetishism,' in *Sexuality and the Psychology of Love* (New York: Collier 1972⁵) 215-16. Here and throughout I have modified the translation.
5 'La castration est ce non-secret de la division séminale qui entame la substitution' writes J. Derrida in 'La Double Séance,' *La Dissémination* (Paris: Editions du Seuil 1972) 300n. 'Non-secret' here suggests that the enigma of castration cannot be determined as a form of meaning, as a hidden *signifié* – just that is what the fetishistic denial of castration seeks to assert – but as a movement of difference which both allows meaning to take place and displaces it, all the same.
6 Freud, *Fetishism* 217.
7 *Ibid.* 218-19.

CHAPTER 13: 'CES RIENS QUI ONT TANT DE PRIX'

1 K. Marx, *Capital*, Vol. I (New York: International Publishers 1970³) 195.
2 It is evident that Marx seeks to describe capital as the true Hegelian absolute subject, which in turn incorporates the theological notion of the (divine, trinitarian) subject. Capital, he writes, 'differentiates itself as original value from itself as surplus-value,

just as God-Father does from God-Son, yet both are the same age and in fact form only one person, for only by virtue of the surplus-value of £10 does the £100 originally advanced become capital, and once this has taken place – once the Son has been begotten, and through him the Father – the difference between the two vanishes once again and both are One: £110 Sterling' (p 162). But Capital is of course not simply the self-sufficient Absolute Subject, culmination of what Heidegger has called the tradition of Ontotheology: it is also a 'living monster.' And this in two ways: first, it lives off the energies of wage-laborers, whose labor-power alone when sold as a commodity can produce surplus value. And second, it lives off the energies not only of living laborers but of the dead as well: 'Capital is dead labor that vivifies itself only by sucking up living labor like a vampire: the more it can suck, the more life it has' (233, translation modified). But its *life*, in turn, consists in nothing but increasing itself (ie, its value) in a spiral without end: 'But capital has only a single life-drive, the drive to produce value (*sich zu verwerten*), to create surplus-value . . . ' (*ibid.*).

3 The question that poses itself here, in conjunction with the foregoing note (see above), is whether the economy of commodity-production as analyzed by Marx and narrated by Balzac does not mark the consummation of the economy of production *tout court*. In other words, whether the obvious narcissism of the movement of capital, consuming all energies in order to produce *more of the same* (ie, value) must not be considered to be the *culmination* of a project inherent in the very notions of *labour* and of *production*, and thus in the practice of Western culture insofar as it has been governed or oriented by these notions and values. There are numerous indications in the writings of Marx that he was well aware of this possibility.

To begin with, his description of the labour process in general – and this may come as a surprise to many, Marxists and non-Marxists – stresses the *idealistic* aspect of labour as an activity that depends essentially upon a projection of *consciousness*. The passage in which Marx describes this is well known, but its idealistic emphasis has, to my knowledge, rarely been noticed. In distinguishing human labour from other forms of purposeful activity, such as that of insects, Marx writes: 'But what distinguishes the worst architect from the best of bees is that the architect has constructed the cell in his head even before he builds it in wax. At the end of the labor-process a result emerges that was present in the imagination [Vorstellung] of the worker – ie, present as an idea [*ideell vorhanden*] from the very first. The worker does not simply effect [bewirkt] a change in the form of natural materials; he also *realizes* [verwirklicht] in the natural material *his own goal*, of which he is fully cognizant' [*seinen Zweck, den er weiß* – Marx's italics]. Labour is thus defined and described as an activity that depends upon *conscious intention*: a description that ultimately goes back to Plato and Aristotle.

Where Marx's discussion of the labour process begins to diverge from the idealistic, metaphysical tradition, however, is in the determination of those ideas: for labour must also, we recall, produce goods capable of fulfilling needs (or desires). Thus, the determination of a positive goal, of the particular objects to be produced, implies the (pre-)determination of the needs (or desires) that such objects will fulfil. Since such determination, like labour in general, is dependent upon the consciousness of the labourer, labour itself cannot be construed as responding directly to 'natural' or 'biological' needs, but rather to *perceptions* of those needs, perceptions which must be mediated by consciousness, and hence by the cultural, social, and historical values that determine a particular consciousness in a particular time and place. This, perhaps, is why Marx was reluctant to determine 'need' more precisely than he did; his deliberate 'imprecision' would be a manner of recognizing, implicitly, the fact that 'need' is inseparable from recognition of need, and hence from all the forces and factors influencing such recognition (which would not be accessible to a discourse on political economy).

In any case, a reading of the German text of *Capital* suggests that Marx's insight into the 'idealistic' component of the labour process may have led him to indulge in a kind of running joke, a double entendre that returns insistently (especially in the first volume) to undermine, or at least to call into question the nature of the reality produced by the labour process. As is well known, the most frequently used example of the labour process in the general discussion of Volume I is that of the fabrication of fabrics (weaving, spinning, carding, etc.). As the text wears on, however, 'fabrication' begins to assume the double meaning it also has in English: the production of a product, on the one hand, but also *an imaginary, deluding, and deluded activity* on the other. For instance, in the following passage: 'In the labor process the activity of man effects, through the means of labor, a transformation of the object of labor that was intended from the beginning. The process disappears in the product: the latter is a use-value. ... What appeared in the laborer in the form of agitation (*Unruhe*) now appears in stable form (*als ruhende Eigenschaft*) as part of the product. *The blacksmith forges and the product is a forging*' (my italics). The English translation, which bravely takes considerable liberties with Marx's text in its last phrase, might well have gone even farther; it might have read, 'The blacksmith has *forged*, and the product is a *forgery*.' For what Marx wrote could easily be taken in this direction (albeit at a connotative level): 'Er hat gesponnen und das Produkt ist ein Gespinst.' *Gespinst* means literally 'something that has been spun' (Marx's example of the labourer is not the blacksmith, but the 'spinner,' about whom more below). But it also can mean a *figment*, as in 'Hirngespinst' (figment of the imagination), Marx's term for money that is hoarded, and by thus being kept to itself and for itself, *loses* its Self (which requires money to disappear into circulation). If this seems contrived, the connotation is strengthened by Marx's (inevitable) reference to the *Spinner*, which, in addition to its denotative meaning, also signifies: *madman*. This running joke – a *Witz* that does not simply negate or abolish the denotative meaning, but rather undermines it – would hardly be inappropriate to a conception of the labour process as one that establishes reality, but also as one that consumes the individuals engaged in it at least as much as it fulfils them.

It is this conception of labour as a dubious if necessary trade-off that leads Marx to demand not merely the *reappropriation* of the products of labour by the labourers; not merely the increase of productivity and its more rational and more equitable organization, but its *reduction*: that is, the reduction of the length of the workday, and ultimately, the reduction of the 'realm of necessity' which even the least 'exploited' wage labour partakes in. It is a measure of our social condition today that the duration of the workday has, in the past half-century at least and despite the overwhelming increase in productivity, scarcely been reduced. Another reason, perhaps, why reading Marx – and Balzac – is still very much on the agenda.

CHAPTER 15: GOING (FOR) BROKE

1 Cf. J. Derrida, 'La Double Séance,' *La Dissémination* (Paris: Editions du Seuil 1972) passim.
2 J. Derrida, 'La Voix et le phénomène' (Paris: Presses Universitaires de France 1966).
3 Karl Abraham, 'Die Spinne als Traumsymbol' (The Spider as Dream Symbol), in *Psychoanalytische Studien zur Charakterbildung* (Frankfurt: S. Fischer Verlag 1969) 248.

CHAPTER 16: THE 'DISSIPATIONAL SYSTEM'

1 See note 2, chap. 13.
2 See J. Derrida, *De la Grammatologie* (Paris: Editions de Minuit 1967) 203-34.

CHAPTER 17: THE SIGNATURE AND THE VOICE

1 The structural importance, and ambivalence, of the *signature* with regard to the subject has recently been explored by Derrida (cf. 'Signature, événement, contexte' in *Marges* [Paris: Editions de Minuit 1971] 390ff; 'Signéponge' in *Digraphe 8* [Paris: 1976 17-39]). What a reading of Balzac suggests in this context is that the development of commodity-production in the eighteenth and nineteenth centuries stands in intimate relation to the structural ambivalence of the signature as analyzed by Derrida. The correlative ambivalence of commodity-production, as discussed in notes 2 and 3 of Chapter 13, consists in the ever-increasing determination of reality as a process of circulation and of exchange on the one hand; and on the other, the confinement of that process within a restricted economy of production, appropriation, and property: that of capital as the autonomous subject-object. In any case, the emergence of the latter sounds the knell of the subject as *individual*: nothing is more *divided* by the circulation and production of commodities than the 'individual,' as the fate of Raphael's signature here demonstrates.

In this connection, reference should be made, if only in passing, to Kafka: not merely to the obvious case of the *Penal Colony* (in which the penalty consists in an inscription of the name), but to his writings in general. Walter Benjamin begins his essay on Kafka by retelling a story from Pushkin: Potemkin, Chancellor under Catherine the Great, suffered from habitual depressions. During a particularly long attack, documents requiring his signature piled up while the affairs of government fell ever deeper into disarray. Finally, 'an unimportant little clerk named Shuvalkin' devised the following strategem: gathering up a sheaf of papers, he boldly entered the darkened room in which Potemkin had closed himself, placed the papers in front of the Chancellor, pressed a pen into his hand, and waited. Mechanically, as though in a trance, Potemkin began to sign the papers, continuing until all were done. Triumphantly Shuvalkin gathered them up, returned to the assembled courtiers, who could scarcely believe their eyes as they read, signed on each of the documents, 'Shuvalkin ... Shuvalkin ... Shuvalkin' (W. Benjamin, 'Franz Kafka,' in *Illuminations* [New York: Schocken 1969] 111-12).

2　For a discussion of the Proustian version of this maternal porosity, see S. Weber, 'The Madrepore,' *Modern Language Notes* LXXXVII 7 (December 1972) 915-61.

3　Martin Heidegger, 'Language,' in *Poetry, Language, Thought* (New York: Harper & Row 1975) 199 (translation modified).

CHAPTER 18: ANTIPHRASIS

1　J. Derrida, *De la Grammatologie* (Paris: Editions de Minuit 1967) 420.

2　F. Rabelais, *Gargantua*, Book I, Chap. 17. See also *Maistre Pierre Pathelin*, verse 614.

CHAPTER 22: REVUE 2: DIAGNOSIS

1　The effort to use history, here the etymological history of a word, to recover its original (and presumably still effective, essential) meaning, should be considered as yet another attempt to cope with the ambivalence of exchange discussed earlier; to 'cope,' that is, from the point of view of the subject seeking to recover (reappropriate) its (threatened) property. Indeed, as a ubiquitous process and medium of exchange and of circulation, *language* (and, in the more general sense, all symbolic systems of articulation, non-verbal as well as verbal) may well have acquired much of its fascination in the twentieth century as a result of its capacity to display this ambivalence. Again, it is in a text of Kafka that Balzac's parodic description finds its 'modern' culmination. 'The Cares of a Family Man' (*Sorge des Hausvaters*) begins thus: 'Some say the word Odradek is of Slavonic origin, and try to account for it on that basis. Others again believe it to be of German origin, only influenced by Slavonic. The uncertainty of both interpretations allows one to assume with justice that neither is accurate, especially as neither of them provides an intelligent meaning of the word.' Despite the obvious differences, the *Sorge* that leads the *Hausvater* to such etymological speculations is not so very far removed from that of Raphael, as the final phrase of Kafka's short text indicates: 'He (Odradek) does no harm to anyone that one can see; but the idea that he is likely to survive me I find almost painful' (Franz Kafka, *The Complete Stories* (New York: Random House, Inc. 1976) 427-9.

CHAPTER 23: HOMECOMING

1 This passage was first published in the 1833 edition of the novel.
2 S. Freud, 'Fetishism,' in *Sexuality and the Psychology of Love* (New York: Collier 1972⁵) 217.
3 Cf. R. Gessain, ' "Vagina Dentata" dans la clinique et la mythologie,' in *La Psychanalyse* III (Paris 1957) 247-95.
4 J. Laplanche and J.-B. Pontalis, 'Fantasme originaire, fantasmes des origines, origine du fantasme,' in *Le Temps modernes* XIX/II (1963/4) 1868.
5 *Ibid.*
6 André Green, 'Le Narcissisme primaire,' Part II, *L'Inconscient* II (April-June 1967) 116.

CHAPTER 24: FINALE: PROJECTION

1 Green, 'Le Narcissisme primaire,' Part II, *L'Inconscient* II (April-June 1967) 108ff.
2 *Ibid.* 109.
3 *Ibid.* 108. In the first printing of the novel, Raphael cries out to Pauline: 'Je veux mourir *en* toi' (my italics), which, already one month later, in the second edition, reads: 'Je veux mourir à toi.' (I thank Professor A.G. Falconer for calling this to my attention.)

CHAPTER 25: EPILOGUE

1 W. Benjamin, 'The Storyteller,' *Illuminations* (New York: Schocken 1969) 99 (translation modified).
2 *Ibid.* 87.
3 *Ibid.* 99.
4 *Ibid.* 87.
5 *Ibid.* 87. Although Benjamin's discussion of story-telling emphasizes the oral tradition, it is with characteristic ambiguity: thus, only in forsaking 'the realm of living speech' does the art of story-telling, or of narration, make 'it possible to see a new beauty in what is vanishing.' Story-telling for Benjamin is not so much an activity of the voice, as one of the *body*, and as such it must share the fate of artisanal forms of

production. Cf. *ibid*. 108. (I have discussed the question of Benjamin's complex attitude towards language in my 'Lecture de Benjamin,' in *Critique* 267-8 [August-
September 1969] 699-712.)

6 *Ibid*. 100.
7 *Ibid*. 101.
8 *Ibid*. 100.
9 *Ibid*. 91.
10 Freud, *Fetishism* in *Sexuality and the Psychology of Love* (New York: Collier
1972⁵) 214.
11 Benjamin, 'The Storyteller' 86.
12 Freud, *Fetishism* 214.

POSTFACE: ET QUE DEVINT *S/Z*?

1 *Barthes par lui-même* (Paris: Editions du Seuil 1975) 170-1.
2 See A.G. Falconer, 'Le Travail de style dans les révisions de *La Peau de chagrin*,'
L'Année balzacienne (1969) 71-106.
3 *S/Z* (Paris 1970), back cover. Future references to this book will be given in parentheses within the text.
4 'Par rapport aux systèmes qui l'entourent, qu'est-il? Plutôt une chambre d'échos: il
reproduit mal les pensées, il suit les mots; il rend visite, c'est-à-dire hommage, aux
vocabulaires, il *invoque* les notions, il les répète sous un nom; il se sert de ce nom
comme d'un emblème ... et cet emblème le dispense d'approfondir le système dont
il est le signifiant. ... La raison de cela est sans doute qu'on ne peut en même temps
approfondir et désirer un mot: chez lui, le désir du mot l'emporte ... ' (*Barthes par
lui-même* 78).

Index of Proper Names

UNIVERSITY OF TORONTO ROMANCE SERIES

This book

was designed by

A N T J E   L I N G N E R

University of

Toronto

Press